Comparing English Worldwide

Comparing English Worldwide

The International Corpus of English

Edited by
Sidney Greenbaum

CLARENDON PRESS · OXFORD
1996

Oxford University Press, Walton Street, Oxford OX2 6DP

Oxford New York
Athens Auckland Bangkok Bombay
Calcutta Cape Town Dar es Salaam Delhi
Florence Hong Kong Istanbul Karachi
Kuala Lumpur Madras Madrid Melbourne
Mexico City Nairobi Paris Singapore
Taipei Tokyo Toronto
and associated companies in
Berlin Ibadan

Oxford is a trade mark of Oxford University Press

Published in the United States
by Oxford University Press Inc., New York

British Library Cataloguing in Publication Data
Data available

Library of Congress Cataloging in Publication Data
Data available

ISBN 0–19–823582–8

1 3 5 7 9 10 8 6 4 2

Typeset by Graphicraft Typesetters Ltd, Hong Kong
Printed in Great Britain
on acid-free paper by
Biddles Ltd., Guildford and King's Lynn

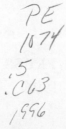

For Sholem and Wendy
Jonathan, David, Sima, and Daniella

PREFACE

This volume introduces the International Corpus of English (ICE). It serves as a reference work for researchers and students using ICE or any of its components. More generally, it presents a conspectus of what is involved in compiling and annotating a corpus and suggests a range of applications for corpora. The recent surge of interest in corpus linguistics ensures that this volume will attract readers other than potential users of ICE—all those who wish to exploit the exciting possibilities for linguistic and related studies that are offered by the many computer corpora that are becoming publicly available.

Part I provides a general introduction to the ICE project and to ICLE, a sub-project devoted to the language of foreign learners of English. The bulk of Part II is devoted to the ICE annotation schemes and the software employed to implement them. Part III discusses the problems of compiling the ICE corpora in a first-language country (New Zealand) and in various second-language countries in Africa and Asia. Finally, Part IV demonstrates the value of the corpora for research, teaching, language planning, establishment of language norms, and information technology.

This is an appropriate place to record my gratitude to the dozens of researchers in the ICE community, who have joined me in developing a major resource for the study of the English language internationally. In particular, I am indebted to my collaborators in the Survey of English Usage, the co-ordinating centre of the ICE project.

S.G.

University College London

CONTENTS

List of Contributors   xi

List of Figures   xiii

List of Tables   xv

Abbreviations   xvi

Part I. Introduction   1

1. Introducing ICE   3
   SIDNEY GREENBAUM

2. Learner English around the World   13
   SYLVIANE GRANGER

Part II. Compilation and Annotation   25

3. The Design of the Corpus   27
   GERALD NELSON

4. Markup Systems   36
   GERALD NELSON

5. The UMB Intelligent ICE Markup Assistant   54
   EDWARD M. BLACHMAN, CHARLES F. MEYER and
   ROBERT A. MORRIS

6. ICE Annotation Tools   65
   AKIVA QUINN and NICK PORTER

7. Developing the ICE Corpus Utility Program   79
   NICK PORTER and AKIVA QUINN

8. About the ICE Tagset   92
   SIDNEY GREENBAUM and NI YIBIN

9. AUTASYS: Grammatical Tagging and Cross-Tagset Mapping   110
   ALEX CHENGYU FANG

10. An Outline of the Survey's ICE Parsing Scheme   125
    JUSTIN BUCKLEY

11. The Survey Parser: Design and Development   142
    ALEX CHENGYU FANG

Contents

Part III. Problems of Implementation   161

12. The New Zealand Spoken Component of ICE:
    Some Methodological Challenges   163
    JANET HOLMES

13. Second-Language Corpora   182
    JOSEF SCHMIED

14. The International Corpus of English in Hong Kong   197
    PHILIP BOLT and KINGSLEY BOLTON

Part IV. Applications   215

15. The Corpus as a Research Domain   217
    GRAEME KENNEDY

16. ICE and Teaching   227
    JOHN M. KIRK

17. The Sociolinguistics of English in Nigeria and the ICE project   239
    AYO BANJO

18. Why a Fiji Corpus?   249
    JAN TENT and FRANCE MUGLER

19. PROSICE: A Spoken English Database for Prosody Research   262
    MARK HUCKVALE and ALEX CHENGYU FANG

Index   281

LIST OF CONTRIBUTORS

AYO BANJO is Professor of English Language and former Vice-Chancellor at the University of Ibadan, Nigeria.

EDWARD M. BLACHMAN is a member of the technical staff of Interleaf Inc., Waltham, Massachussetts.

PHILIP BOLT is Senior Lecturer in English at Hong Kong Polytechnic University.

KINGSLEY BOLTON is Lecturer in English at the University of Hong Kong.

JUSTIN BUCKLEY was a Research Assistant on the Survey of English Usage at University College London.

ALEX CHENGYU FANG is a Research Fellow on the Survey of English Usage, University College London.

SYLVIANE GRANGER is Professor of English Language and Linguistics and Director of the Centre for Computer Linguistics at the Université Catholique de Louvain, Belgium.

SIDNEY GREENBAUM is Research Professor of English and Director of the Survey of English Usage, University College London.

JANET HOLMES is Professor of Linguistics at Victoria University of Wellington, New Zealand.

MARK HUCKVALE is Lecturer in Speech Sciences at University College London.

GRAEME KENNEDY is Professor of Applied Linguistics at the Victoria University of Wellington, New Zealand.

JOHN M. KIRK is Lecturer in English at the Queen's University, Belfast.

CHARLES F. MEYER is Associate Professor of English at the University of Massachussetts at Boston.

ROBERT A. MORRIS is Professor of Mathematics and Computer Science at the University of Massachussetts at Boston.

FRANCE MUGLER is Senior Lecturer in Linguistics at the University of the South Pacific.

GERALD NELSON is a Research Fellow on the Survey of English Usage at University College London.

NICK PORTER was formerly a Research Fellow on the Survey of English Usage at University College London and is now a Software Development Coordinator at Dorling Kindersley Multimedia plc.

AKIVA QUINN was formerly a Research Fellow on the Survey of English Usage at University College London and is now Senior Software Engineer at Imaging Systems and Solutions, Kodak Australia.

List of Contributors

JOSEF SCHMIED holds the Chair of English Language and Linguistics and is Director of the Research in English and Applied Linguistics Centre at the Technische Universität, Chemnitz, Germany.

JAN TENT is Lecturer in Linguistics at the University of the South Pacific.

NI YIBIN is a Research Assistant on the Survey of English Usage at University College London.

LIST OF FIGURES

2.1.	Varieties of English	14
2.2.	An integrated contrastive model	18
3.1.	A schematic representation of the categories of spoken texts	29
3.2.	A schematic representation of the categories of written texts	30
4.A1.	ICECUP's text info screen	53
5.1.	The Create menu in the absence of prior markup	59
5.2.	The Create menu as constrained by prior markup	60
6.1a.	Tag selection: hides alternative tags for already selected words	68
6.1b.	Tag selection: constructing a verbal tag	69
6.1c.	Tag selection: automatically tagging compounds	70
6.1d.	Tag selection: progress report	70
6.2a.	Syntactic marking: displays, words, tags, and markers	71
6.2b.	Syntactic marking with only conjoin markers shown	72
6.2c.	Syntactic marking: edited sentence with normative markup	73
6.3a.	The tree and sentence windows	76
6.3b.	The function and category edit dialog box	76
6.3c.	The feature edit dialog box	77
6.3d.	Overview	78
7.1.	The query dialog box	82
7.2.	A list of the matches to the partial *ly	82
7.3.	A search display for the query working used as an adjective	83
7.4.	The concordance display	84
7.5.	Extra context: previous and following	85
7.6.	Extra context: viewing a whole text	86
7.7.	Text information	86
7.8.	Markup stripping	87
7.9.	Markup selection	87
7.10.	Subcorpus selection: browsing the hierarchy of features	88
7.11.	An example of a Help screen	90
10.1.	The tree for the parsing unit This is an example	126
10.2.	The root of a tree for a clause cluster, showing the highest level of the tree and the clausal top-level functions	127
10.3.	Adding features for a clause	128
10.4.	The tree for a prepositional phrase standing alone as an entire parsing unit	130
10.5.	The tree for a non-clause expressed by a discourse marker	130

List of Figures

10.6. The tree for coordinated stand-alone prepositional phrases   132
10.7. A tree showing coordination modified by adverbials   132
10.8. The tree for disparate co-ordinated elements   134
10.9. A tree containing a predicate group   134
10.10. A tree for coordination of verb phrases where coordination of
       predicates does not apply   136
10.11. A tree for a noun phrase with its primary functional constituents   136
10.12. The complete tree for a noun phrase   137
10.13. Tree containing *parataxis*. Punctuation has been omitted   137

11.1. Verb transitivity types in the ICE tagging scheme   145
11.2. Top-down retrieval for the constituents in an infinitival clause   149
11.3. Bottom-up retrieval for the governing node of specified items   149
11.4. A graphic tree representation of *Tom, John, and Mary*   150
11.5. A graphic tree representation of *Tom loves Mary*   151
11.6. The graphic representation of example [20]   153

14.1. Output from AUTASYS 3.0 for standard and non-standard
       written text   210

19.1. (*Opposite*) A short section of a recorded passage showing (*A*)
       speech pressure signal (*B*) spectrogram (*C*) aligned word
       annotations (*D*) laryngograph signal and (*E*) pitch
       period annotations   268
19.2. (*Opposite*) A long section of a recorded passage showing (*A*)
       speech pressure signal (*B*) 26-channel filterbank output (*C*)
       aligned word annotations (*D*) major pause and alignment region
       annotation and (*E*) fundamental frequency contour   270

LIST OF TABLES

2.1. Factors to consider when collecting samples of learner language   15
2.2. Variables controlled in ICLE   15
2.3. Concordances of *possibility* in ENL and EFL writing   20
2.4. Frequency of sequences of 3–5 words occurring at least twenty times in two similar-sized corpora of EFL and ENL writing   21

5.1. ICE markup 'structural' grammar   58
5.2. ICE markup 'speech' grammar   61
5.3. Table-based visual formalism of the authors   62

7.1. Example of the string description language   81

11.1. Success rates of the Survey Parser for training data   155
11.2. Success rate of the Survey Parser for unseen data   155
11.3. Overall performance of the Survey Parser   155

14.1. Knowledge of English in Hong Kong, 1983–93   200
14.2. ICE text types and data collection in Hong Kong   202
14.3. Language use in Hong Kong colleges and universities   203
14.4. The use of local and foreign reporters in selected English-language dailies   205

15.1. A classification of corpus-based research (1960–93) listed in the ICAME bibliographies 1–3   220–21
15.2. An outline of the units and structures from morpheme to discourse which can be investigated in the ICE corpora   223

18.1. Fiji serials: average circulation per issue at March 1995   253

19.1. A list of texts in broadcast talks   266
19.2. A sample of time-word and syntactic tree files   273
19.3. Frequency distribution of pauses among major syntactic categories   275

ABBREVIATIONS

AUTASYS	Automatic Text Annotation System
BROWN	Brown Corpus of American Printed English
CA	Contrastive Analysis
CIA	Contrastive Interlanguage Analysis
CSAE	Corpus of Spoken American English
DTD	Document Type Definition
EFL	English as a Foreign Language
EIL	English as an International Language
ENL	English as a Native Language
EOL	English as an Official Language
ESL	English as a Second Language
ICAME	International Computer Archive of Modern English
ICE	International Corpus of English
ICECUBE	International Corpus of English Corpus Utility for Building and Enhancing
ICECUP	International Corpus of English Corpus Utility Program
ICE-GB	International Corpus of English, the British Corpus
ICLE	International Corpus of Learner English
KWIC	Keyword in Context
LLC	London-Lund Corpus
LOB	London-Oslo/Bergen Corpus of British Printed English
MB	Megabytes
NLP	Natural Language Processing
PROSICE	A Speech Database Derived from ICE for Studies in Prosody
RAM	Random Access Memory
SDL	String Description Language
SEU	Survey of English Usage
SGML	Standard Generalized Markup Language
SLA	Second Language Acquisition
TEI	Text Encoding Initiative
TOSCA	Tools for Syntactic Corpus Analysis (name of research group at University of Nijmegen)
UCL	University College London
UMB/IMA	University of Massachusetts at Boston/Intelligent Markup Assistant
WCSNZE	Wellington Corpus of Spoken New Zealand English

PART I

Introduction

1

Introducing ICE

SIDNEY GREENBAUM

1. THE ICE COUNTRIES

ICE (the International Corpus of English) is an ambitious project, drawing on researchers located in over twenty countries. Its principal aim is to provide the resources for comparative studies of the English used in countries where it is either a majority first language (for example, Canada and Australia) or an official additional language (for example, India and Nigeria). In both language situations, English serves as a means of communication between those who live in these countries.

The resources that ICE is providing for comparative studies are computer corpora, collections of samples of written and spoken English from each of the countries that are participating in the project. For most of the countries, the ICE project is stimulating the first systematic study of the English used in their country.

I published the original proposal for ICE in 1988 (Greenbaum, 1988a) after preliminary discussions on the scope of the project. Since its inception I have been co-ordinating the project, and the Survey of English Usage (of which I am Director) has been providing guidance to participating research teams and dealing with their queries. The Survey has distributed manuals on the compilation and annotation of the ICE corpora and has created much of the software for these purposes. We have sent out newsletters and accompanying discussion documents. Most of the ICE participants have visited the Survey to view our work on ICE-GB (the British ICE corpus) and to discuss work on their corpora. Since many of them attend annual conferences of ICAME (the International Computer Archive of Modern English), the conferences provide an opportunity for meetings to report progress.

ICE-GB was the first ICE component to be started.[1] At the time of writing, commitments have been received from researchers for eighteen national or regional corpora. When completed, these corpora will constitute the components of ICE—the International Corpus of English:

1. Australia
2. Cameroon
3. Canada
4. Caribbean: Jamaica

5. East Africa
   Kenya
   Malawi
   Tanzania

6. Fiji	12. New Zealand
7. Ghana	13. Nigeria
8. Great Britain	14. Philippines
9. Ireland	15. Sierra Leone
Eire	16. Singapore
Northern Ireland	17. South Africa
10. Hong Kong	18. USA
11. India	

Additional countries are represented in the project by researchers assisting in the compilation and annotation of the corpora (Germany) and in the development of software for grammatical annotation (the Netherlands).

Contributing to the ICE project are the four major countries where English is predominantly the first language: the United States (with over 216 million first-language speakers), the United Kingdom (about 53 million), Canada (over 17 million), and Australia (about 14 million). But also included in ICE are Ireland and Jamaica. The language situation in Jamaica is particularly complex for English: most speak some variety of Jamaican Creole (an English-based creole), English generally being reserved for print and for formal public occasions.

As an official additional language, English is most conspicuous in the public sector: the sole or major language for communication in government administration, at least in central government; the medium of education in the state system, especially in higher education and most of all in science and technology; a major language in radio, television, and the national press. English often serves as a link language for interpersonal communication, particularly in the major cities, where ethnic mixing is greatest. It is also used creatively in the writing of fiction and poetry; some writers for whom English is not a first language have achieved international acclaim, prominent among them the Nigerians Chinua Achebe and Wole Soyinka.

For both first-language and second-language countries, the ICE project has to take account of the numerous bilingual or multilingual speakers and those who do not use or understand English. These may include native inhabitants as well as immigrant communities. The sociolinguistics of English in multilinguistic contexts is the concern of several chapters in this volume—those by Ayo Banjo, Philip Bolt and Kingsley Bolton, Josef Schmied, and Jan Tent and France Mugler. Limitations on the uses to which English is put have raised problems for the compilation of ICE corpora in second-language countries (see the chapters by Philip Bolt and Kingsley Bolton and by Josef Schmied). The compilation of first-language corpora also poses challenges, particularly in collecting the spoken material and more generally on who counts as a speaker of the national variety (see the chapter by Janet Holmes).

Excluded from ICE is the English used in countries where it is not a medium for communication between natives of the country. In those countries (for example, Germany and Japan) English is a foreign language, medium for international—but not intranational—communications. Germans and Japanese resort to English when they are communicating with foreigners who know English but do not understand German or Japanese, or when they are talking with their compatriots in the presence of such foreigners.

The English of foreign speakers has been catered for to some extent in a subproject of ICE: ICLE (the International Corpus of Learner English). For the ICLE project, computer corpora are being compiled that sample the essay writing of advanced learners of English from (at present) ten language backgrounds. Analysis of their writing will reveal which errors can be attributed to interference from native languages and which are common to all foreign learners of English. The ICLE project is outlined in the chapter by Sylviane Granger.

In the early stages of the ICE project various other sub-projects were envisaged: translations into English from European languages, the English used in documents produced by the European Commission, conversations in which the participants are from different countries (including foreign speakers of English). These have not materialized so far because of lack of funding.[2]

2. The ICE Corpora

The ICE project views as the basis for international comparisons the provision of parallel corpora that sample the English used in the participating countries. For valid comparative studies the components of ICE need to follow the same design, to date from the same period, and to be processed and analysed in similar ways.

The project has attempted to achieve conformity, but complete identity between corpora is not possible. Inevitably, there are differences in topics in the samples taken from speech and writing. In a few countries certain categories of language data are unavailable or difficult to obtain, and it may then be necessary to resort to the nearest substitutes. It is unreasonable to expect compilers of the corpora to match speakers or writers exactly in the whole range of biographical features, such as sex, age, educational level, occupation, or to replicate the types of relationships between speakers in conversations in each corpus in exactly the same proportions. Some research teams have joined the project later than others and so there will be discrepancies in the dating of the material, though a difference of a few years can be discounted as insignificant. However, the corpora will be sufficiently similar to justify global comparisons. For detailed comparisons it will be possible to employ the resources of ICECUP, the ICE retrieval software package that pinpoints identities in features of situation or participants (see Chapter 7).

The common design of the ICE corpora is detailed in the chapter on this topic by Gerald Nelson. Here it is sufficient to enumerate the major features of the design:

1. Each corpus contains about one million words.
2. Each corpus consists of 500 texts (samples), each text having about 2,000 words.

3. The texts are drawn from specified text categories and the number of texts in a category is also specified.
4. The major text category division is between spoken and written. Spoken texts are further divided into dialogues and monologues, and some monologues are scripted (read aloud from scripts). Written texts are manuscript or printed.
5. Texts generally date from the period 1990–4 inclusive. A few corpora are likely to include material (particularly spoken material) from a later date.
6. ICE is investigating 'educated' or 'standard' English. However, we do not examine the texts to decide whether they conform to our conception of 'educated' or 'standard' English. To do so would introduce a subjective circularity that would downplay the variability among educated speakers and the variation due to situational factors. Our criterion for inclusion is not the language used in the texts but who uses the language. The people whose language is represented in the corpora are adults (18 or over) who have received formal education through the medium of English to the completion of secondary school, but we also include some who do not meet the education criterion if their public status (for example, as politicians, broadcasters, or writers) makes their inclusion appropriate.

It is intended that the ICE corpora will be published. For that reason, copyright permissions are obtained for all texts.

Inevitably the corpora will be ready for distribution at different times and at different stages of annotation, depending on the rates of progress achieved by the ICE teams. I envisage simultaneous editions of ICE in various formats: lexical ICE (without grammatical annotation), tagged ICE, and parsed ICE. Updated editions will be published at intervals, to include newly completed corpora and corpora that have been newly annotated.

The first editions of ICE will probably appear in 1996 or 1997. The most likely candidates for inclusion in the earliest editions are the corpora from Australia, Great Britain, Hong Kong, India, New Zealand, and Singapore.

3. The Core Corpus and Extensions

What has been described in the previous section is the *core corpus*. The core corpora are the components of ICE and therefore must follow the same design and methods of processing. However, each corpus also serves independently as a resource for research into the particular national variety of English. Some research teams may want to extend their corpus in various respects. These optional extensions are not part of ICE, though if more than one research team undertakes the same extension their extensions will invite comparisons. Possible extensions of data are:

1. an *expanded corpus*, in which all the text categories in the core corpus are increased in size proportionately.

2. a *specialized corpus* for particular text categories, either expansions of categories in the core corpus (e.g. telephone conversations) or additions of categories (e.g. email messages).
3. *non-standard corpora*, in which the population sampled is restricted to (*a*) speakers of non-standard sociolects, (*b*) speakers of regional dialects, (*c*) children, or (*d*) immigrants from countries where English is a foreign language.
4. a *monitor corpus*, in which vast amounts of material that are easily obtainable are deposited and are continually replaced by newer material, so that the corpus is always current. A monitor corpus is not intended to be representative of the language as a whole. It is particularly useful for lexicographers, who are interested in capturing new words and new meanings.

Some teams may want to undertake additional processing. For example:

1. prosodic transcription
2. semantic marking
3. marking of discourse features
4. indexation of the sound recordings to the transcriptions (planned for the American and British corpora)
5. indexation of the video recordings (audio and visual) to the transcriptions

4. ANNOTATION OF THE CORPORA

Several annotation systems have been created for the ICE project. At the primary level are the two markup systems, textual markup and bibliographic and biographical markup, which are the topic of a chapter in this volume by Gerald Nelson.

Textual markup indicates features of the original text that would otherwise be lost. For the written texts, they include paragraph boundaries, headings, and various typefaces; for the spoken texts, they include pauses and overlapping speech. Markup is also required to separate and number the text units that constitute the basis for textual references. We have found it necessary to introduce normalization markup, to enable automatic parsers to cope with the text. In spoken texts normalization involves unparsable phenomena such as word partials, repetitions, and false starts—unparsable at least in the present state of parsers (cf. Stenström and Svartvik, 1994). The original text is preserved in the corpus, but it is the normalized version that is analysed by the parser.

Spoken texts are transcribed orthographically and not phonetically. Transcriptions include a binary system of brief and longer pauses; otherwise, no prosodic information is given. We decided not to mark intonational features for a number of reasons. Our overriding concern was practical: prosodic transcription takes an inordinate amount of time and requires expert assistants. Its inclusion would be costly in time and money. We had conducted some pilot tests at the Survey and these had produced evidence of substantial inconsistencies between transcribers, even for major intonational features such as tone unit boundaries and location of tones. Consistency is undoubtedly even more difficult to achieve when transcribers are located in different countries and therefore cannot check each other's work. Nor were we confident that one intonation system could be applied to all the national varieties of English. Furthermore, past experience has shown that experts in intonation prefer to use their own system. A computer corpus enables them to mark their system at their required level of delicacy on the sections they wish to study, for which purpose they will have access to the sound recordings. It will be much easier to study intonation and the relationship between intonation and syntax when the recordings are indexed to the transcriptions.

Bibliographic and biographical markup records a description of each text and information about the writers or speakers. The markup is stored in a database for which a common ICE structure has been devised.

Two types of grammatical annotation are envisaged for ICE: tagging and parsing. At the time of writing, these have been implemented only for ICE-GB, the British component of ICE.

The ICE tagset was created by the Survey of English Usage. It is based on the tagset developed by the TOSCA Research Group at the University of Nijmegen, but differs from it substantially. Each word in the corpus is assigned a tag indicating its word class. The tag may be accompanied by one or more features. For example, *shouldn't* is tagged AUX(modal,past,neg), denoting that it is a modal past negative auxiliary, and *'s* in *let's* is tagged PRON(pers,plu,encl), denoting that it is an enclitic plural personal pronoun. In all, about 270 tag combinations have been identified. The ICE tagset is described in a chapter in this volume by Sidney Greenbaum and Ni Yibin, and the tag combinations are listed in the Appendix to that chapter.

The TOSCA semi-automatic parsing system was applied to ICE-GB, and most of the corpus was analysed through that system. However, the TOSCA parser failed to produce parses for a substantial minority of the corpus. As a consequence, the Survey of English Usage has been devising a scheme to cope with the failures, and that scheme will be extended to the parts already analysed by the TOSCA parser in an automatic global revision. An outline of the revised ICE parsing scheme appears in the chapter by Justin Buckley.

5. ICE SOFTWARE

Computer programs have been compiled for the annotation of the ICE corpora. Two programs have been developed for assisting the task of inserting textual markup: the Markup Assistant at the Survey of English Usage is described in the chapter by Akiva Quinn and Nick Porter, and the UMB Intelligent ICE Markup Assistant at the University of Massachusetts at Boston is described in the chapter by Edward M. Blachman, Charles F. Meyer, and Robert A. Morris.

The TOSCA tagger, originally created to generate tags from the TOSCA tagset, was adapted to the ICE tagset and it was used to tag ICE-GB. AUTASYS, a tagger which originally generated CLAWS1 tags (the tagset employed on the LOB corpus), was also adapted by Alex Chengyu Fang to the ICE tagset. At the time of writing, the TOSCA tagger is claimed to have an accuracy of 90–4 per cent and AUTASYS an accuracy of about 96 per cent. AUTASYS is described in the chapter by Alex Fang.

Several ICE annotation tools are discussed in the chapter by Akiva Quinn and Nick Porter. Apart from the Markup Assistant, mentioned above, three programs have been developed at the Survey of English Usage to assist annotation: TAGSELECT, ICEMARK, and ICETREE. TAGSELECT is used to check and correct tags. ICEMARK assists the pre-editing required by the TOSCA semi-automatic parsing system to prevent multiple ambiguities; for example, all co-ordination structures and postmodifiers of noun phrases must be manually marked. Finally, ICETREE is intended for use with the Survey parser. It is a tree-editing program that is being employed to check and correct the parses generated by the Survey parser. ICETREE is provided with a hypertext HELP system that explains and exemplifies the ICE parsing system.

ICECUP is a software retrieval package, and ICECUBE is the package for installing it (see the chapter by Nick Porter and Akiva Quinn). ICECUP has search and concordance facilities for retrieving words, markup, and grammatical annotation, including combinations of items. Particularly important for the ICE project is the provision for creating subcorpora that draw on the bibliographic and biographical information about the texts. ICECUP comes with a context-sensitive hypertext help system that explains and exemplifies the markup and the ICE tagset.

The TOSCA semi-automatic parsing system was adapted by the TOSCA Research Group to take account of the ICE tags. It requires pre-editing (the syntactic marking noted above) and usually for each parsing unit more than one analysis (sometimes extending into tens and even hundreds and occasionally thousands of analyses) is offered from which a manual selection is made if there is a correct analysis. Manual interaction, such as changing tags, is often necessary to secure a parse. We have calculated that for our million-word ICE-GB corpus we spent the equivalent of about ten researcher-years on the TOSCA parsing. We were left with about 22 per cent of the utterances and 37.5 per cent of the words in the corpus for which the TOSCA parser failed to produced an analysis.[3] To deal with the parsing of the remainder of the corpus, Alex Chengyu Fang is developing a parser at the Survey of English Usage that offers just one parse. The parser does not require pre-editing, but may require correction with the assistance of ICETREE. Fang has created TQuery, a program for retrieving data from the parsed material. At the time of writing, the tagged corpus and the parsed ICE-GB corpus are separate. We intend to merge the two corpora and to use a new version of ICECUP, incorporating facilities from TQuery, for the merged corpus. The Survey parser and TQuery are described in the chapter by Fang.

The Survey of English Usage has been developing a program for indexing the sound recordings to the transcriptions to enable users of ICECUP to listen at will to the spoken material when searching the corpus. We expect to publish ICE-GB separately at some stage in the indexed format together with the grammatical annotation.

6. THE USES OF THE ICE CORPORA

The ICE project is in its infancy. This is the period when the ICE corpora are being assembled, computerized, and annotated. Overlapping to some extent with this preparatory work are the initial exploitations of the corpora. At the time of writing, none of the corpora are in the public domain, though some material has been exchanged between ICE participants. Once the corpora are distributed internationally, a new era of English corpus linguistics will begin, opening up new directions for applications.

For descriptive linguistics, ICE offers the first systematic collections for many national varieties of English. The tagged and parsed corpora will present unique opportunities for detailed grammatical studies of a range of written and spoken text categories. The richness of the ICE grammatical annotation in those corpora that are tagged and parsed will attract scholars researching even American and British English, the national varieties that have until now received the most attention. Searched in conjunction with ICECUP, the corpora will yield a wealth of data for sociolinguistic research on situational and biographic factors affecting variability in language use.

As the parallel corpora become available, new possibilities open up for rigorous comparative and contrastive studies. I envisage the search for typologies of national varieties of English: first-language versus second-language English, British-type versus American-type English, African versus Asian English, East African versus West African English. Researchers might explore what is common to English in all countries where it is used for internal communication, demonstrating how far it is legitimate to speak of a common core for English or of an international written standard.

Graeme Kennedy (in this volume) outlines possible exploitations of the ICE corpora for linguistic research. Some of the corpora are already being used for this purpose. The Leverhulme project, currently in progress at the Survey, explores clause relationships in spoken and written English, drawing on a selection of text categories in ICE-GB (cf. Greenbaum and Nelson, 1995*a*, 1995*b*, 1996; Greenbaum, Nelson, and Weitzman 1996). A special issue of *World Englishes* (1996, vol. 15, no. 1), edited by Greenbaum and Nelson, is devoted to studies of ICE corpora— including, in some instances, data from more than one corpus.

The compilation of the Hong Kong corpus comes at a crucial stage in the history of English in that British colony, just before the return of the territory to China (see the chapter by Philip Bolt and Kingsley Bolton). The political change is likely to affect the status of English in Hong Kong, the domains in which it is used, and the extent to which it is taught in the public school system. As a consequence, there could well be changes in the forms of Hong Kong English. It would obviously be interesting linguistically and sociolinguistically to compile another Hong Kong corpus in (say) twenty or thirty years to discover the changes that have taken place. More generally, repetition of ICE at regular intervals would provide invaluable data for historical studies. We have no parallel corpora for past periods of English. The ICE project presents an exciting opportunity for future linguists.

The ICE corpora can be exploited in teaching. In this volume John Kirk discusses uses of ICE-GB in introductory courses on corpus linguistics, where he requires students to compile their own mini-corpora for research projects. We can imagine the development of self-study programs at various levels that utilize the corpora for learning about English or improving English proficiency. Several of the ICE programs devised to assist the annotation of the corpora can be adapted as teaching tools (cf. Quinn and Quinn, 1993, 1994). To take one example, the Survey's hypertext help system for parsing lends itself to adaption as a tool for teaching syntax at various levels. It would be possible to add exercises to the system; errors in exercises could then be corrected, followed by remedial instruction and further exercises.

Political independence is a precursor of linguistic independence. In the last few decades several English-speaking countries—some of them second-language countries—have been diverging from British or American norms and establishing their own norms for language teaching and for grammars, dictionaries, and usage handbooks. Nigeria is a prominent example, discussed in this volume by Ayo Banjo (see also the chapter by Jan Tent and France Mugler). Teachers need to know what kind of English to teach, and examinations should test candidates realistically, accepting the language that educated Nigerian speakers of English commonly use. Research on the Nigerian corpus can provide scholars and educationalists with reliable information for formulating a standard language that will also take account of other national varieties (cf. Greenbaum, 1988*b*). Studies based on the corpus can also help in language planning by revealing the extent to which English is being used and its roles in the various regions of the country.

Finally, the chapter on PROSICE by Mark Huckvale and Alex Chengyu Fang points to other areas of application. Corpus-based research is increasingly influencing work in various aspects of natural language processing and speech technology. The wealth of grammatical information and the range of text categories in ICE-GB have made it an obvious resource for the PROSICE project. In this connection, it is appropriate to refer again to the chapter by Fang on the development of the Survey parser, which uses ICE-GB as a knowledge base.

Notes

1. The initial period for the ICE project was supported in part by a grant R000 23 2077 from the Economic and Social Research Council.
2. The early history of the project is outlined in Greenbaum, 1991.
3. The discrepancy between the two methods of calculating the successes of the parser

arises because many of the utterances in dialogue are short, often consisting of just one or two words.

REFERENCES

GREENBAUM, S. (1988*a*), 'A Proposal for an International Corpus of English', *World Englishes* 7: 315.

—— (1988*b*), 'Language Spread and the Writing of Grammars', in P. H. LOWENBERG (ed.), *Georgetown University Round Table on Language and Linguistics*, 133–9 (Washington, DC: Georgetown University Press).

—— (1991), 'The Development of the International Corpus of English', in K. AIJMER and B. ALTENBERG (eds.), *English Corpus Linguistics: Studies in Honour of Jan Svartvik*, 83–91 (London: Longman).

—— and NELSON, G. (1995*a*), 'Nuclear and Peripheral Clauses in Speech and Writing', in G. MELCHERS and B. WARREN (eds.), *Studies in Anglistics*, 181–90 (Stockholm: Almqvist & Wiksell).

—— —— (1995b), 'Clause Relationships in Spoken and Written English', *Functions of Language*, 2: 1–21.

—— —— (1996), 'Positions of Adverbial Clauses in British English', *World Englishes*, 15: 71–83.

—— —— and WEITZMAN, M. (1996), 'Complement Clauses in English', in M. SHORT and J. A. THOMAS (eds.), *Using Corpora for Language Research: Essays in Honour of Geoffrey Leech*, 76–91 (London: Longman).

QUINN, A. and QUINN, D. (1993), 'CORTEX: A Corpus-Based Teaching Expert', in C. ROWLES, H. LIU and N. FOO (eds.), *AI '93 Proceedings of the 6th Australian Joint Conference on Artificial Intelligence, Melbourne, Australia, 17–19 November 1993*, 377–82 (Singapore: World Scientific).

QUINN, D. and QUINN, A. (1994), 'Linguistic Modelling for a Corpus-Based CALL System', in A. WILSON and T. MCENERY (eds.), *Corpora in Language Education and Research: A Selection of Papers from Talc 94*, 87–98 (Lancaster: UCREL, Lancaster University).

STENSTRÖM, A.-B. and SVARTVIK, J. (1994), 'Imparsable Speech: Repeats and other Nonfluencies in Spoken English', in N. OOSTDIJK and P. DE HAAN (eds.), *Corpus-based Research into Language*, 241–54 (Amsterdam: Rodopi).

2

Learner English around the World

SYLVIANE GRANGER

1. INTRODUCTION

Though there is no general agreement on the exact figures, everybody now recognizes that there are now more non-native speakers of English in the world than native speakers. McArthur (1992: 355) speaks of a '2-to-1 ratio of non-natives to natives'. In this context, a project such as The International Corpus of English (ICE) is particularly welcome, as in addition to featuring different native varieties of English, it gives non-native varieties of English the place they deserve. However, ICE only covers institutionalized varieties of non-native English such as Indian English or Nigerian English. It leaves out a sizeable—arguably the largest—group of non-native users of English in the world, i.e. foreign learners of English. It was to do justice to this rapidly expanding group of English speakers that I put forward a proposal to complement ICE with a corpus of learner English, a suggestion which was welcomed by Sidney Greenbaum. This resulted in the launch of The International Corpus of Learner English (ICLE) in late 1990. In this paper I will first situate the corpus within the other non-native varieties of English. Then I will describe the corpus in detail, paying particular attention to issues of methodology. I will briefly illustrate the insights to be derived from a computer-based investigation of learner lexis, grammar, and discourse features. Finally, I will highlight the pedagogical advantages of a corpus-based approach to EFL.

2. NON-NATIVE ENGLISHES

In the World Englishes (WE) tradition, the concept of non-native English is well-established. Kachru (1985: 12) represents the spread of English in the world as three concentric circles:

1. the *inner circle*, which contains the native English-speaking countries (UK, USA, Australia, etc.);
2. the *outer circle*, which contains former colonies of the UK and the USA (India, Kenya, Nigeria, etc.). These countries have developed nativized varieties of

Sylviane Granger

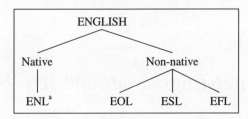

ᵃ Following McArthur (1992: 353), one could further subdivide native English into countries where English is 'profoundly dominant' (e.g. Australia, England, Northern Ireland) and countries where English coexists with at least one other nationally significant language (e.g. Canada, Gibraltar, the Channel Islands).

FIG. 2.1. Varieties of English

English which have achieved the status of official language and/or language of education, administration, etc.;
3. the *expanding circle*, which contains countries where English has no official status and is not used in education or administration (Spain, Sweden, China, etc.).

Within the field of Second Language Acquisition (SLA), non-native English is also an established concept, but unfortunately it is not used in exactly the same way. Whereas WE studies typically refer to the two non-native circles—the outer and the expanding circles—as ESL (English as a Second Language) and EFL (English as a Foreign Language) countries respectively, these same acronyms are used in the SLA tradition with partly different meanings. Because of the importance of setting in language acquisition, SLA specialists often distinguish between ESL learners, who acquire English in an English-speaking country (UK, USA, etc.), and EFL learners, who learn English in a non-English speaking country (Germany, Japan, etc.). To further confuse the issue, the term ESL is often used by American SLA specialists as a cover term for both EFL and ESL learners.

The term ESL is thus potentially ambiguous. To solve this ambiguity one can either subcategorize ESL—e.g. adopt McArthur's (1992: 1035) terms 'Commonwealth ESL' and 'immigrant ESL'—or keep the term ESL to refer to the latter and adopt a different term for the former. In my view, the connotations of the terms 'Commonwealth' and 'immigrant' tip the scales in favour of the latter solution. I would suggest subcategorizing English into the varieties shown in Fig. 2.1.

The non-native varieties comprise (1) English as an Official Language (EOL), a term which covers the indigenized varieties of English (IVEs) in Kachru's outer circle; (2) English as a Second Language (ESL), i.e. English acquired in an English-speaking country (McArthur's Immigrant ESL) and (3) English as a Foreign Language (EFL), i.e. English learned primarily in a classroom setting in a non-English-speaking country (Kachru's expanding circle).

To return to the ICE and ICLE corpora, it is clear that they are highly complementary, ICE covering native and indigenized varieties of English and ICLE focusing exclusively on EFL English.

3. COLLECTING THE ICLE CORPUS

Specialists in second language acquisition are unanimous in deploring the lack of solid empirical foundations for SLA research. In his survey of research on transfer, Odlin (1989: 151) notes 'considerable variation in the numbers of subjects, in the backgrounds of the subjects, and in the empirical data, which come from tape-recorded samples of speech, from student writing, from various types of tests, and from other sources' and concludes that 'improvements in data gathering would be highly desirable'. In collecting the learner corpus I therefore followed two main guiding principles: comparability and size.

To ensure comparability of learner data, it is necessary to control a certain number of factors, which Ellis (1994: 49) presents as shown in Table 2.1. The variables adopted within the framework of ICLE are presented in Table 2.2. The variables pertaining to the type of language covered are:

TABLE 2.1. *Factors to consider when collecting samples of learner language*

Factors	Description
A. *Language*	
Medium	Learner production can be oral or written
Genre	Learner production may take the form of a conversation, a lecture, an essay, a letter, etc.
Content	The topic the learner is communicating about
B. *Learner*	
Level	Elementary, intermediate, or advanced
Mother tongue	The learner's L1
Language learning experience	This may be classroom or naturalistic or a mixture of the two

TABLE 2.2. *Variables controlled in ICLE*

Factors	Description
A. *Language*	
Medium	Written
Genre	Essay
Content	Argumentative; non-technical
B. *Learner*	
Level	Advanced
Mother tongue	French, German, Dutch, Spanish, Swedish, Finnish, Czech, Japanese, Chinese, Polish, Russian
Setting	Classroom

15

1. *medium*: the ICLE corpus consists exclusively of written production data.
2. *genre*: all these written productions represent the same genre, namely essay writing. These essays, which are approximately 500 words long, are unabridged and so lend themselves particularly well to analyses of cohesion (both lexical and syntactic) and coherence.
3. *content*: although the essays cover a wide range of topics, the content is similar in so far as the topics are all non-technical and argumentative in nature.

The variables pertaining to the type of learner are:

1. *level*: ICLE is a corpus of advanced learner English. The notion of 'advanced' is defined on the basis of a purely external criterion, i.e. as the level reached by undergraduates in English Language and Literature in their 3rd or 4th year.
2. *mother tongue*: the corpus covers eleven mother tongue backgrounds both in Europe (French, German, Dutch, Spanish, Swedish, Finnish, Czech, Polish, Russian) and outside Europe (Chinese and Japanese).
3. *setting*: the subjects are all EFL learners, not ESL learners. They have primarily learned English in a classroom context, though some may have improved their knowledge through a stay in an English-speaking country.

When complete, the corpus will contain at least 2 million words, with each 200,000-word subcorpus representative of 300 to 400 different learners. This is an improvement on the slim empirical basis of many SLA studies, but it is still too small for some types of linguistic investigation. A 200,000-word subcorpus is adequate for most studies of grammar and some studies of lexis, but is insufficient, for example, for lexical investigations involving low frequency words.

One limitation of the ICLE corpus is that it covers only one type of production data. Other learner corpora currently being compiled at Louvain should go some way towards complementing the ICLE corpus (a corpus of written English by intermediate learners and a corpus of conversational advanced learner English) but this work is only a drop in the ocean. Much more and varied data need to be collected covering a variety of learners (English for Specific Purposes (ESP) learners, ESL learners, etc.), media, and genres.

A major strength of ICLE is the strict data collection procedure followed, which has ensured that the eleven subcorpora cover the same type of learner language and are thus fully comparable. Of course, this does not mean that there are no other differences, but any major ones are recorded in the learner profile questionnaire which all subjects are required to fill in. This questionnaire contains biographical information (age, sex, years of English at school, prolonged stay in an English-speaking country, knowledge of other foreign languages, etc.) as well as task-related information (whether the essay was timed or untimed, part of an exam or not, whether reference tools were used and if so, which, etc.). This information will be computerized in the form of standardized file-headers, making it possible for researchers to select their own tailor-made subcorpora (a researcher into gender differences for example might wish to have data divided into two corpora, one containing texts written by male students and the other by female students).

4. CONTRASTIVE INTERLANGUAGE ANALYSIS

Once the corpus is collected, the analyst has to opt for a particular method of investigation, which will obviously depend on his research goals. The ICLE project has two main objectives:

(*a*) to uncover the factors of non-nativeness or foreign-soundingness in advanced learner writing, in areas of syntax, lexis, and discourse. To meet this end, it is necessary to compare advanced EFL English with native English;

(*b*) to distinguish between Ll-dependent features (i.e. those features which are due to transfer from the mother tongue) and crosslinguistic invariants, i.e. those features which are common to all advanced learners, irrespective of their mother tongue. To meet this aim, we need to compare the EFL varieties with each other (i.e. the English of German learners with the English of French learners, etc.). These two types of contrastive investigation—NL (native language) vs. IL (interlanguage) and IL vs. IL—constitute a new type of Contrastive Analysis which I have called Contrastive Interlanguage Analysis, or CIA for short.

In fact, our approach to learner data is doubly contrastive. In addition to CIA, it also crucially involves classic CA. Like others in the field, I view transfer as a key phenomenon in SLA. Selinker (1992: 170) views interlingual identifications as 'a basic, if not *the* basic, SLA learning strategy'. Evidence of transfer can only be firmly established, however, if the researcher has access to good contrastive descriptions of the languages involved.

The two contrastive perspectives are combined in the Integrated Contrastive Model (see Granger, forthcoming *a*), which involves constant to-ing and fro-ing between CA and CIA (cf. Fig. 2.2). The researcher can either start from a contrastive description and predict a given output by the learner or start from the learner output and diagnose it with the help of a contrastive description. Needless to say, both prediction and diagnosis are to be interpreted as mere hypotheses to be tested against CA and CIA data. So, for instance, the fact that the passive is twice as frequent in English as in French (see Granger, 1976) may lead one to predict an under-use of the passive by French learners of English. Conversely, if one starts by investigating the use of the passive in learner output and notes an under-use by French learners, one can try and diagnose this phenomenon by looking at contrastive descriptions of English and French. However, for transfer to be unambiguously established, it is not enough to look at CA data. An under-use of the passive may well be an invariant feature of learner English. In this respect, the ICLE corpus provides a particularly safe basis to assess transfer, since it makes it possible to look at a particular feature in several learner Englishes.

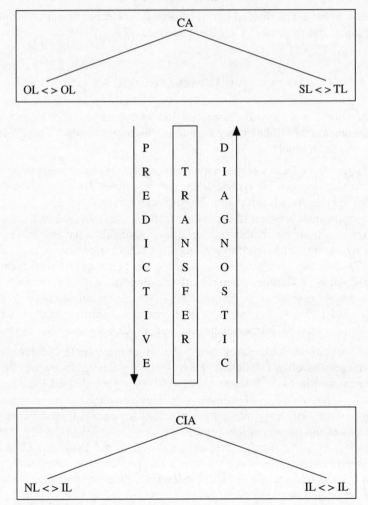

FIG. 2.2. An integrated contrastive model

Other interesting comparisons can be made if the integrated contrastive model is made to include—besides the EFL varieties of ICLE—the EOL varieties of ICE. This rapprochement between the SLA and WE perspectives is called for by Sridhar and Sridhar (1986), who argue that a better understanding of the acquisition of indigenized varieties of English would lead to a more satisfactory theory of SLA. For instance, a comparison of EFL and EOL data would shed new light on the phenomenon of transfer. According to Sridhar and Sridhar (1986: 11), inclusion of EOL data would seriously question the validity of 'putatively universal concepts' such as Kellerman's claim that language-specific items such as idioms are less prone to transfer. In their view 'the fact that such ridiculous propositions remain unchallenged for years is a sad commentary on the narrow theoretical and empirical foundations of current SLA theories'.

5. COMPUTER-BASED APPROACHES TO LEARNER LANGUAGE

The advantage of computerization is that the learner corpus can be analysed using a whole range of computerized methods and tools developed within the framework of corpus linguistics. This computer-based approach to learner language brings out a wealth of quantitative-statistical measures, which make it possible to 'quantify learner language', a hitherto largely unexplored SLA territory. It is particularly useful in exposing patterns of over-use and/or under-use which—arguably more than the presence of overt errors—account for the foreign-soundingness of advanced learners' writing. So, for instance, a recent study of connectors (see Granger and Tyson, 1996) revealed that learners significantly over-used some connectors (such as *moreover* or *for instance*) while significantly under-using some other connectors (such as *however* or *therefore*). This contradicts the view commonly expressed in the EFL literature according to which learner writing is characterized by a general overuse of connectors. It also shows that, although teachers' intuitions are very useful in drawing attention to areas of difficulty, they need to be corroborated by corpus-based investigations of authentic learner data if learners are to receive accurate messages about patterns of language use.

It is worth pointing out that quantitative information is merely a starting-point for more qualitative investigation, which is greatly facilitated by the use of concordances. These show how learners use words in context and highlight erroneous or marked uses. Table 2.3 shows a comparison of the concordances of the word 'possibility' in ENL and EFL writing. One of the learners' recurring errors, namely postmodification with a marked infinitive, is immediately apparent. A look at several ICLE subcorpora shows that this problem is common to learners from various mother-tongue backgrounds.

A computer-based methodology is also particularly useful in investigating learners' phrasal lexicon. Text retrieval software (such as the Collgen facility in TACT) enables the analyst to identify recurring combinations in learner writing. For instance, a search for sequences of three to five words occurring at least twenty times in an 80,000-word EFL corpus and a comparable ENL corpus produced the list shown in Table 2.4. The table suggests that learners significantly over-use some lexical phrases. The over-use of *as far as* (exclusively used in the phrase *as far as X is concerned*) and *point of view* (mainly used in *from the point of view of X*) point to learners' difficulty in introducing topics or arguments (see Granger, Meunier, and Tyson, 1994). Another acute problem for learners, namely the use of collocations, is brought out in a study of amplifier collocations (Granger, forthcoming *b*)

TABLE 2.3. *Concordances of possibility in ENL and EFL writing*

Native corpus (179,822 words)		Non-native corpus (150,595 words)	
(3632)	from the two-fold possibility >for joining the party: was	(2966)	January 1993 on, the possibility >for workers of all kind to
(5292)	popular because of the possibility >for abuse. The second	(3036)	European level, the possibility >for students to move from
(5883)	and sensible possibility >for solving international	(3863)	of employees, the possibility >for professional people to
(482)	you die, there is no possibility >of benefiting from that	(1584)	self-confidence and possibility >of identification. To
(4980)	deduces the possibility >of a relatively increasing	(2107)	already explored the possibility >of forming other such
(6531)	earth. There is no possibility >of his dominant position in	(2896)	argument against the possibility >of an identity
(6860)	that, there is the possibility >of conversion from one	(4909)	there may be a possibility >of reducing the
(7144)	but there is a possibility >of entry for those		
(4513)	There seems every possibility >that the present Queen will	(1292)	is, however, a strong possibility >that our society is still
(7742)	mention the possibility >that one of the motives for		
		(1250)	students have the possibility >to leave for another
		(1253)	culture and have the possibility >to practise their
		(1256)	to young people the possibility >to enrich their
		(3230)	because we have the possibility >to travel more freely all
		(1624)	of life, i.e. the possibility >to be in harmony with

TABLE 2.4. *Frequency of sequences of 3–5 words*
occurring at least 20 times in two similar-sized
(c. 80,000 words) corpora of EFL and ENL writing

Phrase	ENL	EFL
a kind of	3	24
more and more	3	28
as far as	5	36
at the same time	5	31
on the contrary	3	35
a lot of	4	24
point of view	4	50

which reveals that learners have a tendency to over-use general-purpose amplifiers (e.g. *very*, *completely*, or *totally*) but clearly under-use stereotyped combinations (e.g. *readily available*, *keenly felt*, or *vitally important*).

The previous examples illustrate the kind of search that can be made on a learner corpus in its raw form. More sophisticated searches can be carried out on a tagged learner corpus. All the ICLE subcorpora will be grammatically annotated with the TOSCA analysis system which was developed alongside the ICE project. Comparisons of the ICLE corpus with the various NL corpora in ICE will give SLA specialists precise measures of learners' use of tenses, modals, voice, etc. and thereby lead to an enhanced understanding of EFL grammar in general.[1]

6. Pedagogical Implications

The underlying idea behind most recent EFL research is that better descriptions of authentic native English will lead to better EFL tools. In the introduction to the Collins Cobuild English Grammar (1990: x), Sinclair writes: 'We have tried to produce a grammar of real English—the English that people speak and write. It contains detailed information about English, collected from the large corpus we have built up . . . It is designed above all to be really useful to student and teacher.' Kennedy (1992: 335) equally stresses the importance of native English corpora in language teaching: 'Corpus linguistics can tell us not just what is systemically possible but what is actually likely to occur in the language in general or in particular contexts. Without this statistical dimension the unusual elements of a language (including the so-called exceptions) tend to get as much attention as the usual.' This has been convincingly illustrated in a series of studies, notably in Biber, Conrad, and Reppen's (1994) recent analysis of the different types of noun postmodification. This study shows among other things that pedagogical grammars devote much more space to relative clauses than to prepositional postmodifiers while the latter are considerably more frequent in all registers of English.

The EFL world has much to gain from a more solid ENL foundation. But is this native foundation enough to ensure effective EFL material? To Kjellmer (1992: 375) the answer is clearly 'No'. In his opinion, when selecting which elements to teach and in what order, one should strike a balance between two types of elements: '(*a*) the elements the learner is likely to mistreat because they are different, maybe insidiously different, from those in his native language, and (*b*) the elements he is likely to meet and to require. Information on (*a*) is supplied by contrastive work, corpus or non-corpus, information on (*b*) is supplied by corpus work.' Kjellmer (1992: 376) concludes that teaching would benefit from a compromise between the 'emphasis-on-typicality' approach typical of recent trends in EFL and a contrastive 'emphasis-on-difference' approach.

In view of the now universally recognized importance of transfer in SLA, one has to agree with Kjellmer that a contrastive perspective is useful and indeed necessary. However, the strong version of CA—the 'difference equals problem' hypothesis—is a thing of the past. Learner language is not only characterized by interlingual errors but also by a whole range of intralingual and developmental features. What we need, therefore, is a combination of authentic native data and authentic learner data. The former will ensure that the materials used reflect authentic native usage and the latter will enable the EFL specialist to choose the items to be included in the syllabus and the weighting they will be given on the basis of learners' attested needs. The learner perspective is essential because, as acknowledged by Kennedy (1991: 110), 'it is, of course, not easy to predict what particular quantitative information can be of pedagogic significance'. The Collins Cobuild English Guides series provides a very comprehensive view of the authentic use of words (prepositions, reporting expressions, linking words, etc.) but before we can hope to turn this mass of information into useful EFL tools, we need to know what particular problems learners have at different levels of proficiency. Only a close investigation of learner data will tell us, for instance, that learners have a tendency to over-use sentence initial connectors (cf. Granger and Tyson, 1996), something which could then give rise to effective remedial exercises. Indeed, the typicality approach may sometimes run counter to sound pedagogic practice. Verb forms are a case in point. Kennedy (1992: 342) reports that where 'now' is the time reference 95.4 per cent of verb forms are the simple present and only 4.6 per cent are present progressive. On this basis he suggests introducing the present progressive later in the syllabus. However, in the case of French mother-tongue learners, it is the present progressive that is difficult to acquire, not the simple present. Even advanced learners are prone to use the simple present where a present progressive is necessary and this amply justifies the space allotted to the progressive in pedagogical grammars. A recent investigation of grammar checkers (Granger and Meunier, 1994) shows that electronic tools also suffer from a native speaker bias and can only be improved if learners' attested problems are addressed.

7. Conclusion

In a somewhat nostalgic article Kingscott (1990: 75) reflects that 'Mother-tongue English will soon cease to be the predominant form of English' and expresses his concern about the spread of unidiomatic 'Foreigners' English'. It is likely that the vast numbers of non-native speakers of English who now use English as a language of communication will have some effect upon the evolution of the language. Nevertheless, there are ways of countering this spread of unidiomatic English, not least of which is finding out what it is that makes EFL English unidiomatic. Results gained from computer learner corpora are already producing some interesting findings and changing some of our preconceived ideas about learner language. If these findings are translated into new learning materials, better adapted to the learner's needs, maybe we will be able to make the pendulum swing back the other way!

Acknowledgments

I gratefully acknowledge the support of the Belgian National Scientific Research Council and the University of Louvain Research Fund who helped to fund the ICLE project.

Note

1. On the tagging of interlanguage data, see Meunier (1995).

References

AIJMER, K. and ALTENBERG, B. (1991) (eds.), *English Corpus Linguistics* (London: Longman).

BIBER, D., CONRAD, S. and REPPEN, R. (1994), 'Corpus-based Approaches to Issues in Applied Linguistics', *Applied Linguistics* 15/2: 169–89.

Collins Cobuild English Grammar (1990) (London/Glasgow: Collins ELT).

Collins Cobuild English Guides, Prepositions (1991) (London: HarperCollins).

ELLIS, R. (1994), *The Study of Second Language Acquisition* (Oxford: Oxford University Press).

FLOWERDEW, L. and TONG, A. K. K. (1994) (eds.), *Entering Text* (Hong Kong: The Hong Kong University of Science and Technology).

FRIES, U., TOTTIE, G. and SCHNEIDER, P. (1994) (eds.), *Creating and using English Language Corpora* (Amsterdam/Atlanta: Rodopi).

GRANGER, S. (1976), 'Why the Passive?', in J. VAN ROEY (ed.), 23–57.

—— (1994), 'The Learner Corpus: A Revolution in Applied Linguistics', *English Today* 10/3: 25–9.

—— (forthcoming *a*), 'From CA to CIA and Back: An Integrated Contrastive Approach to Computerized Bilingual and Learner Corpora', in K. AIJMER, B. ALTENBERG, and JOHANSSON (eds.), *Languages in Contrast: Papers from a Symposium on Text-based Cross-Linguistic Studies Lund, 4–5 March 1994*, Lund Studies in English 85 (Lund: Lund University Press).

—— (forthcoming *b*), 'Prefabricated Patterns in Advanced EFL Writing: Collocations and Lexical Phrases', in A. COWIE (ed.), *Phraseology* (Oxford: Oxford University Press).

—— and MEUNIER, F. (1994), 'Towards a Grammar Checker for Learners of English', in U. FRIES *et al.* (eds.), 79–91.

—— MEUNIER, F. and TYSON, S. (1994), 'New Insights into the Learner Lexicon: A Preliminary Report from the International Corpus of Learner English', in L. FLOWERDEW and A. K. K. TONG (eds.), 102–13.

—— and TYSON, S. (1996), 'Connector Usage in the English Essay Writing of Native and Non-Native EFL Speakers of English', *World Englishes*, 15/1: 19–29.

KACHRU, B. (1985), 'Standards, Codification and Sociolinguistic Realism: The English Language in the Outer Circle', in R. QUIRK and H. G. WIDDOWSON (eds), 11–30.

KENNEDY, G. (1991), '*Between* and *Through*: The Company they Keep and the Functions they Serve', in K. AIJMER and B. ALTENBERG (eds), 95–110.

—— (1992), 'Preferred Ways of Putting Things with Implications for Language Teaching', in J. SVARTVIK (ed.), 335–73.

KINGSCOTT, G. (1990), 'Exiguities of Pertaining Criticism', *English Today* 21/6.1: 74–75.

KJELLMER, G. (1992), 'Comments', in J. SVARTVIK (ed.), 375–8.

McARTHUR, T. (1992), *The Oxford Companion to the English Language* (Oxford: Oxford University Press).

MEUNIER, F. (1995), 'Tagging and Parsing Interlanguage', in L. BEHEYDT (ed.), *Linguistique appliquée dans les années nonante*, ABLA Papers no. 16: 21–9.

ODLIN, T. (1989), *Language Transfer: Cross-Linguistic Influence in Language Learning* (Cambridge: Cambridge University Press).

QUIRK, R. and WIDDOWSON, H. G. (1985) (eds.), *English in the World: Teaching and Learning the Language and Literatures* (Cambridge: Cambridge University Press).

SELINKER, L. (1992), *Rediscovering Interlanguage* (Oxford/New York: Longman).

SRIDHAR, K. K. and SRIDHAR, S. N. (1986), 'Bridging the Paradigm Gap: Second Language Acquisition Theory and Indigenized Varieties of English', *World Englishes*, 5/1: 3–14.

SVARTVIK, J. (1992) (ed.), *Directions in Corpus Linguistics* (Berlin/New York: Mouton de Gruyter).

VAN ROEY, J. (1976) (ed.), *English-French Contrastive Analyses* (Leuven: Acco).

PART II

Compilation and Annotation

3

The Design of the Corpus

GERALD NELSON

1. INTRODUCTION

The International Corpus of English is at present envisaged to comprise eighteen national or regional corpora compiled in countries where English is spoken as a first language or as a second official language (Greenbaum, 1992). While each component corpus can exist independently as a valuable resource for investigations into individual national or regional varieties, the value of the corpora is enhanced by their compatibility with each other. They have been compiled according to a common design, using the same criteria for text selection and the same time-frame. This level of standardization ensures that the corpora can be used for direct comparative studies of varieties of English throughout the world. The design of the corpus emerged after extensive discussions among participants in the project, which centred on the range of text categories to be included and on the textual and social variables to be taken into account in the selection and documentation of samples (Leitner, 1992; Peters, 1991; Schmied, 1990).

2. THE BASIC STRUCTURE OF THE CORPUS

Each national or regional corpus consists of 500 texts of approximately 2,000 words each, giving a total of approximately one million words. Many of the texts are composite, since they consist of two or more different samples of the same type which are combined to make up 2,000 words. Since in some categories, such as business letters and press news reports, almost all the 2,000-word texts are composite, all the corpora contain more than 500 samples. As far as possible, the texts are self-contained. Extracts from printed works were taken from the beginning of a chapter, and spoken extracts begin at the start of a topic and at a new speaker turn. The end of a text coincides with a paragraph ending in printed texts, and with the end of an exchange or topic in spoken ones. We have omitted texts which contain large numbers of quotations, foreign words, or mathematical formulae. We have avoided certain types of creative writing in which the use of English is intentionally idiosyncratic. For the same reason, poetry has been excluded from the corpus. Before looking at the categories of texts in the corpus, I will discuss the general criteria for text selection.

3. TEXT SELECTION

The texts in the corpus generally date from 1990 to 1994 inclusive. This means that the printed texts were originally published, and the spoken texts originally recorded, during this period.[1] The corpus does not include reprints, second or later editions, or repeat broadcasts. For handwritten material, these dates refer to the date of composition.

The authors and speakers of the texts are aged 18 or over, and have been educated through the medium of English to at least the end of secondary schooling. We use these two criteria because they are quantifiable. We do not attempt an evaluation of the language in a text as a criterion for inclusion or exclusion. Age and educational level can be accurately measured, and they can be applied in the same way in every country. The project, then, is not based on any prior notion of what 'educated' or 'standard' English is. We do expect, however, that studies of the corpus will contribute towards a more robust definition of such concepts.

All speakers and writers are natives of the country in whose corpus they are included. 'Native' for our purposes means either that they were born in the country concerned, or if not, that they moved there at an early age and received their school education through the medium of English in that country. In the British corpus, for example, the authors and speakers were born in England, Scotland, or Wales. Those who were born elsewhere have been living in Britain for most of their lives and were educated in Britain.

The component corpora are intended to be representative of the English used in each participating country. We have therefore attempted to include as full a range as possible of the social variables which define the population. In each category we have sampled both males and females, and included people from a wide range of age-groups. In dialogues, for example, we have male–female, female–female and male–male exchanges. Similarly the speakers come from different age-groups and from different regional backgrounds. However, we have not attempted to ensure that the proportions of these social variables are the same in the corpus as in the population as a whole. Men and women are not equally represented in many professions such as technology, politics, and law, so they do not produce equal amounts of discourse in these fields. Similarly, the various age-groups found in the population as a whole are not found in the same proportions among students or academic authors.

4. THE TEXT CATEGORIES

The choice of text categories for the corpus was influenced by the need to sample as many as possible of the various uses of English in each participating country. The international nature of the corpus had important implications for its overall

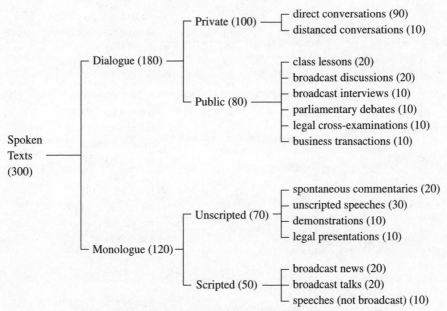

FIG. 3.1. A schematic representation of the categories of spoken texts

design. A corpus dealing exclusively with British English, for example, might include many more text types than are represented in ICE. We might wish to include electronic mail messages, faxes, and answer-phone messages, for example, in order to give a more complete view of British English in use in the 1990s. However, these text types are not available in all the ICE countries, and indeed still have restricted use even in Britain. For these reasons, they have been excluded from the general design.

The ICE text categories are shown in Figs. 3.1 and 3.2. The numbers in parentheses indicate the number of 2,000-word texts in each category. These categories have been included in every component corpus, and may be referred to as the 'core' corpus. All ICE teams are collecting the core categories, but are also free to include other types as well. The component corpora may be extended to include particular text types or particular sections of the population which are not found in the core corpus. The American team, for instance, intend to collect a larger amount of spoken material than in the core corpus. Other possible extensions of the core corpus are specialized corpora of, say, newspaper English, and the language of immigrant communities and children (Greenbaum, 1991).

The text categories are arranged in a hierarchical structure. It should be emphasized that this structure is not irrevocably fixed, and is intended only as an initial classification of the texts. It is partly based on our intuitions about the differences between text types. However, studies of the corpora may reveal that some categories will have to be conflated, or that some will require further sub-classification. For

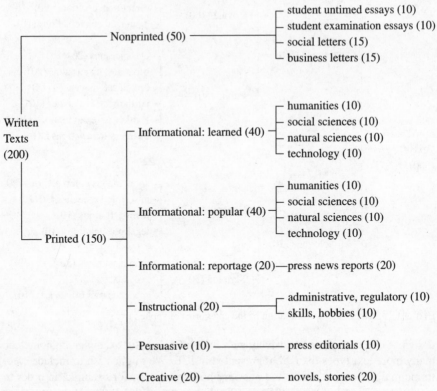

FIG. 3.2. A schematic representation of the categories of written texts

this reason, the retrieval software, ICECUP, has been designed to create subcorpora which cut across the original classifications, as well as taking account of other parameters, such as speakers' ages, educational levels, and regional backgrounds.

The first major division in the corpus is between the two modes of speech and writing. There are 300 spoken texts and 200 written, giving 600,000 words of speech and 400,000 words of writing. However, 50 of the spoken texts are scripted. These have some of the attributes of both spoken and written English, and as such provide an overlap between the two modes.

4.1. *Spoken Texts*

For ethical and legal reasons, the recording of spoken texts was non-surreptitious. Permission was received from the speakers in non-broadcast material before the recordings were made. In cases where pre-recorded material was used, such as parliamentary debates and legal proceedings, permission was received afterwards, though in all cases the speakers were aware that their speech was being recorded. It is possible that non-surreptitious recording can lead to self-consciousness on the part of speakers. To eliminate any possible distortion of the data which this might cause, we decided not to use the first fifteen minutes of recorded conversations. 2,000 words corresponds to about fifteen minutes of conversation, so in most cases at least twice this amount was actually recorded.

The spoken texts are divided into dialogues and monologues. The dialogues consist of both private and public types. This distinction is based on the settings in which the interactions take place. Private dialogues—face-to-face conversations and telephone calls—are ones in which there is no audience. Though the exchange may be overheard, the speakers only address each other; in general they do not speak for the benefit of anyone else who may be present. In contrast with this, public dialogues are specifically intended to be heard by others who are present and who are not participating in the exchange. Legal cross-examinations and parliamentary debates provide the clearest examples of this type. In both cases the speakers address an individual—a witness, a lawyer, or a fellow politician—but the exchange is intended to be heard by everyone present. In some cases, the speakers are aware of an even larger audience, in that the proceedings are recorded for public broadcasting. Two of the categories in the core corpus consist of broadcast material. These are discussions, which involve a chairman and a panel, and interviews, which involve two speakers.

In public dialogues, the topic of discussion is known in advance by all the participants. For business meetings and parliamentary debates, there may even be a written agenda or schedule to guide the proceedings. For broadcast discussions and classroom lessons, the general topic is known in advance, and the speaker turns are guided by the chairman or teacher. In contrast, private dialogues range freely over unprepared subjects.

In monologues, the chief distinction is between unscripted and scripted material. Unscripted texts include spontaneous commentaries, lectures, demonstrations, and legal presentations. In spontaneous commentaries, the commentators describe what they see—a sports event or a formal ceremony, for example—as it occurs. They have no opportunity to prepare their speech, since they must react instantly to events over which they have no control. Most of the other types, however, do permit some degree of planning. In lectures and legal presentations, we can expect the speakers to refer from time to time to prepared notes, but the speech itself is extempore. In contrast, scripted texts are fully scripted. That is, they are lectures and talks in which the speaker reads directly from a prepared script. For these texts, we have used the spoken version rather than the written script, since even a very faithful reading from a script will contain speech phenomena such as pauses, hesitations, and false starts which are not in the written version.

4.2. Written Texts

The major distinction in the written component of the corpus is between printed and non-printed texts. There are 150 printed texts and 50 non-printed ones. The two

31

types differ in their intended readership and in their mode of composition. Printed material is written for a large, unrestricted audience that the writer does not know. In some cases, such as newspapers, popular writing, and fiction, this audience is the general public. Academic writing reaches a smaller, more well-defined readership, but the exact individual readership is unknown to the writer at the time of composition. The intended readership for non-printed material is much smaller. For social letters, it is usually one individual who is personally known to the writer. On the other hand, the addressee is not necessarily known personally to the writer of business letters. Student essays are generally written for one teacher and examination scripts for one or two examiners (whose identity may not be known to the students).

In their modes of composition, the distinction between printed and non-printed material is also clear. Non-printed texts are a direct product of the individual writer. They are usually not edited by anyone else and, especially in the case of examination scripts, they afford the writer little time for revision. In contrast with this, writers of printed works are usually required to follow the house style of the publisher or newspaper for which they are writing. Printed material may have been edited by a number of different people, and the final version is often the product of several earlier revisions. Some non-printed texts, of course, are now regularly produced on wordprocessors (business letters, for example), and can benefit from the use of automatic spelling, grammar, and style checkers. In all cases, these facts about the mode of composition have been recorded with each text.

Informational writing has been divided into learned writing, popular writing, and press reportage. Within learned and popular writing ten texts are taken from each of the following subject areas: humanities, social science, natural science, and technology. Learned writing is produced by specialists for specialists. In the humanities, for example, it may include journal articles by academic historians written for other academic historians. The equivalent of this in popular writing would be a work written for readers who may not have any formal qualifications in history but who none the less have an interest in, and some knowledge of, the subject. In general, popular writing has a wider and more varied readership than learned writing, though the subject areas within it can still be quite specialized. The British corpus, for instance, includes an article entitled 'Digital Compact Cassette: The Whole Story', published in *Hi-Fi News & Record Review*. This was clearly intended for a relatively restricted readership with specialized interests, but it is a readership which is drawn from the general public, and not from experts in technology.

The category of press news reports includes leading articles, general domestic and foreign news, sports reports, and business news. It does not include editorials, which are in the 'persuasive writing' category of the corpus. The news reports were written by staff reporters and journalists; we have been careful to exclude reports provided by international news agencies such as Reuters and Associated Press. We have sampled both daily and weekly newspapers, and have attempted to achieve a good geographical spread by including national, regional, and local newspapers.

Instructional writing is divided into administrative and regulatory texts and publications dealing with skills and hobbies. Administrative and regulatory writing is corporate in origin. It is written on behalf of, for example, government departments or other administrative bodies and it aims to provide information for the general public on such matters as social welfare and health benefits, together with instructions on how to apply for these. It also includes printed regulations such as library membership rules and regulations for university entry. This category does not include Acts of Parliament or legal documents. We excluded these because of their highly specialized use of language.

Texts in the skills and hobbies category also offer instruction, but these are directed towards a smaller and more specialized readership. They include publications such as car manuals, cookery books, and gardening manuals. They often present instructions in a step-by-step format and may rely heavily on diagrams and other illustrations.

Press editorials have been distinguished from general news reports on the grounds that their main intention is to persuade rather than to inform. They are less directly tied to current events, and they afford the writer the opportunity to be discursive in a way that news journalism does not.

The last category in the corpus is creative writing—novels and short stories. It includes a variety of fiction types, such as science fiction, thrillers, and detective novels. In addition, we have included both narrative or descriptive prose and passages of dialogue.

5. COPYRIGHT AND TEXT COLLECTION

Copyright permission was obtained for all the texts in the corpus. Although this added greatly to the time needed to compile the corpora, it was necessary because of the international nature of the project. The texts will be distributed worldwide in computerized form, together with the various stages of annotation which have been added to them. Our copyright permission allows the texts to be used for research purposes only. A copyright statement and full acknowledgement of source are included with every text in the corpus.

The experience of most ICE teams has been that copyright holders—authors, speakers, publishers, and broadcasting companies—were generally very willing to grant permission for the use of their output in academic research. In Britain, a small number of them gave blanket permission to use any of their output. However, all the teams have had to collect many more texts than are required in most categories, since some copyright holders are slow to respond to requests for permission. In general, it was more difficult to obtain permission from copyright holders in the commercial sector, where confidentiality is a major concern. For spoken data, we offered speakers the option of remaining anonymous in the corpus. This meant that their real names would not appear in our records, and identifying names occurring in the recording would be changed, with appropriate markup, by the transcriber.

The written categories in the corpus were the easiest to obtain, not least because they could be collected retrospectively. Material published in 1990, say, could be collected and computerized at a later date. The computerization was also relatively straightforward; printed works were optically scanned onto computers, and in some cases, such as newspapers, the texts were already in computerized form when we acquired them. Handwritten material presented greater difficulties. The social letters, in particular, were difficult to obtain in the quantities required, since most personal communication is now carried out by telephone. To collect the social letters, we used a mailshot of 500 names taken from a social survey.

Of all the categories in the corpus, conversations were by far the most difficult to collect. This was mainly because of the number of different texts needed (90). To ensure a good range of speakers and situations, a large number of people were enlisted to make recordings. Inevitably, these speakers appear in several texts, but we never used the same combination of speakers in more than one text. Some of the recordings had to be rejected, either because of poor quality or because they contained extensive contributions by foreign speakers. The number of speakers in the conversations proved to be a major consideration. We intended to include interactions involving four, five, and six speakers, as well as smaller groups. In practice, however, we found that if a text contains a large number of speakers, it will also contain a great deal of overlapping speech. This means that long sections of the recording will be unclear and therefore untranscribable. As well as this, the more speakers there are, the more difficult it is to identify them accurately. We concluded that for practical reasons the conversations should be limited to a maximum of four speakers.

Pre-recorded material was the easiest to collect, and it had many other advantages from our point of view. In general, the recording quality was very good, since it was made by specialists using professional equipment. The parliamentary debates in the British corpus were obtained directly from the House of Commons, where each day's proceedings are recorded as a matter of course. By using these, we were not restricted to the edited versions which are broadcast on television and radio. It also allowed us to sample the speech of less prominent politicians; the more well-known ones were already well represented in other categories of the corpus, such as broadcast interviews and broadcast news. The speakers were not always named in the recordings, and in these cases their identities were established by consulting the relevant transcripts in Hansard.

We also obtained pre-recorded material from the law courts. These were only available for cases in open court, to which members of the public have access, and which may be freely reported in the press. Cases in the family courts, and ones involving minors, were not available. In the British corpus, the proceedings deal with commercial law, compensation claims, and libel actions. Each recording was accompanied by a court log-book, in which details of participants were given.

The time required to compile the corpora was determined not only by copyright problems, but also by the number of different samples and the range of sources required. In comparison with other corpora, the individual components of ICE, with one million words each, are relatively small. However, one million words could be compiled very quickly if they were taken from a small number of sources. In contrast, the ICE corpora sample a very wide range of different sources. The corpus design dictates that we use at least 500 different texts, and because many of these are composite, the actual number of individual samples is much greater. The British corpus, for example, contains a total of 989 different samples. Though it makes the compilation stage much more time-consuming, our broad sampling procedure ensures that the corpora are representative of the English in general use in each participating country.

NOTE

1. A few teams who joined the project at a late stage may have some texts from a later period.

REFERENCES

GREENBAUM, S. (1991), 'The Compilation of the International Corpus of English and its Components' (London: Survey of English Usage, University College London).

—— (1992), 'A New Corpus of English: ICE', in J. SVARTVIK (ed.), *Directions in Corpus Linguistics: Proceedings of Nobel Symposium 82*, Stockholm, 4–8 August 1991 (Berlin: Mouton de Gruyter).

LEITNER, G. (1992), 'International Corpus of English: Corpus Design—Problems and Suggested Solutions', in G. LEITNER (ed.), *New Directions in English Language Corpora: Methodology, Results, Software Developments*, 75–96 (Berlin: Mouton de Gruyter).

PETERS, P. (1991), 'ICE Issues in the Collecting and Transcribing of Texts', unpublished discussion paper.

SCHMIED, J. (1990), 'Corpus Linguistics and Non-native Varieties of English', *World Englishes*, 9: 255–68.

4

Markup Systems

GERALD NELSON

INTRODUCTION

Markup is the first level of annotation applied to the component corpora in ICE. It may be divided into two distinct types: textual markup, which is added to the texts themselves, and bibliographical and biographical markup, which is stored externally in the form of a file header for each text. The system for textual markup is based on a proposal by Rosta (1990) and is fully described in two manuals, one each for spoken and written texts (Nelson, 1991*a*, 1991*b*). The system for encoding bibliographical and biographical information is described in Nelson (1991*c*). In this paper I will discuss both markup types in turn, giving examples from the British ICE corpus (ICE-GB). Finally, I will discuss some of the ways in which markup is used in text retrieval.

1. TEXTUAL MARKUP

Textual markup encodes features of the original text that are lost when it is converted into a computerized text file. The texts are stored as plain ASCII files, so in written texts, for example, typographic features such as boldface, italics, and underlining are lost during computerization. In spoken texts, the transcription must be marked up to indicate such features as pauses, speaker turns, and overlapping segments. These textual features are encoded by adding markup symbols to the text. All markup symbols are enclosed within angled brackets. In most cases they appear in pairs, with an opening symbol *<symbol>* and a closing symbol *</symbol>*. For example, if the word 'every' appears in boldface in the original printed text, then it will appear as *<bold>every</bold>* in the corpus. Similarly headings are enclosed within *<h>* and *</h>*, while paragraphs are enclosed within *<p>* and *</p>*. The markup symbols are inserted manually, but the process is partially automated by the Markup Assistant program. This is a set of WordPerfect macros which assigns whole markup symbols to single keys. When the markup has been applied, the CHECKMUP program in ICECUBE checks that all the symbols are valid and that every opening symbol has a corresponding closing one. A complete list of the ICE markup symbols, with a brief explanation of their meaning, is given in Appendix 1. This list is the minimum set which has been applied by all the ICE teams. Some teams have extended the set in order to mark additional features. In the American corpus, prosodic markers have been added to the spoken transcriptions.

A small number of markup symbols indicate locations in the text. That is, they do not extend over any words, and so they are indicated by a single symbol rather than by a pair of symbols. An example of this is the markup for the position of a line-break, <*l*>, which is indicated if it occurs within a word. Thus *im*<*l*>*possible* shows that this word was originally split by a hyphen over two lines, and that the hyphen appeared after the prefix.

The most common location marker is the text unit marker <#>. The text unit is the basic unit of every text. In written texts it corresponds to the orthographic sentence. In spoken texts it is the approximate equivalent of an orthographic sentence, though in many cases this is syntactically incomplete. The beginning of every text unit is marked with <#>. These are numbered in sequence throughout the text and they provide a reference system for citations from the corpus. In ICECUP, the retrieval software, the text unit is the default setting for the display of search results.[1] This means that if the user searches for a particular word, it will be displayed in the context of the complete text unit in which it appears. Extract [1] shows the title, authors' names, and the first paragraph of a printed academic paper. As well as text unit markers, it displays markup for headings, boldface, underlining, footnote references, superscript, and paragraph boundaries.[2]

[1] <#1:1> <h> <bold> AI TECHNIQUES APPLIED TO THE CLASSIFICA-
TION OF WELDING DEFECTS FROM AUTOMATED NDT DATA
</h> </bold> <#2:1> <bold> <h> Dr A McNab and Iain Dunlop </bold> </h>
<#3:1> <h> <ul> <bold> 1. <#4:1> <sent> Introduction </bold> </ul> </h>
 <#5:1> Automated NDT using specialised mechanical scanners or ROVs
has a number of attractions for land-based and offshore application. <#6:1>
These include the permanent recording of position and measured flaw data,
improved test speed, accuracy, and reliability of data collection. <#7:1> This
is particularly true in hostile environments where operator access is difficult
and large areas of the structure must be scanned <fnr> <sp> (1) </sp> </fnr>.
 [ICE-GB-W2A-036-1]

1.1. *Foreign and Indigenous Words*

Since ICE deals exclusively with varieties of English, special attention has been paid to instances of foreign and indigenous words which appear in the corpora. Foreign and non-naturalized words are marked as in [2]:

[2] And the Latin word for those huge lengths of papyrus glued together which you
have to unroll in other words a scroll is a <foreign> volumen </foreign> so this
gives us our word volute [ICE-GB-S2A-024-50]

Of course many foreign words, such as *staccato*, *maelstrom*, *rouge*, and *genre*, have become naturalized over time, and are now considered part of the English lexicon. These require no markup in ICE.

In some ICE countries, such as India and Cameroon, English is used as a second official language, and may coexist with several local ones. In these countries, words from local languages are marked as *<indig>* (indigenous) rather than *<foreign>*, though they will be marked as foreign words in every other ICE corpus in which they appear. If words from more than one indigenous language appear in a corpus, the specific language from which they come can be incorporated into the markup symbol, e.g. *<indig=Urdu>*.

Foreign and indigenous words are grammatically analysed according to the word class of their English equivalents. Apart from recording their use in English, the markup also ensures that we produce accurate counts for English words and word classes in the corpus. Many foreign and indigenous words have the same form as English ones, and must be clearly distinguished from them in frequency lists.

1.2. *Extra-Corpus Text and Quotations*

In some texts, material has to be excluded from analysis. An example of this might be a speech by an American politician in a British news broadcast. Since the British corpus only samples British speakers and writers, the words of foreign speakers are transcribed with the rest of the text to provide context, but they are enclosed within extra-corpus markup <X> and </X> to exclude them from further analysis. Words marked in this way will not appear in frequency counts and will not be grammatically or syntactically analysed. Similarly, words by British speakers are excluded from all the other component corpora in ICE.

Quotations are treated in a similar way, since they are not usually the writer's or speaker's own words, and may date from before the ICE sampling period, 1990–4. In the following example, the quotation is in the writer's own words, but it is taken from his 1987 diary. It is marked as a quotation and as extra-corpus material, in order to distinguish it from the rest of the text, which dates from 1990.

[3] <#116:1> In case I was tempted to gloss over certain thoughts, I decided to share the diary which had helped me admit to myself what I was now admitting to the listeners.
<#117:1> <sent> Here are some of those thoughts. <X> <quote>
<#X118:1> <sent> 6 November 1987:
<#X119:1> <sent> Today I went home and, having been asked to be chairman of my local comprehensive school's annual quiz, I felt rather dubious, rather frightened that I might let myself down by not being able to speak the words clearly [. . .] </quote> </X> [ICE-GB-W2B-001-116 ff.]

In some cases a quotation may be integrated into the syntax of a writer's own sentence:

[4] THERE was a time during the 1970s when the buses in West Yorkshire carried an advertisement for an independent airline which read: <quote> 'Fly via Schiphol, London's third airport.' </quote> [ICE-GB-W2E-008-23]

Here the quotation—even though it dates from the 1970s—forms part of the syntax, and to exclude it would result in a syntactically incomplete text unit. For this reason, it is marked only as a quotation, and not, as in [3], as extra-corpus material. For the purposes of parsing, integrated quotations like these are retained, though the fact that they are quotations is clearly marked.

1.3. *Written texts*

In general, written texts require relatively little markup. Most of the markup which is applied is for typographic features such as boldface, italics, and underlining, and for aspects of the layout, such as paragraph boundaries, headings, and footnotes. The beginning of each sentence is marked, but this can be done automatically with a good degree of accuracy by globally inserting the symbol after each period, question mark, and exclamation mark. Any errors which may occur, because of decimal points, for example, can be manually corrected when the markup is being checked. In handwritten texts, deletions and insertions made by the writer are marked where they occur.

1.4. *Spoken texts*

Spoken texts, and especially dialogues, require much more markup than written ones. The markup is applied during transcription; see Nelson (1995). The transcription scheme is orthographic. It observes the normal conventions of orthographic spelling, capitalization, word-spacing, and hyphenation. To improve readability, capital letters are used at the beginning of text units and for words that are normally capitalized in writing. No punctuation is included. The transcription takes no account of phonetics, and the only prosodic features marked are pauses. These are indicated using a binary system of short and long pauses. The short pause <,> is defined as a perceptible break in phonation equivalent in length to a single syllable uttered at the speaker's tempo. The long pause <,,> is the equivalent of two or more syllables, again measured at the speaker's tempo. Extract [5] is taken from a scripted monologue and illustrates some of these transcription conventions:

[5] <#32:1> <sent> I do not regard it <,> as in any sense wrong for Britain to make criticisms of that kind <,> plainly and courteously <,> nor in any sense wrong <,> for us to do so if necessary alone <,> <#33:1> <sent> As <w> I've </w> already made clear <,> I have like the Prime Minister and other right honourable friends <,> fought too many European battles in a minority of one to have any illusions on that score <,> <#34:1> <sent> But it is crucially important <,> that we should conduct those arguments <,> upon the basis of a clear understanding <,> of the true relationship between this country <,> the Community

<,> and our Community partners <,> <#35:1> <sent> And it is here I fear <,> that my right honourable friend <,> increasingly risks leading herself and others astray <,> in matters of substance <,> as well as of style <,,>

[ICE-GB-S2A-050-32-35]

1.4.1. *Overlapping Speech*

In dialogues, speaker turns are indicated by speaker identifications <$A>, <$B>, etc. Very often there is overlap between all or part of these turns, especially in informal conversations, when speakers talk simultaneously and interrupt each other. This means that the strings to be transcribed occur simultaneously in the recording, and it is the task of the markup scheme to represent this phenomenon in a linear transcription. To achieve this, each overlapping string is separately enclosed within <[> and </[>:

[6*a*] <$A> Is that because you've got lots or <,> <[>nothing stands out</[>
<$B> <[>Yeah I suppose</[> No I can't say anything really stands out in mind [ICE-GB-S1A-016-126-128]

Then the overlapping pair of strings is enclosed within <{> and </{>:

[6*b*] <$A> Is that because you've got lots or <,> <{> <[>nothing stands out</[>
<$B> <[>Yeah I suppose</[> </{> No I can't say anything really stands out in mind

In this example, speaker A's *nothing stands out* overlaps with speaker B's *Yeah I suppose*. This is a rather simple case. A more complex example is shown in [7], where there are two overlaps within a single turn. The individual overlaps are transcribed after speaker B's complete turn. Then they are numbered in sequence to show the corresponding overlapping pairs:

[7] <$A> And what about uhm holidays just you and her Would she do that
<$B> Uhm well I <{1> <[1> suggested </[1> that but she didn't want to and somebody else said well maybe that was a bit of a mouthful and you know try just an <{2> <[2> evening on your own </[2> together
<$A> <[1> Like skiing or something </[1> </{1>
<$A> <[2> Or a day trip </[2> </{2>
[ICE-GB-S1A-031-157-61]

The overlapping pairs in this sequence are: (1) B's *suggested* and A's *Like skiing or something*, and (2) B's *evening on your own* and A's *Or a day trip*.

A frequent phenomenon in dialogue is overlapping with a pause. Speakers often pause just long enough to allow another person to interject a very brief utterance such as *uhm, yes, oh,* or *right*. In the ICE markup scheme, these overlaps are treated in the same way as overlapping words. In [8] speaker A pauses after *worked out,* allowing speaker B to interject *Uhm* into the silence. Speaker A's short pause is indicated by <,> in the first line:

[8] <$A> The maintenance for the children that you've worked out <,> <{> <[> uhm <,> is something that you and I have discussed on the phone I mean <,> <$B> <[> Uhm </[> </{> [ICE-GB-S1B-072-1-2]

The opening symbol <[> has no corresponding closing symbol, since the overlap has no scope over any words.

This system for marking overlaps was adopted because complete speaker turns are essential for parsing. The marking scheme indicates the overlapping without making the turns discontinuous. In [8], for example, speaker A's turn is transcribed as a single syntactic unit, despite the fact that it is interrupted immediately after the subject, *The maintenance for the children that you've worked out.*

1.4.2. *Normalizing the Text*

Spoken English is characterized by a wide range of nonfluencies which are not found in writing. Among these are repetitions [9], self-corrections [10], and hesitations [11].

[9] If one's gone through *those those* uh procedures then it wouldn't take very long I think to uh clean up the rest <,> [ICE-GB-S1A-024-56]

[10] Unfortunately there *is tends to be* a bias towards publishing only positive results [ICE-GB-S2A-033-29]

[11] *A a and* more likely I suppose primary because your first degree has got to relate pretty closely if you're going to get on a course in most cases
[ICE-GB-S1A-033-145]

These phenomena are transcribed as they occur, and the markup for them will be of particular interest to researchers studying interaction between speakers. However, they may be seen as disruptions of the underlying syntax, and as such are problematic from the point of view of automatic parsing. We use the general term 'normalization' to describe the method of using markup to deal with them. Repetitions are marked for normative deletion. The first instance is enclosed in <-> and </->, and the second in <=> and </=>. Then the whole sequence is enclosed in <}> and </}>, to show that the two lexical items form a repetition.

[9a] If one's gone through <}> <-> those </-> <=> those </=> </}> uh procedures then it wouldn't take very long I think to uh clean up the rest <,>

Repetitions are only marked when they disrupt the syntax. Repetitions which are used for emphasis, such as *no no no* and *really really*, need no markup.

The same markup is used for self-corrections. The first version is marked <-> and </-> and the 'correct' version is marked <=> and </=>. Again the whole sequence is enclosed within <}> and </}>.

[9*b*] Unfortunately there <}> <-> is </-> <=> tends to be </=> </}> a bias towards
publishing only positive results

We mark hesitations in a similar way, but since they also involve at least one incomplete word, they require extra markup for this. Incomplete words are enclosed
within <.> and </.>:

[11*a*] <}> <-> <.> A a </.> </-> <=> and </=> </}> more likely I suppose primary
because your first degree has got to relate pretty closely if you're going to
get on a course in most cases

Normalization is mainly used in spoken texts, though it can also be applied to
written ones. Misspellings, for example, may occur in handwritten texts such as
student essays, and to a lesser extent in printed material. In these cases, the original
misspelling is retained but it is marked for normative deletion. The correct form is
then supplied by the annotator and is enclosed within <+> and </+>:

[12] This seems to have <}> <-> occured </-> <+> occurred</+> </}> throughout
the period with several localities (Wales, Loire, Normandy and Brittany) as
the ultimate destination of the Britons. [ICE-GB-W1A-001-70]

Items marked for normative deletion do not form part of the input to the automatic
parser, though the fact that they were in the original is recorded by the markup. Our
principle has been to normalize the original text as little as possible, and to do so
only when it was essential for parsing.

1.5. *Special Characters*

Some characters, such as accents and typographical symbols, cannot easily be reproduced on a computer screen and have been automatically converted to SGML
(Standard Generalized Markup Language). In this format, a brief description of the
character appears between an ampersand (&) and a semi-colon (;). Thus the character δ becomes *δ*. Accents are treated in the same way. For example, the *é*
in *blasé* is converted to *&e-acute;* and the whole word becomes *blas&e-acute;*.
These special symbols can be selected for retrieval from a list in ICECUP.

2. BIBLIOGRAPHICAL AND BIOGRAPHICAL DATA

Unlike the textual markup we have discussed so far, bibliographical and biographical markup is not stored with the corpus texts themselves. It is stored separately
in the form of a file header, of which there is one for each text. The purpose of
the file header is to give a complete description of each text in the corpus. The
information is stored in the file header in separate fields such as 'category', 'date',
'publisher', etc. These details were initially entered into a standard, commercial

database such as dBase IV or Paradox. Each ICE team is using a common database structure to ensure compatibility across the corpora. The file headers were produced automatically using the EXTRACT program, which was specially written for this purpose. Like the textual markup, the data in the file headers is enclosed within opening and closing symbols, e.g. *<date>1991</date>*.

The information in the file headers may be divided into the following levels:

1. Text Description
2. Text Source
3. Text Internals
4. Biographical Information

A complete list of the fields in the file headers is shown in Appendix 2. Appendix 3 shows a sample header for a printed text. In the following sections I give a brief overview of the kinds of information in each of the four levels.

2.1. *Text Description*

The Text Description locates the text in the hierarchy of the corpus as a whole by specifying its text category and subcategories. If the text is a social letter from the British corpus, then its category will be:

> *ICE-GB—Written—Non-printed—Nonprofessional Writing—Correspondence—Social Letters*

For details of the text categories, see Chapter 3. This level also specifies the version of each text, for example whether it is lexical, tagged, or parsed.

2.2. *Text Source*

Text Source information records bibliographical data about the sources of texts in the corpus. In this level we include the source title and publisher of printed texts, and their place and date of publication. For spoken texts, we record the TV or radio channel on which it was broadcast, as well as the date and time of broadcasting or recording. This level also includes a copyright statement for every text.

2.3. *Text Internals*

This level contains information about the specific extract used in the corpus. The specific extract may be an article taken from an edited book, for example. The title of the book will appear in Text Source, while the title of the article, with its page numbers, will appear in Text Internals. In the case of dialogues, this level also indicates the relationship between the speakers. Two possible values are available for this field: *equals* and *disparates*. Conversations among friends or members of a family may be said to be between equals, while in a doctor–patient or teacher–student dialogue, the relationship is between disparates.

2.4. *Biographical Information*

The file headers contain biographical details about each speaker and author in the corpus, where these are known. These details include sex, birthplace, nationality, occupation, and age or age-range. The following age-ranges are noted: *18–25, 26–45, 46–65*, and *Over 65*. The educational level of our informants is an important parameter in the corpus, and this has been catered for in two fields in the file header. An 'Educational Level' field contains one of the values *secondary* or *university*, meaning that the author or speaker has completed secondary or university education. A further descriptive field, 'Education', allows the annotator to give more specific details, e.g. the university attended and the type of degree held.

3. Markup and Text Retrieval

Textual markup greatly enhances the value of the corpus as a research tool, but from the point of view of the ordinary user, it can make the individual texts difficult to read. This is particularly true of dialogues, which often have extensive markup for overlapping speech and normalization. Extract [13*a*] shows one text unit from a fully marked-up conversation:

[13*a*] <$A> <#208:2:A> <sent> Well I think uhm that <}> <-> he </-> <=> he </=> </}> sings with a choir <,> <{1> <[1> and the </[1> choir and this is the <{2> <[2> Baroque singers of York </[2> or something or the Bach Choir the York Bach Choir <,> <{3> <[3> and uh <}> <-> he he <.> arran </.> </-> <=> the leader arranges </=> </}> uhm venues and gigs <,,> [ICE-GB- S1A-032]

To improve the readability of the text, ICECUP has been designed with a default setting for the display of citations. The default display is the original version of the text, prior to markup. It does, however, include text unit markers for reference. So the user who retrieves [13*a*] will see only the following display:

[13*b*] <#207:2:A> Well I think uhm that he he sings with a choir and the choir and this is the Baroque Singers of York or something or the Bach Choir the York Bach Choir and uh he he arran the leader arranges uhm venues and gigs

The user can, however, choose to override the default display and see all the markup, or he can specify one or more types of markup to display.

The file headers can be read by using the 'Text Info' feature in ICECUP. As the example in Appendix 3 shows, file headers can be quite complex, and may contain more information than individual researchers will normally require. For this reason, the complete file headers are only read by ICECUP itself during the creation of subcorpora. The user does not read the file header in the format shown in Appendix 3. Instead, ICECUP displays by default only a selected set of the most important fields in the header. These include biographical details, text category, source title, and date. Appendix 4 shows the Text Info screen corresponding to the file header in Appendix 3. Both the bibliographical and the biographical information windows can be scrolled to reveal the full set of fields.

All the markup symbols can be retrieved from the corpus using ICECUP. They can be retrieved individually or in any combination. Students of dialogue can retrieve overlapping segments and all of the nonfluencies which have been discussed. Those interested in written discourse may wish to study how paragraphs begin and end, for example, or the language of newspaper headlines. These searches can be carried out by specifying the appropriate markup symbol from a complete list provided in ICECUP. File header information is used in creating subcorpora, that is, in isolating parts of the corpus for analysis. Researchers can restrict their analysis to a particular national corpus or to part of a national corpus. In addition, they can create a subcorpus which cuts across national corpora, for example, a subcorpus of scripted monologues in British and American English. The two types of markup can also be combined with each other in more sophisticated searches. For example, a researcher interested in overlapping speech in conversation might wish to see if the relationship between the speakers has any significant effect on the amount or type of overlapping which they produce. To retrieve the relevant data for this, a subcorpus of conversations must first be created. The user can then create two further subcorpora derived from this: one in which the speakers are equals, and one in which they are disparates. Finally, the markup symbols for overlapping speech can be retrieved separately from each of these subcorpora.

NOTES

1. Many texts in the corpus are composite, that is, they comprise separate samples combined to create a single 2,000-word text. These shorter samples are referred to as *subtexts*. The text units are numbered in a continuous sequence throughout the text, whether it is composite or not. A second number indicates the number of the subtext, for example: *<#65:2>*. This is text unit 65, and it occurs in the second subtext. By convention, all texts have at least one subtext, so the subtext number is always at least 1. In spoken texts, the text unit numbers include additionally the speaker identification, e.g. *<#12:3:A>*. If the text unit occurs within extra-corpus material (see Sect. 1.2), then the text unit number has the form <#X:34:1>.
2. To improve the readability of some citations, I have omitted markup symbols which are not relevant to the type under discussion.

REFERENCES

NELSON, G. (1991*a*), 'Manual for Spoken Texts' (London: Survey of English Usage, University College London).

—— (1991*b*), 'Manual for Written Texts' (London: Survey of English Usage, University College London).

—— (1991*c*), 'File Header Information' (London: Survey of English Usage, University College London).

—— (1995), 'The International Corpus of English: Markup for Spoken Language', in G. LEECH and J. MYERS (eds.), *Spoken English on Computer: Transcription, Markup and Application*, 220–3 (London: Longman).

ROSTA, A. (1990), 'The System for Preparation and Annotation of ICE Texts' (London: Survey of English Usage, University College London).

Appendix 1: ICE Markup Symbols

<#>	Text unit marker
<sent>	Sentence marker
<I>.....</I>	Subtext markers. All texts, whether they are composite or not, are enclosed in these symbols
<space>	Marks unusual spacing, e.g. within a word
<l>	Line-break, if it occurs within a word
<p>.....</p>	Paragraph
<h>.....</h>	Heading
<sb>.....</sb>	Subscript
<sp>.....</sp>	Superscript
<ul>.....</ul>	Underlining
<bold>.....</bold>	Boldface
<it>.....</it>	Italics
<smallcaps>.....</smallcaps>	Small capital
<typeface>.....</typeface>	A major change of typeface
...	Marginalia appear immediately after the sentence(s) to which they refer
<footnote>.....</footnote>	Footnotes appear immediately after the footnote reference
<fnr>.....</fnr>	Footnote reference
<mention>.....</mention>	A word cited as a word, e.g. '*Never* is an adverb'
<foreign>.....</foreign>	Foreign word
<indig>.....</indig>	Indigenous word
<quote>.....</quote>	Quotation
<X>.....</X>	Extra-corpus text
<O>.....</O>	Untranscribed text, e.g. diagrams, graphs, laughter
<?>.....</?>	Uncertain transcription
<unclear>.....</unclear>	Unclear word or syllable
<del>.....</del>	Text deleted by the author (handwritten texts only)
<&>.....</&>	An editorial comment by the corpus annotator
<@>.....</@>	A name or word changed by the corpus annotator to provide anonymity for speakers
<w>.....</w>	Encloses a word with an internal or external apostrophe, e.g. *John's, we're, boys'*, unless the word receives a single grammatical tag, *e.g. can't, won't, mightn't*, which are tagged as negative modals
<(>.....</(>	Discontinuous word, e.g. *fan-bloody-tastic*
<)>.....</)>	The normalized version of a discontinuous word, e.g. *bloody fantastic*
<.>.....</.>	Incomplete word
<->.....</->	Normative deletion
<+>.....</+>	Normative insertion
<=>.....</=>	Part of a repetition or self-correction which is retained for parsing

<}>.....</}>	These symbols enclose every instance of normalization
<[>.....</[>	Overlapping string
<{>.....</{>	Two or more overlapping string sets
<$>	Speaker identification; they are identified as <$A>, <$B> etc.
<,>	Short pause
<,,>	Long pause

The following table lists all the data fields which are included in the file headers. Some of the fields are specific to written or spoken sources. They do not appear in the file header if they are inapplicable to a particular text type.

Field name	Description
address	Full address of publisher or radio/TV channel.
affiliations	Affiliations, memberships etc., of authors and speakers, e.g. 'Member of the Royal Academy'.
age	The age of an author or speaker. If the exact age is not known, one of the following ranges is used: *18–25; 26–45; 46–65; Over 65.*
audience	A brief description of the audience being addressed, e.g. *public, students.*
audience.size	A number or approximate number for the size of the audience.
birthplace	Birthplace of author or speaker.
category	The text category. For a complete list, see Chapter 3.
channel	Full name of radio or TV channel.
circulation	The circulation figure, at the time of publication of the text, of a newspaper.
communicative.role	The role of a speaker in a communicative situation e.g. *interviewer, chairman.* In written texts this is *author* or *co-author.*
copyright.statement	This is usually in the form 'Reproduced by permission of . . .', but many publishers insist on their own wording.
course	Title of the course for which a student essay or examination script was written.
date	Date of publication, composition, or broadcasting.
editor	Editor of a collection of essays, papers, articles, etc.
education	A descriptive field in which a speaker's educational background is given e.g. 'Ph.D. Chemistry, Bristol University'.
educational.level	A specific value field in which one of the following must appear: *secondary, university.*
examination	Name of the examination for which a script was written.
examining.body	Title of the examining body for which a script was written.
forenames	Forenames of authors or speakers. If the name has been changed to preserve anonymity, it is enclosed in 'changed name' markup symbols, e.g. <@>John</@>.
format	This applies only to non-printed texts. It specifies whether the text was *handwritten, typed,* or *wordprocessed.*
free.comments	This field allows the annotator to add extra relevant information if necessary. It only contains information which cannot be accommodated in any other field.
frequency	The frequency of publication of a periodical or newspaper e.g. *daily, weekly, quarterly.*
gender	*Male, female.*
ISBN	International Standard Book Number.

Field name	Description
ISSN	International Standard Serial Number.
main.title	Full title of a subtext.
mother.tongue	A speaker or author's first language.
nationality	Nationality of author or speaker.
no.	The number of a periodical.
no.of.participants	The number of speakers taking part in a communicative situation. It includes extra-corpus speakers.
occupation	Occupation of author or speaker.
organising.body	The name of the group or body responsible for organising a lecture, debate etc.
other.languages	Languages, apart from the mother tongue, which are spoken fluently by an author or speaker.
place	Place of publication or recording.
publisher	Full name of publisher.
relationship	Relationship between speakers. The only permitted values are *equals* and *disparates*.
scope	This field specifies whether a newspaper is national, regional, or local in its readership.
series	The title of the series in which a monograph, collection etc, was published.
source.subtitle	Subtitle of the source of a subtext.
source.title	Full title of the source of a subtext.
source.type	One of the following: *monograph, collection, periodical, newspaper, student essay, examination script, letter, miscellaneous.*
specific.type	The type of source from which the subtext has been taken is specified in this field, e.g. brochure, leaflet. It is used only if the source type is *miscellaneous*.
subtext name	Each text has a unique mnemonic name. It is in the form 'ICE-GB-' (for the British corpus) followed by the mnemonic name. Example: ICE-GB-Coleridge.
subtext no.	If a corpus text is composite, each subtext is identified by the addition of a number to the textcode, e.g. W1A-001-1.
textcode	The code number of the text, e.g. ICE-GB-W1A-001.

APPENDIX 3: FILE HEADER SAMPLE

This is the header for *Dickens* by Peter Ackroyd (Sinclair-Stevenson, 1990), pp.12–16, which has been included in the British corpus.

```
<text.info>
  <file.description>
    <textcode>ICE-GB-W2B-008</textcode>
    <number.of.subtexts>1</number.of.subtexts>
    <category>printed:informational:popular:humanities</category>
    <wordcount>2101</wordcount>
    <version>tagged by the TOSCA tagger using the ICE tagset </version>
    <free.comments>           </free.comments>
  </file.description>
  <subtext.source=W2B-008>
    <source.type=monograph>
      <source.title>Dickens</source.title>
      <source.subtitle>           </source.subtitle>
      <series>           </series>
      <publication.statement>
        <publisher>Sinclair-Stevenson Ltd</publisher>
        <address>7/8 Kendrick Mews, London SW7 3HG</address>
        <place>London</place>
        <date>1990</date>
        <ISBN>1-85619-000-5</ISBN>
      </publication.statement>
      <copyright.statement>reproduced by permission Sinclair-Stevenson Ltd</copyright.statement>
      <free.comments>Biography of Charles Dickens</free.comments>
    </source.type>
  </subtext.source>
```

```
<subtext.internals=ICE-GB-W2B-008>
  <subtext.name>ICE-GB-Dickens</subtext.name>
    <main.title>              </main.title>
    <subtitle>              </subtitle>
    <page.nos>12-16</page.nos>
  <free.comments>              </free.comments>
</subtext.internals>
<biography=ICE-GB-W2B-008>
  <speaker.id>A</speaker.id>
    <communicative.role>author</communicative.role>
    <surname>Ackroyd</surname>
    <forenames>Peter</forenames>
    <age>42</age>
    <gender>male</gender>
    <nationality>British</nationality>
    <birthplace>London</birthplace>
    <education>Master's Degree, Cambridge University</education>
    <educational.level>university</educational.level>
    <occupation>novelist, biographer</occupation>
    <affiliations>Fellow Royal Society of Literature</affiliations>
    <mother.tongue>English</mother.tongue>
    <other.languages>not known</other.languages>
  <free.comments>              </free.comments>
</biography>

</text.info>
```

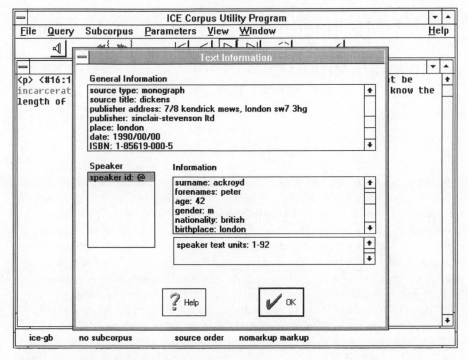

FIG. 4.A1. ICECUP's text info screen

5

The UMB Intelligent ICE Markup Assistant

EDWARD M. BLACHMAN, CHARLES F. MEYER and ROBERT A. MORRIS

1. INTRODUCTION

We have developed an editor, the UMB Intelligent ICE Markup Assistant (UMB/ IMA), that greatly eases the task of adding ICE markup to samples of written or (especially) spoken English. The editor brings to ICE ease-of-use innovations developed in other areas of computer application, particularly in 'What You See Is What You Get' (WYSIWYG) document editing. There are many such interactive programs familiar to scholars and desktop publishers, and there is a sense in which these programs can be considered markup systems. Certainly the documents they create can be expressed in markup languages for interchange and other purposes; yet these editors allow users to create and edit those documents without ever having to see or understand the intricacies of the interchange markup. With the UMB/ IMA, a sample's markup can be seen and edited via a presentation that is easier to understand than ICE markup, yet with constraints and filters that make the effort completely compatible with the SEU Markup Assistant (see Chapter 6) and ICE in general. Finally, we know that linguists deal with many varieties of markup, so we strove to build a system whose concepts could be applied not only to ICE but also to other markup schemes.

From the outside, a markup system is not very different from any other kind of editor: it requires import and export facilities (or Open and Save, if you prefer), as well as support in the user interface for making new objects, and for selecting and manipulating existing objects. It is at the next level of detail that markup concerns enter into the picture—determining the objects to be made and selected, finding the places where a judicious amount of programming can ease the job of adding markup, and determining the appropriate import and export facilities.

We built our editor atop an extensible document processing system from Interleaf, Inc. (English *et al.*, 1990). Interleaf is typical of high-end WYSIWYG word processing packages, offering users pulldown and popup menus, dialogs, and keyboard shortcuts by which they can perform file manipulation, style modification and imposition, and text, table, graphics, and equation editing. The system runs on many Unix platforms, as well as on DOS and Windows; by working in its extension language, we freed ourselves from having to worry directly about hardware and operating system issues. Instead, we focused on our primary goal: extending this user interface to make it useful for ICE corpus preparation.

2. CONTEXT SENSITIVITY

Computer users should not be presented with a myriad meaningless choices as they put their software to work. Instead, intelligent software offers the user choices that make sense given the current state of the data (in this case a document being edited and the point at which the edit takes place). From experience with other interactive editors and from general user interface principles, we knew that reducing the choices presented would make users more accurate and more comfortable in preparing ICE samples. We therefore focused on context sensitivity as a goal for our extended user interface: our software simplifies the user's task by allowing only actions consistent with the markup that has already been placed in the sample.

2.1. *Elements*

For a user, the typical job starts with a sample that is incomplete according to the desired markup scheme and ends with a sample that is at least more nearly complete. Adding markup is the goal, and so the objects that first come to mind for creation are markup codes. We saw three alternative approaches to code creation.

1. *Markup as data.* One way to look at markup is as data no different, except in its internal syntax, from the text of the samples being prepared. The simplest software would simply allow the user to type into the sample, creating markup codes one character at a time. This is clearly a least-common-denominator approach. While it can work, it requires an immense amount of knowledge and discipline on the part of the user, and intimate familiarity with the details of the particular markup scheme being used.

2. *Markup codes as objects.* One step up from seeing markup as data is to see its codes as objects that can be manipulated, or perhaps even edited, but that are usually created and left unmodified. There are two advantages here. One is that the user is freed from the need to know the internal syntax of the markup codes, at least when creating them. The SEU Markup Assistant (see Chapter 6) implements this approach by associating codes with function keys. Another advantage is that markup presentation need not be limited to the way the codes appear in the target markup scheme, but can be enhanced for readability. Such enhancement makes it more likely that a user can look at a sample and quickly understand its markup, which in turn makes it more likely that the markup will turn out correct in the end.

This approach, however, is limited too. Recall that one of the problems associated with ICE and similar markup schemes is the large number of codes they include. Simply treating codes as objects fails to address complexity due to the size of the code universe. SGML-based schemes are built around markup grammars that effectively constrain code placement; the scheme may contain a universe of codes, but for any given location in a document, only a subset of those codes are valid. ICE markup has no officially specified coding grammar; yet it is clear from reading the ICE specification that some sequences of markup make more sense than others. (For instance, if a given range of text is correctly coded as an orthographic sentence, it would make no sense to put a paragraph code inside it.) We believe that SGML-style grammars can be imposed on ICE markup, and that users of markup software succeed by mentally generating a rudimentary grammar of this sort.

Unfortunately, whether the markup grammar is mental or embedded in the markup system, the codes-as-objects model is difficult to integrate with markup-grammatical editing. In both cases, the problem is that small manipulations (such as the deletion of a single end-marker) can have surprisingly large markup-grammatical implications, changing the validity status of large stretches of a document outside of or even physically far from those manipulations. When the user's markup grammar is mental, as for users of the SEU Markup Assistant, it falls to proofreaders to detect such problems. But when the markup grammar is embedded in the software, as it is in our efforts, the codes-as-objects model (which we initially implemented) can lead to software behaviour that proves mystifying to the user.

3. *Elements as objects*. Here we borrowed terminology from SGML, and inspiration from SGML editors such as Author/Editor (SoftQuad, 1994). An element is a range of a document bounded at the beginning by a start-marker and at the end by the corresponding end-marker. Some elements are defined to have no content. For instance, this happens when an element marks a position in the text, rather than a range of text. In ICE, for example, a pause is such an element. It is indicated with a single, 'self-closing', marker. ICE also includes implicit markup (as does SGML, with a somewhat different formalism); for example, the marker that starts one speaker's turn implicitly ends the turn started by the preceding speaker turn marker. For simplicity's sake, we decided to present the user with an environment in which all start-markers (except for those that are self-closing) have explicit end-markers.

Treating elements as objects means that if a start-marker is present, its corresponding end-marker is always present as well, and this is true both at initial creation and after editing. As a result, the user's location in the document is always well-defined from the perspective of an SGML-like markup grammar. Our software unambiguously presents the user with the current structure of the document and dynamically tailors the interface accordingly. The SEU Markup Assistant embodies limited facilities of this sort: function keys which deposit markers having explicit ends toggle their behaviour between the start- and end-markers, thus generally insuring that constructions are closed.

2.2. *The Hierarchy*

As discussed above, while there is no formal grammar associated with ICE markup, we felt none the less that there would be value in discovering an informal grammar inherent in ICE markup so that it could then be incorporated into our system and enable context-sensitive element creation and pasting. To discover this grammar, we started by positing a set of conceptual categories for ICE elements. Each category consists of elements whose effect on the structure is similar, in that those elements allow the same content and are permissible in the same places (Morris, Blachman, and Meyer, 1993). Table 5.1 shows the grammar[1] for the categories we think of as 'structural'.

For example, suppose the user drops a pair of codes marking a paragraph (<p_> and <p/> in the ICE markup, <PAR_> and <PAR/> in our standard mnemonic presentation). Paragraphs are textblocks, in our grammar, and as such can contain extra-corporal text, utterances, quotations, and pauses. So at any point between these markers, our editor offers the ICE text unit pair (<#_> and <#/> in ICE, <TXU_> and <TXU/> for us), because text units are utterances. In contrast, it does not offer the paragraph markers at this point. Paragraphs logically do not contain one another directly (though they can contain quotations that in turn contain paragraphs), and that can be seen in the fact that the textblocks category is not one of its own subcategories.

Coming up with this grammar was one of the more difficult parts of the development effort, involving much trial and error.[2] But with the grammar in hand, we were able to build an editor that is indeed context-sensitive; this means that the user's prior work on a sample is automatically used to guide and constrain further work on that sample, reducing the complexity of the task and improving the user's accuracy.

2.3. *Create, Select, and Paste*

Context sensitivity comes into play in our software when the user adds elements to the sample, selects a portion of the sample for further manipulation, or pastes a previously cut selection. Selection means the designation of a contiguous portion of the sample for further manipulation. To avoid the presence of dangling markers, selections must be element-complete: for each start-marker contained in a selection, its matching end-marker must also be so contained, and vice versa. For instance, suppose that part of a sample consists of two sentences, tagged <sen_> . . . sentence 1 . . . <sen/><sen_> . . . sentence 2 . . . <sen/>; suppose further (to make this simple) that there is no markup inside either sentence, and that the insertion point is currently within sentence 1. Within sentence 1, the user may extend the selection freely. But any attempt to extend rightward beyond the end of sentence 1 will cause automatic extension leftwards past its start; and further extension past the start of sentence 2 will automatically be extended past the end of sentence 2.

The nature of our markup grammar and the automatic extension to complete markup-grammatical elements mentioned in the previous paragraph ensure that any

TABLE 5.1. *ICE markup 'structural' grammar*

Category	ICE elements		Subcategories
extra-corpus	editorial comment extra corpus text	uncertain transcription untranscribed text	
textblocks	footnote marginalia subtext marker	heading paragraph	extra-corpus utterances quotations pauses
typography	line-break typeface small caps roman italics underlining	subscript superscript unusable character ambiguous hyphen orthographic space	
utterances	text-unit	sentence	extra-corpus quotations words normalizations pauses
quotations	quote	mention	extra-corpus textblocks quotations speech
words	discontinuous orthographic normalized discourse	foreign incomplete footnote reference	typography
changes	names	words	extra-corpus normalizations
normalizations	deletion insertion replacement	preservation original	extra-corpus
speech	speaker-id		extra-corpus utterances quotations words pauses
pauses	short	long	

Note: ICE markup's elements are divided into categories: all elements in a given category can be created in the same places and share the same subcategories of permitted content.

selection can be cut without invalidating the rest of the markup. However, pasting is another matter. A selection may only be pasted if it 'fits' at the point where it would be pasted. Our software does the appropriate check and adjusts the interface accordingly. Thus, in the above example, if one selected sentence 1, cut it, and then moved the insertion point inside sentence 2, then the Paste option would be dimmed (visible but not available) on the Edit menu (because sentences cannot contain other sentences directly).

Element creation can take place either with or without a selection. When it occurs with a selection, it 'wraps' the selection in the start- and end-markers of the new element; with no selection, it places the new element's start- and end-markers adjacent to one another at the editor's insertion point. In either case, element creation is constrained by the other elements in the sample. With no selection, it is constrained by the element containing the insertion point; with a selection, it is also constrained by the requirement that the selected element should 'fit' inside the new one. Following standard practice, we reflect these constraints by dimming categories on the ICE creation menu if they cannot be chosen (Figs. 5.1 and 5.2).

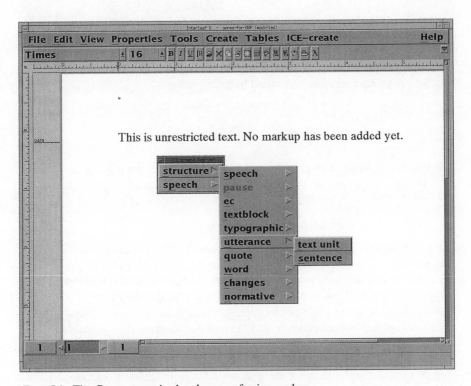

FIG. 5.1. The Create menu in the absence of prior markup

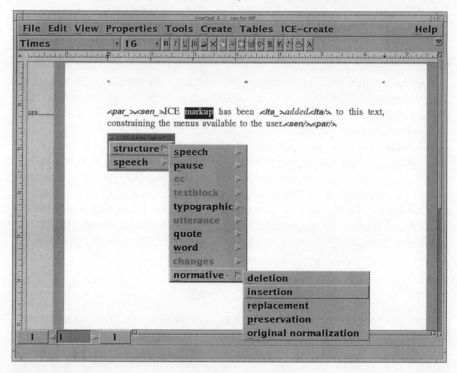

FIG. 5.2. The Create menu as constrained by prior markup

3. OVERLAPPING SPEECH

The knottiest development problems proved to arise from the tagging of overlapping speech—sequences of overlaps within samples of spoken English.

3.1. *Context Sensitivity Revisited*

Categories for overlapping speech do not fit neatly into the 'structural' markup grammar we laid out originally, requiring us to define a second grammar and rewrite our software to work with two markup grammars simultaneously. From an SGML perspective, this took us into uncharted territory. SGML has a feature (CONCUR) that corresponds to our notion of multiple grammars; however, it is found in only one SGML parser implementation, and none of the commercially available SGML editors support it. Table 5.2 sketches our solution; more detail is found in Morris, Blachman, and Meyer (1993). Note that the speech category appears in both the speech grammar and the structural grammar, but with different subcategories in each. This grammar is separate from the structural grammar because there is no

TABLE 5.2. *ICE markup 'speech' grammar*

Category	ICE elements	Subcategories
overlapping sets speech overlapping strings	overlapping set speaker-id overlapping string	speech overlapping strings

way to formulate sensible rules for containment across the two grammars (except for the speech *category*). An overlapping set can begin at a point that is arbitrary from the perspective (for example) of textblocks; similarly, overlapping strings can begin or end at points that are arbitrary from the perspective of words.

3.2. *The Visual Formalism*

The element-oriented user interface based on element selection and context-sensitive creation and pasting proved inadequate to support the markup of overlapping speech. Structural correctness does not address the biggest problem in adding markup for overlapping speech: to correctly mark the points where overlap starts and stops. Even guessing at those points was difficult, and verifying the correctness of any given attempt was nearly impossible.

This problem is familiar to corpus linguists, who traditionally had to choose between readability and descriptive adequacy in representing overlaps (Meyer, Morris, and Blachman, 1994). Readable systems are useful, even indispensable, for books and articles intended for a human audience, but their emphasis on printed form makes them unsuitable for electronic corpus work. The example below shows an iconic markup of speech overlap depending on spacing and vertical alignment.

```
A: it's figure three that we have to edit now
                                  [         ]
B:                                  no it's figure
     four we already did figure three
         [                              ]
A:        oh yeah I remember          we did it before
```

Descriptively adequate systems like ICE markup achieve exquisite precision, but only by sacrificing readability, as in the following example.

```
<$A> it's figure three that we have to <{_1> <[_1> edit now
<[/1>
<$B> <[_1> no it's fig <[/1> <{/1} ure four <{_2> <[_2> we
already did figure three <[/2>
<$A> <[_2> oh yeah I remember <[/2> <{/2> we did it before
```

TABLE 5.3. *Table-based visual formalism of the authors*

A	B
it's figure three that we have to	
edit now	no it's fig
	ure four
oh yeah I remember	we already did figure three
we did it before	

Readability is very important to users, because if they cannot easily see where they have marked overlaps, they cannot verify the correctness of their work, and the cost of obtaining accurate markup will skyrocket. We invented a new representation for overlapping speech (shown in Table 5.3) that combines readability and descriptive adequacy (Meyer, Morris, and Blachman, 1994). As with the rest of our work, it does not replace ICE markup—rather it provides a readable interface to that markup, or to any other scheme that attempts to capture overlaps like those found in speech.

Table 5.3 represents a span of time during which overlapping speech took place. Each column belongs to a single speaker; heavy rules label turn boundaries, while light rules label milestones at which overlap started or stopped. We built this new representation on the tables package of the underlying software, then changed the user interface to reflect the fact that the user is not building generic tables, but rather using a tabular representation to depict overlaps. For instance, we knew that users would find themselves having to add milestones to previously unbroken runs of text, so we added a command—Split—that breaks such a run in two and adds a milestone between them.

4. OTHER EASE-OF-USE ASPECTS

While context sensitivity and overlapping speech are our primary foci, we also address some other areas of ease-of-use, notably visual legibility and automatic processing. One of the virtues of ICE markup is its brevity: codes are always short, which means that the impact of the markup on the size of a sample is minimal, and the keystrokes required of an expert user are minimized as well. However, for non-expert users, this very brevity makes ICE markup hard to read, so beginning and intermediate users are likely to make markup errors.

We put two features into our system to aid such non-expert users. First, instead of showing codes in ICE markup syntax, we show codes (in a different font from the text) with mnemonic labels that are at least somewhat decipherable. (The labels are stored and can be altered separately from the bulk of the system, allowing users to determine their verbosity for themselves.) Second, we make it possible for the markup to be hidden either all or in part, so that a user can examine a particular aspect of the coding with respect to the sample in isolation.

Interactive addition of markup is necessary in many instances, but some kinds of markup can and therefore should be done by machine. Here we have made a beginning by writing code to automatically add codes for paragraphs, to provisionally add codes for quotes and sentence boundaries, and to automatically number text units. Finally, none of the interactive software is of any interest unless the interactive version can be accurately translated to and from the official ICE markup. Our software includes filters to and from ICE markup.

5. FUTURES

We are thinking about broadening our work beyond constrained markup of ICE samples. Much interesting work is done with SGML markup languages developed along the lines specified by the Text Encoding Initiative (Sperberg-McQueen and Burnard, 1994). Our work in context sensitivity has not yet resulted in something suitable for the full range of SGML languages, but we have engineered our software with a view toward SGML applications; we believe that our tabular approach to the markup and display of overlapping speech may have utility in the broad TEI community. More immediately, because many texts from the Corpus of Spoken American English (Chafe, Du Bois, and Thompson, 1991) will be included in the American component of ICE, we intend to write a program to convert CSAE markup to ICE markup.

6. AVAILABILITY OF THE SOFTWARE

Our software is available without charge to anyone who wishes to study or use it. For details on how to retrieve it, send internet mail to the third author as ram@cs.umb.edu. In order to use the program, you must have Interleaf 6.1 installed on a suitable computer, generally one of several Unix workstations or an IBM compatible PC with a Pentium P60 chip or better, running Windows NT 3.5 or better, or Windows 95 and possessing at least 24MB of RAM. Lesser configurations may work but are not recommended. Site licences for Interleaf 6.1 are available at nominal cost to US universities from the UMASS-Boston Software Engineering Laboratory, serl@cs.umb.edu. In the UK, university purchasing consortia also receive substantial discounts on Interleaf 6.1. In other countries, consult local Interleaf sales offices.

NOTES

1. In technical SGML terms, this grammar is simple. Each conceptual category is an or-group whose members share a common content model; that content model is the optional

repeating or-group of #PCDATA (in most cases) or any of the or-groups corresponding to the categories that category can contain. For example, the utterances category might be encoded as follows:

```
<!ENTITY % utterances 'text-unit I sentence'>
<!ELEMENT (%utterances;) - -
(%ec; I %words; I %quotations; I %normalizations; I %pauses; I #PCDATA)+ >
```

This kind and degree of categorization is rarely found in the common run of SGML DTDs, even though it was the natural choice in this case.
2. We are grateful to Eva Hertel and Barbara Kauper, working in Josef Schmied's ICE group, who exercised and refined the current hierarchy in testing our software.

References

AIJMER, K. and ALTENBERG, B. (1991) (eds.), *English Corpus Linguistics* (London: Longman).

CHAFE, W. L., DU BOIS, J. W. and THOMPSON, S. A. (1991), 'Towards a New Corpus of Spoken American English', in K. AIJMER and B. ALTENBERG, 64–82.

ENGLISH, P. M., JACOBSON, E., MORRIS, R. A., MUNDY, K. B., PELLETIER, S. D., POLUCCI, T. A., and SCARBRO, H. D. (1990), 'An Extensible, Object-Oriented System for Active Documents', in R. FURUTA (ed.), 263–76.

FURUTA, R. (1990) (ed.), *Proceedings of the International Conference on Electronic Publishing, Document Manipulation, and Typography* (Cambridge: Cambridge University Press).

MEYER, C. F., MORRIS, R. A. and BLACHMAN, E. (1994), 'Can You See Whose Speech is Overlapping?', *Visible Language*, 28/2: 110–33.

MORRIS, R. A., BLACHMAN, E. M. and MEYER, C. F. (1993), 'A Constraint-Based Editor for Linguistic Scholars', *Electronic Publishing—Origination, Dissemination and Design*, 6/4: 349–59.

SOFTQUAD (1994), Author/Editor, commercial software for SGML editing. SoftQuad can be contacted at 56 Aberfoyle Crescent, Suite 810, Toronto, Canada, M8X 2W4.

SPERBERG-MCQUEEN, C. M. and BURNARD, L. (1994), 'Guidelines for Electronic Text Encoding', available by internet file transfer from tei-ftp.vic.edu

6

ICE Annotation Tools

AKIVA QUINN and NICK PORTER

A key aspect of the International Corpus of English (ICE) is the detailed linguistic annotation it contains. Providing annotations for textual features, word classes, syntactic categories, and functions allows comparisons to be conducted along many axes. Transforming a raw input file into a properly annotated text can involve much work, so software tools have been developed to keep this effort to a minimum. This paper describes three programs produced by the Survey of English Usage for machine-assisted annotation. The Markup Assistant automates the insertion of textual markup, generating ICE markup symbols at a single key press and ensuring that markup symbols are closed. The ICE Tag Selection System automates the selection from the alternative word-class tags generated by an automatic word-class tagger. The ICE Syntactic Marking System automates the addition of syntactic markers to texts prior to parsing by an automatic parser. The ICE Syntactic Tree annotator complements automatic parsing by providing a graphical environment for the manual editing of syntactic analyses.

1. THE ICE MARKUP ASSISTANT

The ICE Markup Assistant automates and simplifies key presses for the insertion of the standard set of ICE markup symbols used throughout the project. ICE uses Standard Generalised Markup Language (SGML) to encode, in a machine-independent manner, a range of typographic and content features, and the structure of a text. Implemented as a set of macros under WordPerfect, the text unit markup is inserted automatically at probable sentence boundaries—after each full stop, question mark, and exclamation mark in the text that is followed by a space or an end of line. Having the majority of text units correctly inserted saves time, and additional text units inserted after abbreviations can easily be deleted.

Reduced key presses are provided for all the standard ICE markup symbols. Most markup types require an open and close symbol for each sequence that forms a paragraph, appears in boldface, and so on. For instance the following sequence represents two words in boldface:

<#25:1> <bold> Retrograde Amnesia </bold>

The first time the key for boldface is pressed the SGML open symbol <bold> is generated, the next time the SGML close symbol </bold> is produced. This system generally ensures that markup symbols are closed, and reminds users to do so should they try opening the same symbol again before closing it. For markup types that do not require closure, separate keys are provided to generate a single entity markup symbol without requiring explicit closure. This applies to atomic entities in the text such as pauses or line breaks, and to markup types that are closed by the next symbol of that type (for instance, the text unit markup <#25:1> is closed by the start of text unit <#26:1>).

As an indication of the detailed markup applied in the International Corpus of English, an extract from a text with a not unusual amount of markup is reproduced below (ICE-GB-S1A-009-63-72).

```
<$A> <#63:1:A> <sent> <w> I've </w> still got those things
which Shar brought back <,> <{> <-> in </-> <=> in </=>
</{> the summer
<#64:1:A> <sent> I must <{> <[> <,> eat them </[>
<#65:1:A> <sent> Yes

<$B> <#66:1:B> <sent> <[> You ought to use them </[> </{>

<$B> <#67:1:B> <sent> <w> They've </w> got <}> <-> sell-
by dates </-> uh <=> use-by </=> </}> dates on them

<$A> <#68:1:A> <sent> Yes
<#69:1:A><sent> Well <w> that's </w> all about three
years in advance
<#70:1:A> <sent> I don't know why but uh <w> it's </w>
sitting there
<#71:1:A> <sent> I was sort of saving it for a rainy day
<}> <-> and the rainy </->
<#72:1:A> <sent> <=> Well touch wood the rainy </=> </}>
<?> <w> day's </w> never come </?> <,,>
```

Besides the range of orthographic features that are marked up, a range of textual markup is applied in anticipation of parsing. Normative deletions remove repetitions or false starts from the sentence to allow parsing, while retaining the extra words. Normative insertions fill in missing words, while normative replacements provide the correct form of a word to allow parsing, for instance replacing 'dessert' with 'desert' in the following sentence:

Shan did not <}> <-> dessert </-> <+> desert </+> </}> him.

The replacement opens with <}> and closes with </}> and pairs of symbols are also used to indicate the deletion <-> and insertion <+>, which illustrates the utility of the markup closure key presses. For spoken texts, a greater number of normative emendations are required, and short and long pauses are marked up. Given that several hundred markup symbols are added to each 2,000 plus word text, the Markup Assistant can save tens of minutes per text being marked up.

2. THE ICE TAG SELECTION SYSTEM

TAGSELECT automates selection from the alternative word-class tags generated by the TOSCA tagger, AUTASYS, or other automatic taggers. The alternative tags for each word are displayed with the most likely tags first. The user need only intervene if the first tag is not the correct one. This is done by simply highlighting the correct tag. Where the correct alternative is not shown, a new tag can be added from the list of possible tags. TAGSELECT runs under Microsoft Windows and all functions are available via the Graphical User Interface, using menus, buttons, and scroll bars.

The first operation in TAGSELECT is for users to select the text in which tags will be selected. Available texts are indicated in a list. One text unit is displayed at a time and users can move to the next, previous, or a given sentence number at the click of a button.

The Tag Selection display consists of a window with the alternative word-class tags for each word, a window showing the full text of the current sentence, and a 'Control Panel' with buttons to provide the various tag selection commands. The current word and its tags are highlighted with a grey background and the currently selected tags are highlighted in blue. Once a word-class tag is selected for a word the alternative tags are hidden from view (see Fig. 6.1a). If the highlighted tag is the correct one for the current word, users need simply press 'Select Tag' to move on to the next word. Otherwise 'Next Tag' and 'Previous Tag' are used to highlight the appropriate tag before pressing 'Select Tag'.

Where the correct tag is not one of the alternatives provided by the tagger it can be added. The new tag is constructed by selecting the word class and each required and optional feature for it. For example Fig. 6.1b shows the first stage of adding a verb. If the user is unsure about the choice of tag, a query can be left alongside the word to alert checkers. This is very helpful for checkers who can then skip from one queried tag to another to audit the selections that the tag selector was unsure about. Another time-saving feature allows the rest of a compound to be tagged

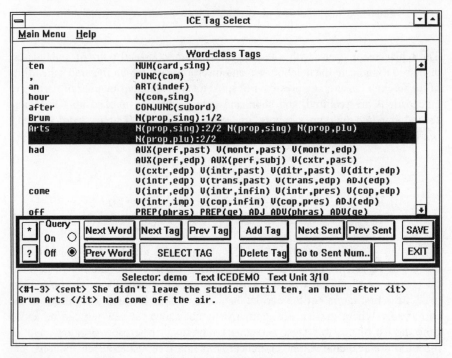

FIG. 6.1a. Tag selection: hides alternative tags for already selected words

automatically once the first part of a compound is tagged. On selecting or adding the initial part of a compound such as N(com,plu):1/2 you will be given the option to 'Automatically tag the rest of the compound?' as shown in Fig. 6.1c.

Along with searching for queries in the text, users can also search for words, tags, or word-tag combinations. This allows repeated or similar examples to be viewed and consistency maintained within and across texts. There is also a facility to mark tags that should be deleted as alternatives for a particular word. These deletions are recorded and passed on to the maintainers of the Automatic Tagger being used, so that appropriate changes can be made to the Tagger's lexicon. This option is only for use by the tagset manager as it affects which legitimate word-class tags a word can have.

Although designed for use with ICE, the Tag Selection System is flexible enough to operate on any set of word-class tags. The tagset file contains a full list of all the ICE tags. The tagset manager can modify the set of tags by editing this file, which consists of word-class descriptions followed by the alternative tags for that class. Optional features, such as compound, are enclosed in square brackets; required features, such as form for verbs, are enclosed in parentheses. For example:

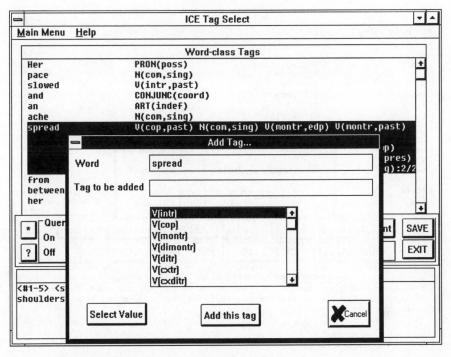

FIG. 6.1b. Tag selection: constructing a verbal tag

Adjective
ADJ(ge)
ADJ(comp)
ADJ(edp)
ADJ(ingp)
ADJ(sup)

TAGSELECT also provides process control, keeping track of who is working on each text and its stage of completion. Texts are classified as unselected, selection in progress, ready for checking, ready for second check, or finished. A progress report showing the status of each text can be viewed at any time (see Fig. 6.1*d*).

The ICE Tag Selection System also has facilities for preparing texts before tag selection and producing disambiguated texts after tag selection, which are not discussed here. In summary, graphical display, selecting tags, queries, searching for words, tags, or queries, and automatic tagging of compounds all go towards a system that greatly enhances the productivity of linguists selecting the contextually appropriate word-class for every word in a text.

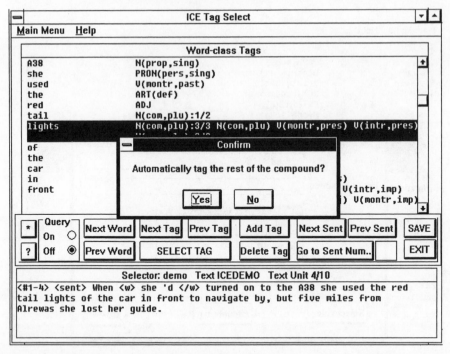

F IG . 6.1c. Tag selection: automatically tagging compounds

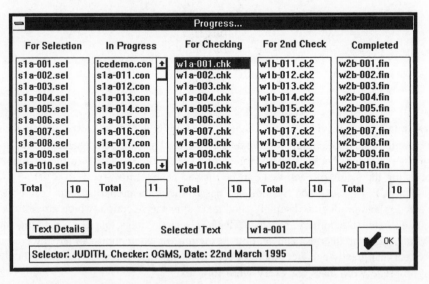

F IG . 6.1d. Tag selection: progress report

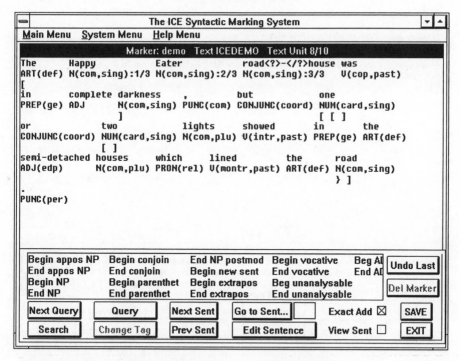

FIG. 6.2a. Syntactic marking: displays, words, tags, and markers

3. THE ICE SYNTACTIC MARKING SYSTEM

ICEMARK is used to add syntactic markers to tagged texts prior to parsing by the TOSCA parser or any other parser that requires such pre-editing. Syntactic markers help disambiguate the input to the parser and restrict the number of alternative syntax trees generated. The text is displayed one text unit at a time and markers are added by selecting one from the list and pointing to the word before or after which the marker should be added. Similar 'point and click' functions are used to delete a marker, to move to other sentences, to query a sentence, and so on.

The syntactic-marking screen consists of a main window containing the current sentence, plus a 'Control Panel' with the list of syntactic markers and the marking functions situated below. The sentence is shown across the screen with the selected word-class tag under each word, and syntactic markers below that. Different colours are used to help focus on the words (in black), word-class tags (in blue), or syntactic markers (in red, or green for co-ordination markers) (see Fig. 6.2a).

By default ICEMARK handles the ordering of markers applied to the same word automatically, placing beginning markers immediately before the word and end markers immediately after it. For example the beginning and end of an appositive NP are marked as follows in ICEMARK (with word-class tags omitted):

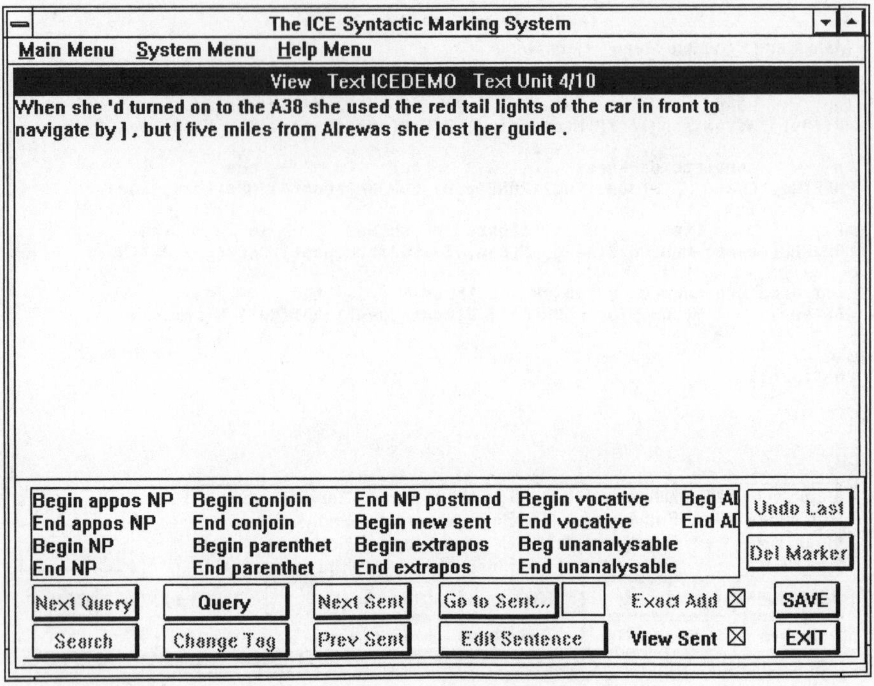

The ICE Syntactic Marking System	▼	▲

Main Menu   System Menu   Help Menu

View   Text ICEDEMO   Text Unit 4/10

When she 'd turned on to the A38 she used the red tail lights of the car in front to
navigate by] , but [five miles from Alrewas she lost her guide .

Begin appos NP	Begin conjoin	End NP postmod	Begin vocative	Beg Al	Undo Last
End appos NP	End conjoin	Begin new sent	End vocative	End Al	
Begin NP	Begin parenthet	Begin extrapos	Beg unanalysable		Del Marker
End NP	End parenthet	End extrapos	End unanalysable		

Next Query	Query	Next Sent	Go to Sent...	Exact Add ☒	SAVE
Search	Change Tag	Prev Sent	Edit Sentence	View Sent ☒	EXIT

FIG. 6.2b. Syntactic marking with only conjoin markers shown

> Our president, Nelson Mandela, will . . .
>   bA   eA

This is transformed into the following output:

> Our president, <bA> Nelson Mandela <eA>, will . . .

Where the order of syntactic markers on a particular word is significant, for example if there are markers for two different syntactic features, users can select to
have full control over the ordering. Markers can be deleted by pointing at the appropriate marker and clicking on the 'Delete Marker' button. There is also an undo
facility to remove the last marker added to the sentence. Users can record queries
on the marking of a sentence, and search for queries, words, and tags in a text.

     Besides the use of colour, another visual mechanism to help users is to view the
sentence with no word-class tags and only conjoin markers shown. This is particularly useful for long sentences with complex co-ordination (see Fig. 6.2*b*). Word-
class tags are carefully checked during the tag selection process, but there could
be new tagging decisions or simply unnoticed errors to repair while applying syntactic

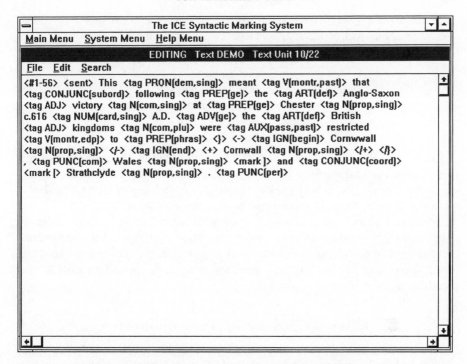

FIG. 6.2c. Syntactic marking: edited sentence with normative markup

markers. Tags can be changed by selecting the tag in the marking window, and clicking on 'Change Tag'. This presents the list of word-classes and feature-values for the subclasses, from which the required tag is constructed.

A sentence-editing window is provided to correct textual errors in the current sentence. Markup symbols (not displayed in the syntactic-marking window), lexical items, and punctuation can be changed, along with word-class tags and syntactic markers if required. Use of this function is restricted to corpus supervisors, as reference must be made to the original text, manuscript, or recording to ensure that the changes are in line with the original. For example, while marking ICE-GB some further normative emendations were added to sentences which otherwise would not conform to the formal grammar (see Fig. 6.2c).

As mentioned above, textual markup symbols are not displayed in the syntactic-marking window. This is because features like boldface, paragraphs, and orthographic words do not affect syntactic structure. Markup for normative emendations (see Section 1) is also not displayed, but rather interpreted so that the contents of normative insertions, being part of the sentence to be parsed, are displayed while the contents of normative deletions are not.

ICEMARK can operate on any set of syntactic markers, defined in a file with one syntactic marker per line. Along with the syntactic marker, each line contains a brief description of the marker which will appear in the list of markers to be added. As an example, part of the ICE syntactic marker set is listed here:

> bA   Begin Appositive
>
> eA   End Appositive
>
> bADV   Begin ADV phrase
>
> eADV   End ADV phrase
>
> bN   Begin NP
>
> eN   End NP

Like the Tag Selection System, the ICE Syntactic Marking System can use any set of word-class tags defined in the tagset file. ICEMARK provides process control, again like TAGSELECT, to keep track of the stage of completion of each text and who is working on it. Progress reports can be viewed on demand.

ICEMARK also runs under Windows, again providing a familiar, easy-to-use interface. In some ways ICEMARK is the 'super annotation' tool as it can be used to alter textual markup and change word-class tags as well as apply syntactic markers, but the Markup Assistant and Tag Selection System are more specialized tools for the first two tasks.

4. THE ICE SYNTACTIC TREE ANNOTATOR

As automatic parsers become more effective, their use will become more widespread and the need for an efficient method of parsing the material that the parser fails to cope with will become increasingly important. Within the ICE community the problem is addressed through the use of two programs: a parser that can produce a partial as well as a complete analysis and an editor that enables the analyses to be corrected or completed. The common graphical representation for a parse analysis is the 'tree' form. ICETREE is an editor that allows for the manipulation of such a form. Material that remains unparsed after automatic analysis is passed to the partial parser, which provides a partial analysis for all of the remaining unparsed material. The ICETREE program then provides an efficient graphical environment for the manual correction and completion of the partial analyses. In addition, it allows parse trees to be built from scratch, and can be used as a viewer for complete analyses.

A partial or full analysis that is to be edited or viewed using ICETREE must be in the indented format, a format produced by several of the automatic parsers currently available. The indented form is a DOS text representation of a parse analysis, where the various levels are represented by indentation in the file, as in the following example.

```
PU,CL(main,act,decl,indic,montr,pres,unm)
 SU,NP()
  NPHD,PN(pers,plu){we}
 VB,VP(act,indic,montr,pres,prog)
```

```
OP,AUX(pres,prog,encl){'re}
MVB,V(montr,ingp){doing}
OD,NP()
 NPPR,AJP(attru)
  AJPR,AVP(int)
   AVHD,ADV(int){very}
  AJHD,ADJ(){similar}
 NPHD,N(com,plu){kinds}
 NPPO,PP()
  P,PREP(ge){of}
  PC,NP()
   NPHD,N(com,plu){things}
A,PP()
 P,PREP(ge){at}
 PC,NP()
  NPHD,N(com,sing){work}
A,PP()
 P,PREP(ge){at}
 PC,NP()
  DT,DTP()
   DTCE,ART(def){the}
  NPHD,N(com,sing){moment}
```

The main window of ICETREE contains a grid on which the analysis is displayed. Each word in the sentence is displayed down the right hand side of the window with the grammatical analysis displayed to the left as a tree. The full sentence is also displayed in a second window beneath the main one, as in Fig. 6.3*a*. To add a node, the user double clicks with the mouse at the location where the node is required. A dialog box then appears, as in Fig. 6.3*b*. The appropriate function and category values can then be selected from the drop-down lists. Clicking on the EDIT FEATURES ... button produces a further dialog box, shown in Fig. 6.3*c*, which allows for the selection of feature values.

The values in both dialog boxes are linked so that the selection of a function value limits appropriately, in terms of the grammar, the selection of a category value and they both in turn limit the possibilities for feature values. These values, together with their links, are determined by five DOS files. Modification of these files allow ICETREE to be used with any grammar and any notation system.

The tree is edited by cutting and pasting nodes and unlinking and re-linking them. Two nodes are linked by simply clicking on one and dragging the mouse between them. To cut a node, first highlight it by clicking on it with the mouse, then select the CUT option from the edit menu. Once a node has been cut, the node disappears. Clicking on a grid position currently unoccupied by a node and selecting PASTE inserts the recently cut or copied node to the new position.

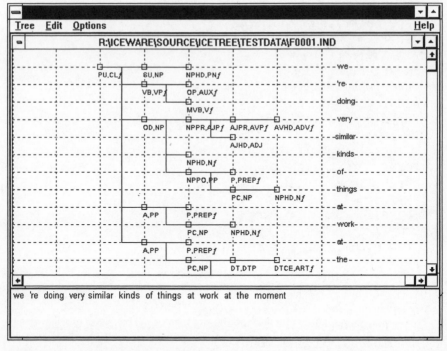

FIG. 6.3a. The tree and sentence windows

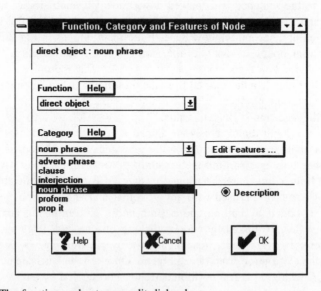

FIG. 6.3b. The function and category edit dialog box

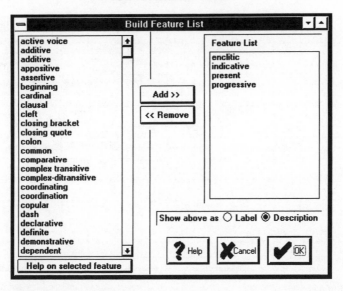

FIG. 6.3c. The feature edit dialog box

The windows are re-sizeable, moveable, and scrollable so the users can create their own best view. The tree branches can be changed from a square to diagonal format. An overview feature is provided (see Fig. 6.3*d*), which zooms out from the tree, so that more of the tree can be seen in the window, particularly useful when editing large trees.

At the time of writing the ICETREE program is just approaching its first version. Later versions may include integration with the Survey parser, to provide a complete parsing environment.

5. WINDOWS INTERFACE STANDARDS

Following the Windows user interface standard provides a user with a recognizable interface that does not require relearning basic concepts for each program. Hence TAGSELECT, ICEMARK, and ICETREE will be familiar to anyone who has used other Windows applications. A number of specific interface design standards have been followed in both of these ICE Annotation Tools for Windows. Firstly IBM's Customer User Access (CUA) defines the mouse actions for selecting an item and performing an action, among other things. This forms part of the Windows interface standard along with the naming and ordering of menu items, the positioning of child windows, the use of dialog boxes, and scroll bars. These are all features that Windows users take for granted and hence little training is required to use a new application that follows the interface standards.

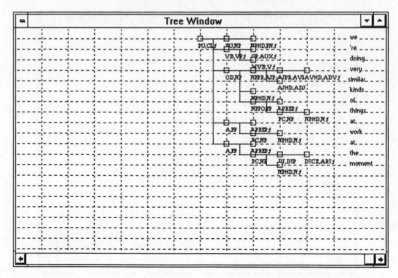

F<small>IG</small>. 6.3d. Overview

6. C<small>ONCLUSIONS</small>

In recent years not only have corpora increased in number and size, but users now expect detailed annotation of textual, grammatical, prosodic, semantic, pragmatic, and discoursal features. Most of these annotations cannot be fully automated if a high degree of accuracy is required, so providing tools to apply and check annotations is a key to successful corpus development. The tools presented here make the annotation of the International Corpus of English much more efficient, and could be used with equal effect on other corpora with similar annotation requirements.

R<small>EFERENCES</small>

G<small>REENBAUM</small>, S. and Y<small>IBIN</small>, N. (1994), 'Tagging the British ICE Corpus: English Word Classes', in N. O<small>OSTDIJK</small> and P. <small>DE</small> H<small>AAN</small> (eds.), *Corpus-Based Research into Language*, 33–45 (Amsterdam: Rodopi).

Microsoft Press (1992), *The Windows Interface: An Application Design Guide* (Redmond, Wash.: Microsoft Press).

N<small>ELSON</small>, G. (1991*a*), *Markup Manual for Spoken Texts* (London: Survey of English Usage, University College London).

—— (1991*b*), *Markup Manual for Written Texts* (London: Survey of English Usage, University College London).

V<small>AN</small> H<small>ERWIJNEN</small>, E. (1990), *Practical SGML* (Dortrecht: Kluwer Academic Publishers).

Y<small>IBIN</small>, N. (1993), *ICE Syntactic Markers Manual* (London: Survey of English Usage, University College London).

7

Developing the ICE Corpus Utility Program

NICK PORTER and AKIVA QUINN

1. DEVELOPMENT

1.1. *Motivation and Requirements*

Soon after the Survey of English Usage initiated the project, it was realized that there was a need for a general corpus processing and analysis tool for the International Corpus of English. In its broadest conception, this tool was to cover the central requirements for corpus preparation and study, including corpus annotation, markup conversion and filtering, searching, concordancing, statistical analyses, subcorpus information, and subcorpus selection. The system would primarily target ICE corpora, yet would provide a range of general corpus utilities equally applicable to other corpora.

The requirements for ICECUP were determined by the design and content of ICE and the corpus utilities that were to be provided. The International Corpus exists primarily to allow comparison between national and regional varieties of English, but further, each component corpus is structured according to medium (spoken, manuscript, and printed) and genre (news, business, natural sciences, novels, and so on). Describing and quantifying linguistic features within national, medium, and genre categories is a key requirement.

ICE corpora use Standard Generalized Markup Language (SGML) to encode typographic and content features of a text, as well as word-classes, syntactic structures, and functions. Searches and concordances should be able to include any combination of these markup symbols in their search arguments, together with lexical items, punctuation, and wildcards. The citations or concordance lines shown should be able to focus attention on relevant annotations by selectively filtering out markup symbols. Making functions easy to find, and providing help to explain the options at any point in the program, are also key parts of the specification. Besides providing facilities to support linguistic research, ICECUP has to be easy to use and accessible to potential users.

1.2. *Design Issues*

A modular programming language that is widely used, and available on a popular platform, would enhance the program's flexibility and reusability. Languages such as ICON or LEX that are geared towards text processing were rejected in favour of the C++ programming language. C++ is the object-oriented version of C, a language that is universal within the academic community. The object-oriented qualities of C++ allow for the production of a modular design, essential if the program code is to be flexible and reusable.

The IBM-compatible Personal Computer (PC) system and the Microsoft DOS operating system were initially chosen as the preferred platform since they were both predominant and cheap—important considerations, especially within the ICE community, where certain members may have limited access to computer technology. However, in the early stages of the project the decision was made to develop a Windows version of ICECUP, and it is this version that has become the standard. The Windows GUI environment (the most popular operating system world-wide) had obvious advantages over the DOS operating system. A new program which runs under Windows™ needs no special training, familiarity with any Microsoft Windows™ application will map readily into an understanding of the new software's menus and dialogs.

The main overriding concern throughout the construction of the software was to keep it general, to avoid tailoring the software to the specific needs of the ICE format. Consequently, the SGML markup system was adopted as the standard for ICE, allowing for variety in markup systems, and universality with special symbols. As long as the markup is enclosed within the standard SGML form, the markup can be as idiosyncratic as one likes, without resulting in incompatibility with ICE. Avoiding such specialization has meant that the software can, with the minimum of alteration, be used on any text, with any markup system and any linguistic database.

2. THE ICE CORPUS UTILITY PROGRAM VERSION 2.0

. . . easy to use and accessible to potential users.

ICECUP Version 2.0 is the second incarnation of ICECUP and is the first to be released outside the ICE community. The system includes facilities to perform complex searches, produce concordances, select subcorpora according to a range of features, and filter markup to maintain text readability. It comes complete with a context-sensitive hypertext help system.

2.1. *Querying the Corpus*

. . . typographic and content features of a text, as well as word-classes, syntactic structures and functions. Searches and concordances should be able to include any combination of these markup symbols in their search arguments, together with lexical items, punctuation, and wildcards.

TABLE 7.1. *Example of the string description language*

SDL Expression	What it matches
<N(com,sing)><ADJ>	All common singular nouns followed by an adjective
<h><V(imp)>	Headings that start with an imperative verb
John Major ## affair	*John Major* with *affair* in the same text unit
look {1-3}# up_<PREP(phras)>	*look* and *up* separated by one to three words where *up* is used as a phrasal preposition

2.1.1. *The String Description Language*

Complex queries can be formulated using a specially designed String Description Language (SDL). SDL allows queries for words used as specific word-classes, sequences of tags, textual markup with tags, grammatical patterns, phrases, co-occurring words, or any other combination of lexical items, tags, and wildcards. SDL queries can also include prefixes, suffixes, and infixes, e.g.

$$*tion\ <N(com,sing)>$$

selects all words ending in 'tion' that belong to the word class common singular noun. Combining lexical items with tags and wildcards allows more complex queries to be constructed. These include queries for words belonging to specific word classes, sequences of tags, textual markup with tags, grammatical patterns, phrases, co-occurring words, or any combination of these. The examples given in Table 7.1 illustrate the range of possible queries using the String Description Language (SDL).

2.1.2. *Building a Query*

The SDL query is specified in ICECUP by means of a Query Dialog Box. The query is typed into the edit area and then a button is clicked to initiate it (see Fig. 7.1). To ease the formulation of an SDL query that might contain such items as textual markup, word classes, syntactic markers, and other linguistic annotation, users select such items from a list of descriptions and add them directly to the query. Similarly, special symbols used for accented characters (as in *cliché* or *coup de grâce*) or other non-standard characters (such as bullets or degree-signs) can also be selected from a list of descriptions. This explicit representation of the linguistic content of a corpus frees the user from the task of constantly referring to a large set of annotations.

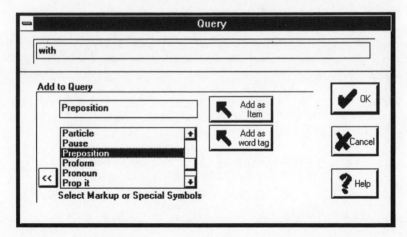

FIG. 7.1. The query dialog box

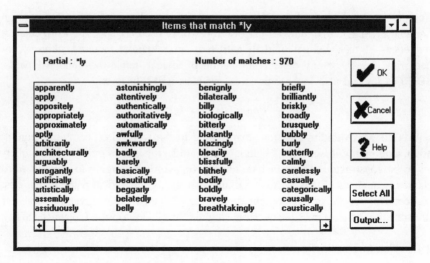

FIG. 7.2. A list of the matches to the partial **ly*

2.1.3. *Multi-queries and Partials*

Another dialog form allows for partial words or markup to be specified with SDL. Prefixes, suffixes and infixes can be specified as follows:

re*   matches words starting with 're', including *re*

*ate   matches words ending with 'ate', including *ate*

act   matches words containing 'act', including *act, acting,* and *reaction*

These word partials (which need not be morphological units) can be freely combined with other SDL elements, allowing queries such as

$$*ly\_<ADV(ge)$$

all words ending in 'ly' that belong to the word class general adverb. The items that match such a specification are displayed as a list; one or more may be selected and searched for in a batch form called a multi-query. For example, Fig. 7.2 shows the first four columns of the matching items for *ly.

2.3. *Displaying the Results*

2.3.1. *Search Display and KWIC Concordances*

We can take as an example a search for the word *working* used as an adjective that has the form of an -ing participle in ICE-GB (the one-million-word British component of ICE) (see Fig. 7.3). The caption displayed at the top of the screen would give the source of the current citation (text S2B-042 text unit 47), the current citation number, and the frequency of this search argument. The word occurring in the context being searched for would be highlighted on screen.

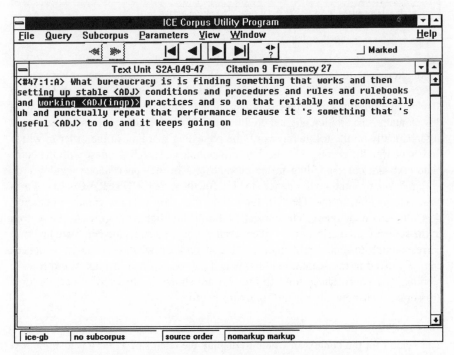

FIG. 7.3. A search display for the query *working* used as an *adjective*

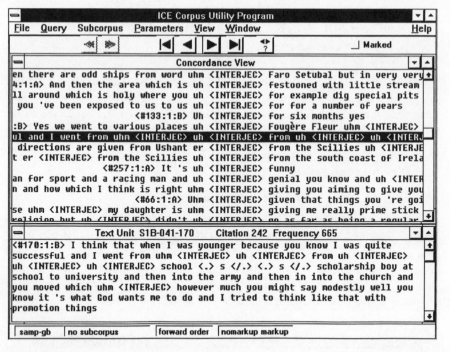

FIG. 7.4. The concordance display

An alternative to the above is the concordance display, sometimes referred to as a Key-word in context (KWIC) display. Concordance output is a useful way to display citations that contain the search argument. Each line of the concordance window contains one citation aligned on the query. The concordance lines can be sorted alphabetically on the following word, the preceding word, or in the order in which they appear in the corpus. The display also contains a search window with the complete text unit corresponding to the current item in the concordance window.

Fig. 7.4 shows the concordance display for the query <INTERJEC> (the word-class interjection) in the ICE-GB. Each line of the top window contains one citation, aligned on the query. The current citation is highlighted in grey. At the bottom of the screen a smaller version of the search window contains the complete text unit corresponding to the current item in the concordance window. Context sentences can be viewed in the search window, which can be scrolled or maximized to ease reading. The concordance lines in Fig. 7.4 are shown in 'forward' order, i.e. they are sorted alphabetically on the following word.

2.3.2. *Context*

The default for the context in which to display the results of a query is a single text unit. However, any amount of context can be specified, from a number of preceding

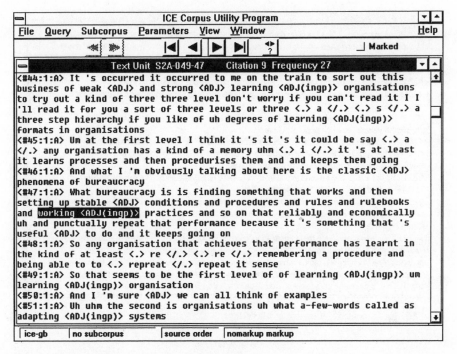

FIG. 7.5. Extra context: previous and following

and following text units to the whole text. Fig. 7.5 shows the same citation as in Fig. 7.3 but with previous and following context. Fig. 7.6 shows the whole text display for the same citation. A different kind of context is provided by the text information facility. Information on the citation source can be requested with details of the publication, unpublished source, oral context, or author/speaker specifics. Fig. 7.7 shows the scrollable View Text Window displaying the information for the text S1A-003. The ICECUP status bar (Fig. 7.8) indicates to the user his or her own context within the ICECUP program. It indicates the corpus being searched (ICE-GB), any subcorpus in use, what markup is being displayed, and the order in which citations are being shown.

2.3.3. *Markup Utilities*

The citations or concordance lines shown should be able to focus attention on relevant annotations by selectively filtering out markup symbols.

Fig. 7.8 shows a citation displayed with all its markup, including word-class tags. If we contrast this with Fig. 7.3 it is easy to appreciate the loss of readability that occurs if a markup filtering facility is not available. Markup display options are vital when searching heavily annotated corpora, such as those used in linguistic research.

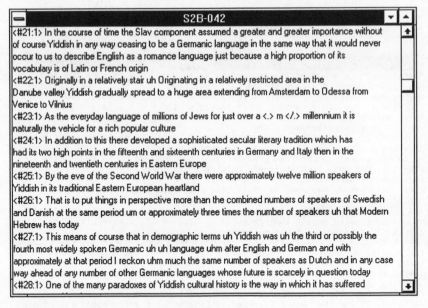

FIG. 7.6. Extra context: viewing a whole text

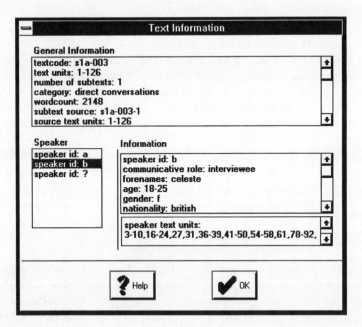

FIG. 7.7. Text information

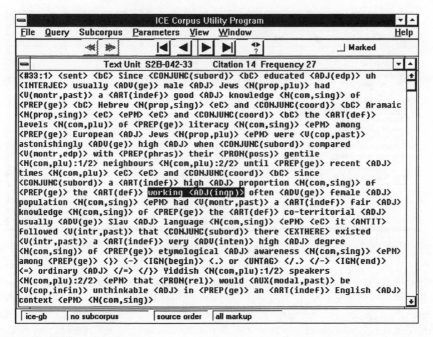

FIG. 7.8. Markup stripping

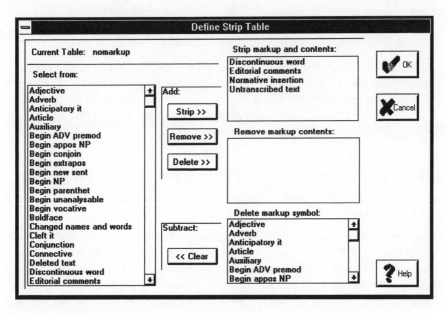

FIG. 7.9. Markup selection

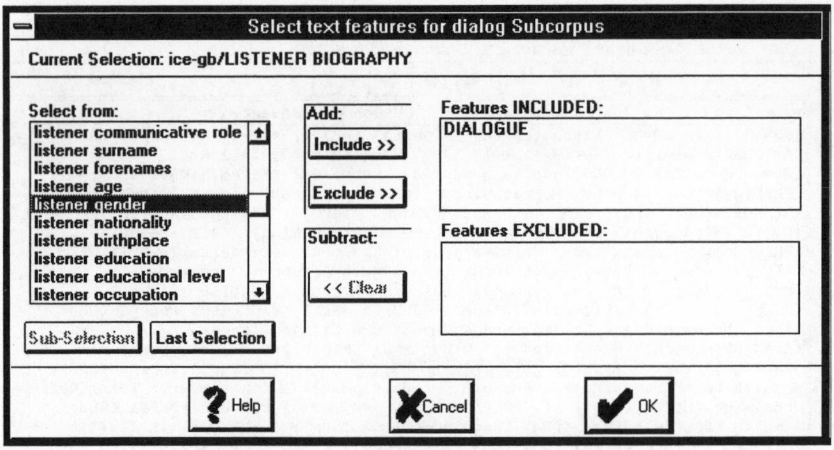

FIG. 7.10. Subcorpus selection: browsing the hierarchy of features

The dialog box shown in Fig. 7.9 illustrates how users can create bespoke markup 'filters' which allow them to focus on information that is relevant to a particular line of research. The list box on the left includes an exhaustive list of markup in the current corpus. Selecting from this list and including the selection in any of the three list boxes on the right-hand side defines how and what markup is removed from the display. Through the use of such filters readability is maintained and the focus remains on the items searched for, which are highlighted.

2.3.4. Saving Results to File

The results of a query in ICECUP can be saved to a file for later printing or editing. The user can determine whether he or she wants to save all the results of the query or simply the current result being viewed. Also, users can mark certain results whilst browsing them with the concordance or search views, and then ask ICECUP to save just the results they have marked.

2.4. Using Subcorpora

Describing and quantifying linguistic features within national, medium and genre categories is a key requirement . . .

Subcorpus information is collected in a bibliographical and biographical database. In the case of ICE this contains four levels of information for each text: general features of the corpus text, details of the subtext source, the subtext internals, and biographical data on each of the speakers or writers. For the purposes of an integrated electronic publication, this information is included as a file header for each corpus text. Otherwise it is kept in a separate database against which queries can be made to select defined subcorpora. Given the levels of textual and socio-linguistic information stored, a subcorpus can be a list of texts, subtexts, or text units which match the required set of feature-values.

Subcorpus selection allows researchers to focus their searches on a particular part of the corpus. Whether the area of interest is a national variety, gender differences in language, a particular medium, or a topic, subcorpora restrict the search to those citations that match the given parameters. Selection criteria can be combined to allow comparative studies across any of the recorded textual and socio-linguistic parameters. Subcorpus selections can be saved, and the mnemonic name used to recall the selection at a later time. The top level of subcorpus selection matches the four levels of information stored for each text. Selections can be made on text details (for instance the text category, indicating medium and genre), source details (such as publisher, audience size), or speaker/writer details (age, mother tongue, etc.), or some other of the over forty subcorpus parameters. Features can be included if a text, subtext, or range of text units matches the given value, or excluded if a particular value is present. Fig. 7.10 illustrates a user in the process of creating subcorpus of dialogue texts from the British component of ICE where the listener(s) gender is to be specified.

In the International Corpus of English, a wide range of textual and socio-linguistic parameters has been defined to capture details about the source, content, and authorship of each text. ICECUP allows researchers to restrict their searches based on these text parameters. This feature is particularly useful in comparative studies of English. It is possible, for example, to restrict the search to one national corpus, to compare corpora of, say, American and Canadian English, or to search for specified text parameters across national corpora.

2.5. ICECUBE

ICECUP has a sister program known as the *ICE Corpus Utility for Building and Enhancing* (ICECUBE)—a set of text-processing and indexing tools for ICE and ICECUP. ICECUBE consists of a set of seven functions—Prepare, CheckMUP, Extract, ReadDB, CreateDAT, Index, and MakeConc.

2.5.1. *Prepare and CheckMUP*

The Prepare function contains five options for processing texts: old ICE Markup can be converted to new SGML style; items in a text can be space separated, including genitive markers; special symbols such as umlauts and bullets can be converted to SGML symbols; and text units can be numbered. Certain of these options are required if the texts are to be used with one or other of the tagging programs currently in use with ICE. Space separation of items and text unit numbering are both required if the texts are to be indexed for use with ICECUP.

Nick Porter and Akiva Quinn

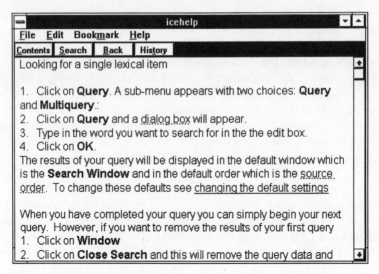

FIG. 7.11. An example of a Help screen

2.5.2. *CreateDAT, ReadDB and Extract*

The three functions CreateDAT, ReadDB, Extract are concerned with creating the files that ICECUP requires for its subcorpus facility, collating information from both the texts themselves and a database of socio-linguistic data.

2.5.3. *Index and MakeConc*

The Index and MakeConc utilities are used to index texts so that they may make use of ICECUP's rapid retrieval system. It is a requirement of ICECUP that data is processed with the Index utility.

2.6. *Help!*

... providing help to explain the options at any point in the program ...

Both ICECUP and ICECUBE come complete with context-sensitive, hypertext help systems. At any point in the program simply clicking on a Help button or hitting the F1 key will provide the user with on-screen information relevant to the current predicament. For example, if the user is formulating a query in ICECUP's query dialog box and is unsure as to the procedure, clicking on the help button or hitting the F1 key initiates the help system and automatically focuses it on the relevant topic. Clicking on a highlighted area initiates a jump to more information concerning the highlighted item—a hypertext link. In this way the information required can be found swiftly and with the minimum of effort.

Fig. 7.11 shows the help topic for a single item query. The underlined items are hypertext jumps to related topics. In addition to being context-sensitive the ICECUP Help system has all of the general qualities of any Hypertext system, such as a contents page, a search facility, backtracking, and the ability to insert bookmarks.

3. CONCLUSIONS

ICECUP was developed in house at the Survey of English Usage from a relatively loose specification that has been constantly updated during its development. This has, at times, made things difficult from a software engineering perspective. However, such a constant change in specification has meant that the software has been fine-tuned to the user's needs. ICECUP is a tool that has been created by those who will use it—the corpus linguists.

ICECUP is under continual development. Current plans include: updating the SDL and query dialog box to allow for morphological generation and analysis facilities; implementing Object Linking and Embedding (OLE) to allow the sharing of data with other Windows™ software, such as statistics packages like SPSS; providing instant access to audio playback of digitized spoken material; and investigating further the use of SGML, Relational databases, and Client/Server technology.

REFERENCES

HERWIJNEN, E. VAN (1990), *Practical SGML* (Dordrecht: Kluwer Academic Publishers).
PORTER, N. C. and QUINN, A. (1994), 'Developing the ICE Corpus Utility Program', in *English Today*, 10/3: 19–24.

8

About the ICE Tagset

SIDNEY GREENBAUM and NI YIBIN

The ICE tagset was devised by the Survey of English Usage. It is based on the tagset that was developed by the TOSCA Research Group at the University of Nijmegen, though the two differ substantially. The ICE tagset distinguishes nineteen word classes:

adjective	ADJ
adverb	ADV
article	ART
auxiliary	AUX
conjunction	CONJUNC
connective	CONNEC
existential *there*	EXTHERE
formulaic expression	FRM
genitive marker	GENM
interjection	INTERJEC
nominal adjective	NADJ
noun	N
numeral	NUM
particle	PRTCL
preposition	PREP
proform	PROFM
pronoun	PRON
reactional signal	REACT
verb	V

One of these classes is confined to just one item: existential *there*.

One or more features may be associated with a word class, and these are shown in parentheses as part of the tag. The tag as a whole is enclosed in angle brackets. For example, *isn't* in [1] is tagged as belonging to the class of verbs <V> and in addition as having the features *present* (*pres*), *copular* (*cop*), and *negative* (*neg*):

[1] Hugo has taken a dislike to Isaac Simons, but it *isn't* <V(cop,pres,neg)> personal. (W2F-016-133)

As [1] illustrates, verbs may have several features attached to their word-class tag. In all, we have found it necessary to assemble a repertoire of eighteen features for verbs to cope with the distinctions we want to preserve. Large sets of features are similarly necessary for auxiliaries and pronouns.

The Appendix to this chapter lists in alphabetic order the nineteen word classes and their associated features. The possible tag combinations (combinations of word classes and features) appearing in the Appendix amount to 262. From time to time we find additional combinations, for example *'s* as an enclitic representing the full forms *does* and *has* (see [3*d*] and [3*k*] below). The final total of possible tag combinations may therefore advance beyond 262.

The description of the ICE tagset is given in the *ICE Tagset Manual* (Greenbaum, 1995) and the *Alphabetical Reference Guide to the ICE Tagset* (Ni, 1995). The *Manual* explains each of the nineteen word classes in the tagset and their accompanying features, and discusses with exemplification the criteria by which they are assigned to lexical items and problem cases. As a further help to users, references are given to sections in *A Comprehensive Grammar of the English Language* (Quirk *et al.*, 1985) and *A Student's Grammar of the English Language* (Greenbaum and Quirk, 1990). For closed classes and subclasses, we attempted to provide exhaustive lists. For example, the *Manual* contains lists of auxiliaries, conjunctions, and pronouns in their various subclasses.

The *Guide* offers a quick reference to tags and closed-class items and an alphabetical list of words and phrases, which include those that posed problems during the tagging of ICE-GB. Each entry is accompanied by illustrative sentences. For example, *best* is noted as being a superlative adjective or adverb (the superlative of the adjective *good* or the adverb *well*) but the reader is also advised that it may be an elliptical past semi-auxiliary (elliptical for *had best*), as we find in:

[2] Best start saving (S1A-061-102)

To take another example, the *Guide* shows that the form *'s* can be tagged in as many as eleven different ways:

[3*a*] Unless something*'s* <AUX(pass,pres,encl)> done about her she'll end up like her mother. (W2F-007-129) [*is*, the enclitic form of the present passive auxiliary]

[3*b*] In the time they've been here he*'s* <AUX(perf,pres,encl)> seen her relax, get into the swing of things. (W2F-016-68) [*has*, the enclitic form of the present perfect auxiliary]

[3*c*] Vernon asked: 'Your Froggie*'s* <AUX(prog,pres,encl)> a-wooing?' (W2F-020-186) [*is*, the enclitic form of the present progressive auxiliary]

[3*d*] What*'s* <AUX(do,pres,encl)> he do? (S1A-058-214) [*does*, the enclitic form of the present *do* auxiliary]

[3*e*] If I haven't passed it*'s* <AUX(semi,pres,encl):1/3> going to cost me a lot of money to come home and re-take. (W1B-005-87) [the first item of the enclitic form of the present semi-auxiliary, *is going to*]

Sidney Greenbaum and Ni Yibin

[3*f*] It*'s* <AUX(semi,pres,encl,disc):1/3> not going to do any harm to anyone (S1A-071-205) [the first item of the enclitic form of the discontinuous present semi-auxiliary *is going to*]

[3*g*] Isobel*'s* <GENM> grief was a terrible grief. (W2F-020-103) [the genitive marker]

[3*h*] Let*'s* <PRON(pers,plu,encl)> see if there are buyers. (W2C-015-9) [*us*, the enclitic form of the plural personal pronoun]

[3*i*] What*'s* <V(cop,pres,encl)> the frightful noise in the background? (W2F-020-152) [*is*, the enclitic form of the present copular verb]

[3*j*] There*'s* <V(intr,pres,encl)> no surer way to lose a good friend than to marry her. (W2F-018-10) [*is*, the enclitic form of the present intransitive verb]

[3*k*] He*'s* <V(montr,pres,encl)> a choice of taking his wife and children away from everything they've ever known, or staying and watching them starve. (W2F-007-83) [*has*, the enclitic form of the present monotransitive verb]

The *Manual* and *Guide* are intended both for the compilers of the ICE corpora and for the users of the corpora. The two documents serve in the first place as a guide to those who check the results of the automatic tagging program. They are permanently a help to those who are searching the corpus for grammatical information (for example, modal auxiliaries) or for lexical items in specific grammatical uses (for example, *that* as a relative pronoun). The two guides to the ICE tag system went through a number of editions. The revisions reflect the experience of researchers at the Survey in checking the output of the automatic tagging.

Quite recently, all the information conveyed in the *Manual* and the *Guide* has been incorporated within a program called TagHelp. For the benefit of those who are annotating the corpora, TagHelp is available within the Help systems of TAGSELECT and ICETREE (see Chapter 6 in this volume). Users of the corpora will be able to access TagHelp through the Help system of ICECUP.

In establishing the ICE tagset, we had in mind several principles. To start with, we wanted our categories and features to conform in general to the analyses in the *Comprehensive Grammar* (which has come to be recognized as the standard reference grammar for English) and in its derivatives: the *Student's Grammar* and *A Communicative Grammar of English* (Leech and Svartvik, 1994). We could then be confident that the ICE tags and their assignment would be recognized by potential users of the ICE corpora.

Secondly, we wanted the labels for the tags to be easily recognizable. We ensured recognition by employing abbreviations for the terms which either are widely used (such as AUX, ADJ, PREP) or can be immediately grasped as related to their full forms (such as *subjun* for subjunctive, *subord* for subordinator, EXTHERE for existential there, INTERJEC for interjection). In distinguishing the two subclasses of semi-auxiliaries, we used *semip* for the smaller subclass of those followed by an *-ing* participle.

Thirdly, we were inclined to include subclasses that comprised a limited number of lexical items that we could list in full. We were therefore happy to establish tags for those subclasses of adverbs whose members can be listed: additive (e.g. *also*), exclusive (e.g. *only*), particularizer (e.g. *especially*), relative (e.g. 'the time *when*'), *wh-* (e.g. *how*). Two other subclasses that did not allow complete listing were distinguished because they are easily identified: intensifiers (e.g. *extremely*) and adverbs used to form phrasal verbs (e.g. 'look *out*', 'make *up* a story'). All other adverbs were labelled ADV(ge), consigned to a heterogeneous set that researchers could subdivide by imposing their own criteria. As a further example, the pronoun/determiner class consists of items most of which could function as pronouns or determiners, such as *some, this, which,* and *all*. We established fifteen subclasses of pronouns/determiners.

Fourthly, we avoided making distinctions that are not formally marked either in the word itself or within the immediate context. For example, we do not distinguish in the tagging between reflexive and emphatic uses of pronouns such as *myself* because the distinction cannot be achieved automatically. Similarly, we treat under the feature *do* all the uses of this dummy operator, including the emphatic functions, as in 'You never *did* get that joke' (S1A-018-145). On the other hand, we tag differently the auxiliary and lexical verb functions of *be, do,* and *have*, since the two functions are clearly differentiated in context.

Some distinctions are in fact difficult for linguists to make. We introduced the feature 'transitive' as a neutral term for verbs that are followed by the sequence NP plus non-finite verb phrase; for example, the sequence 'me to cover up' in 'They asked me to cover up for them' (W2F-006-134), where *asked* is tagged as transitive (abbreviated as 'trans'). 'Transitive' neutralizes the distinction between monotransitive (a verb complemented by just a direct object), ditransitive (a verb complemented by an indirect object and a direct object), and complex transitive (a verb complemented by a direct object and an object complement). By using this tag, we avoid having to decide which type of transitivity the verb has. As Mair has demonstrated, this tripartite distinction ignores 'the gradient transitions between categories' (cf. Mair, 1990: 93–101, 220–2). Since researchers may well differ in their treatment of this area of syntactic gradience, we decided that decisions for more delicate analyses should be left to them. Hence, the italicized verbs in [4a]–[4d] are tagged as 'trans':

[4a] This is a period when she hardly *feels* <V(trans,pres)> herself to exist at all. (W2F-019-16)

[4b] [...] I *remember* <V(trans,pres)> you coming up out of the sea with a dog, carrying your clothes in a bundle. (W2F-018-195)

[4c] Some of them are fairly large and look like one *imagines* <V(trans,pres)> a monkey to look, [...] (W2B-021-26)

[4d] But the Tory party's history *has* <V(trans,pres)> realism engraved at its heart. (W2F-003-35)

There is a familiar distinction between count and non-count (or mass) nouns, but it is not one that is made in the ICE tagging system. Non-count nouns are tagged in exactly the same way as singular count nouns. We did not introduce a separate tag for non-count nouns because the automatic tagger could not be relied on to identify them consistently, and even the human checker would not always be able to tell them apart from singular count nouns. In part, the problem is that the distinction is often blurred. It is hard to say whether the italicized nouns are count or non-count in [5a]–[5d]:

[5a] I heard that some other people from *college* are going to go along [. . .] (S1A-002-101)

[5b] [. . .] there're many projects that they have on *hand* (S1A-003-57)

[5c] Oh what sort of *park* is it (S1A-006-229)

[5d] They think that if you pay it must by *definition* be better (S1A-012-139)

A very different problem led to the creation of UNTAG, a tag that is used where none of the lexical tags are appropriate. Speakers often fail to finish a word and the resulting word partial is assigned UNTAG because it cannot be tagged as belonging to a specific word class. Sometimes, the word partials are a consequence of hesitation [6a], or self-correction [6b], or change of mind [6c]:

[6a] Uh the characters sought leave to appeal against that decision by *su* <UNTAG> uh summons issued on the tenth of January nineteen ninety-one uh (S2A-065-5)

[6b] The <UNTAG> *pant* <UNTAG> the plant was still broken down (S2A-067-69)

[6c] Uh and he told me that he'd felt that he'd felt a pain in the buttock and uh uhm in *hi* <UNTAG> the lower part of his back (S2A-067-58)

Word partials may also occur in handwritten texts, usually when writers change their mind and delete the word instead of completing it, the deletion here indicated by the brackets:

[7] [. . .] so I [apo <UNTAG>] started to apologize in full [. . .] (W1B-007-38)

UNTAG is assigned to words as well as word partials. Self-correction or a false start in speech or deletion in writing may result in ambiguity:

[8] [*it* <UNTAG> *is* <UNTAG> probably <ADV(ge)> tha <UNTAG>] Thus survival, social and curiosity motives are [. . .] (W1A-017-128)

It can have any of three tag combinations: PRON(antit), PRON(cleftit), and PRON(pers, sing). Anticipatory *it* appears in constructions where a clause (usually the subject) is extraposed (cf. Quirk *et al.*, 1985, 18.33–35); cleft *it* is used in cleft sentences (cf. Quirk *et al.*, 1985, 18.25 f.); and PRON(pers,sing) is the tag for other uses of *it*. Similarly, *is* is grammatically ambiguous in the abandoned sentence, since it could be a copular verb, an intransitive verb (if the completed construction were a cleft sentence), the progressive auxiliary, the passive auxiliary, or the first part of one of several semi-auxiliaries (e.g. *is to*, *is going to*, *is about to*).

Finally, we assign UNTAG to a word form that merges two or more grammatical words, as in the tag question *innit*, which has recently been recorded as an alternative to *isn't it*:

[9] Bit cheeky, *innit* <UNTAG> (S1A-078-165)

Another cause of the merger is a misspelling, as in the omission of the apostrophe for *it's*:

[10] But *its* <UNTAG> not the same is it. (W1B-003-145)

Or a misprint may result in two words being printed as one:

[11] Frankenstein's monster is capable of behaviour that is autonomous and not always predictable or imitatable by the builder or *bythe* <UNTAG> experts [. . .] (W2A-035-70)

So far we have been discussing the principles that underline the creation of the ICE tagset. However, in applying the tags we have to decide on the criteria for assigning them to lexical items, and much of the *Manual* and the whole of the *Guide* are devoted to guidance on such decisions.

The distinctions between word classes can be fuzzy even when various criteria are applied. As a guide to the human checker and researchers, we specified which tag should be selected when there is doubt. For example, sometimes there are no clues as to whether a word ending in *-ing* is a noun or a verb. When there is such a doubt, the *Manual* stipulates that the word should be tagged as a verb:

[12a] [. . .] well *learning* <V(intr,ingp)> is what to change and adapt and survive and fit in with changing circumstances (S2A-049-24)

[12b] Uhm right okay *nurturing* <V(intr,ingp)> is what happens to you from your environment uhm (S1B-016-100)

Researchers have to bear this stipulation in mind when they engage in searches.

The *Manual* also advises on the tagging of adverbs and prepositions that might be regarded as part of a multi-word verb, since the collocational links are not always clear. The checker is directed to overcollect them as phrasal adverbs or phrasal prepositions if there is doubt:

[13a] And Ted Hooker-Smith's coming *down* <ADV(phras)> from Preston. (W2F-020-195)

[13b] He lagged *away* <ADV(phras)> a few steps, then came back. (W2F-015-88)

[13c] Adam uhm what did you see as missing *from* <PREP(phras)> other activities for the disabled which might have got you into starting this group (S1A-001-1)

Researchers have to be aware that it is up to them to decide what combinations to recognize as phrasal verbs, prepositional verbs, or phrasal-prepositional verbs.

The *Manual* does not treat these types of verbs as compounds; for example, a prepositional verb such as *look after* is not regarded as one grammatical word. But there are numerous other instances where combinations of various kinds are treated as compounds. The same tag is assigned to each part of the combination but with a different serial number, as with *in other words*:

[14] *In* <CONNEC(ge):1/3> *other* <CONNEC(ge):2/3> *words* <CONNEC(ge):3/3> what Standard Oil does is organise the refiners (S1B-005-21)

Such ditto tags are used for combinations in various word classes, for what are traditionally recognized as grammatical words:

[15*a*] 'Fair enough, lad,' he said, smiling as if this had been his intention *all* <ADV(ge):1/2> *along* <ADV(ge):2/2>. (W2F-001-135)

[15*b*] *In* <PREP(ge):1/4> *the* <PREP(ge):2/4> *event* <PREP(ge):3/4> *of* <PREP(ge): 4/4> an emergency when cleaners are on the premises assistance may be obtained by dialing 222 on any college internal phone. (W1B-028-33)

[15*c*] The Iraqi dictator is benefiting from decades of Arab frustration; frustration at Arab's inability to co-operate, *let* <CONJUNC(coord):1/2> *alone* <CONJUNC (coord):2/2> unite [. . .] (W1B-020-107)

[15*d*] They will be here in *a* <PRON(quant,plu):1/3> *very* <PRON(quant,plu):1/3> *few* <PRON(quant,plu):1/3> moments (S2A-019-31)

Some multi-word expressions that were assigned ditto tags can be interrupted by intervening words. To show the connection between the parts of the multi-word expressions when there were such interruptions, we resorted to the feature 'discontinuous'. For example, in [16] the first and second parts of the semi-auxiliary *'m going to* are separated by the intruding *just* and therefore discontinuous tags are added to all three parts of the semi-auxiliary:

[16] I'*m* <AUX(semi,pres,encl,disc):1/3> just <ADV(excl)> *going* <AUX(semi,pres, encl,disc):2/3> *to* <AUX(semi,pres,encl,disc):3/3> go berserk for a while (S1A-001-18)

Similarly, discontinuous tags are added in [17] to *so as to* to cope with the intervention of *not*:

[17] You'll learn assertiveness *so* <PRTCL(to,disc):1/3> *as* <PRTCL(to,disc):2/3> not <ADV(ge)> *to* <PRTCL(to,disc):3/3> be inhibited by other people's agendas (S2B-029-118)

One of the determinants for the assignment of tags was the requirements of the parser. Sometimes we had to accept what was needed for the parser to produce any analyses rather than what is found in standard treatments. For example, the TOSCA parser (which we were intending to use for the next stage of annotation) required us to assign ditto tags to every sequence of two or more nouns that constitute a unit. In [18] we therefore gave ditto tags to the sequence *breakfast-time vagueness*, though we would have preferred to treat *breakfast-time* as a noun functioning as premodifier of a noun head:

[18] Her office personality is a positive one; but she is not aware of this, any more than she is conscious of *breakfast-time* <N(com,sing):1/2> *vagueness* <N(com, sing):2/2>. (W2F-019-32)

In many instances, the tags were changed during the interactive stage of parsing to enable the parser to operate. Thus, *am* in [19] was correctly tagged in the first instance as a copular verb:

[19] 'Good Lord you are <V(cop,pres)> indispensable'
'Yes well I am <V(intr,pres)> when other people are on holiday' (S1A-095-257f)

However, the *copular* feature was changed to *intransitive*, since otherwise the parser would fail. Similarly, stranded phrasal prepositions in a passive construction had to be tagged as adverbs during interactive parsing, since the TOSCA parser cannot treat words as prepositions when they are without a complement. Hence, we had to change *after* in [20] from the original <PREP(phras)> to <ADV(phras)>:

[20] I am glad to hear that off site locations were well looked *after* <ADV(phras)> by St. John Ambulance personnel. (W1B-018-79)

With is correctly analysed as a type of subordinator, tagged <PRTCL(with)>, when it introduces a non-finite clause that has a subject, as in [21]:

[21*a*] Well, staffs were small and we stayed remarkably busy, *with* <PRTCL(with)> reporters doubling up at times as sub-editors and doing all sorts of other jobs. (W2F-014-81)

[21*b*] He closed the door behind him, then stood inside the porch *with* <PRTCL (with)> his hands clasped behind his back. (W2F-009-61)

[21*c*] For example, if the red-amber-green traffic light signals are used as input, *with* <PRTCL(with)> 110 and 001 to correspond to 1 for advance, and 010 and 100 to correspond to 0 for stop, only three complete cycles through the training data are required to produce a correct response, from a set of weights initially. (W2A-032-73)

However, the parser cannot recognize the use of *with* in analogous verbless clauses, so that *with* in [22] has to be tagged simply as a preposition:

[22] *With* <PREP(ge)> all this death around, she's becoming frightened of exertion anyway. (W2F-016-52)

We hope at a later stage to revert to the tag assignments that we prefer.

REFERENCES

GREENBAUM, S. (1995), *The ICE Tagset Manual* (London: Survey of English Usage, University College London).

—— and QUIRK, R. (1990), *A Student's Grammar of the English Language* (London: Longman).

LEECH, G. and SVARTVIK, J. (1994), *A Communicative Grammar of English* (London: Longman).

MAIR, C. (1990), *Infinitival Complement Clauses in English* (Cambridge: Cambridge University Press).

NI, Y. (1995), *An Alphabetical Reference Guide to the ICE Tagset* (London: Survey of English Usage, University College London).

QUIRK, R., GREENBAUM, S., LEECH, G., and SVARTVIK, J. (1985), *A Comprehensive Grammar of the English Language* (London: Longman).

TAG	EXPLANATION OF TAG	EXAMPLE
ADJ(comp)	adjective, comparative	*thinner*
ADJ(edp)	adjective, -ed participle	*stained* shirt, *talented* person
ADJ(ge)	adjective, general	*happy*
ADJ(ingp)	adjective, -ing participle	*amazing* news, *uninteresting* lesson
ADJ(sup)	adjective, superlative	the *fiercest* dog
ADV(add)	adverb, additive	He is *also* my friend
ADV(excl)	adverb, exclusive	*only* three people
ADV(ge)	adverb, general	Listen *carefully*
ADV(ge,comp)	adverb, comparative	Run *faster*
ADV(ge,sup)	adverb, superlative	He works the *hardest*
ADV(inten)	adverb, intensifier	*very* exciting
ADV(inten,comp)	adverb, intensifier, comparative	*more* interesting
ADV(inten,sup)	adverb, intensifier, superlative	*most* surprising
ADV(partic)	adverb, particularizer	John *in particular* was excellent
ADV(phras)	adverb, phrasal	Look the word *up*
ADV(rel)	adverb, relative	the reason *why* he lied to you
ADV(wh)	adverb, wh-adverb	*Where* did you go?
ART(def)	article, definite	*the* weather
ART(indef)	article, indefinite	*a* cat
AUX(do,imp)	auxiliary, *do* imperative	*Do* sit down
AUX(do,imp,neg)	auxiliary, *do* imperative, negative	*Don't* be silly
AUX(do,past)	auxiliary, *do*, past	*Did* you know that?
AUX(do,past,neg)	auxiliary, *do*, past, negative	You *didn't* lock the door
AUX(do,pres)	auxiliary, *do*, present	I *do* like you
AUX(do,pres,encl)	auxiliary, *do*, present, enclitic	What*'s* he want to prove?
AUX(do,pres,neg)	auxiliary, *do*, present, negative	You just *don't* understand
AUX(do,pres,procl)	auxiliary, *do*, present, proclitic	*D'*you like ice-cream?
AUX(let,imp)	auxiliary, *let* imperative	*Let's* go
AUX(modal,past)	auxiliary, modal, past	I *could* have done that
AUX(modal,past,encl)	auxiliary, modal, past, enclitic	I*'d* love one
AUX(modal,past,neg)	auxiliary, modal, past, negative	You *shouldn't* do it

TAG	*EXPLANATION OF TAG*	*EXAMPLE*
AUX(**modal,pres**)	auxiliary, modal, present	If I *may*
AUX(**modal,pres,encl**)	auxiliary, modal, present, enclitic	I*'ll* let you know
AUX(**modal,pres,neg**)	auxiliary, modal, present, negative	If it *can't* be done, it *can't* be done
AUX(**pass,edp**)	auxiliary, passive, *-ed* participle	I've *been* cheated
AUX(**pass,imp**)	auxiliary, passive, imperative	*Be* seated!
AUX(**pass,infin**)	auxiliary, passive, infinitive	Do you want to *be* relieved?
AUX(**pass,ingp**)	auxiliary, passive, *-ing* participle	I don't like *being* teased
AUX(**pass,past**)	auxiliary, passive, past	It *was* created in 1956
AUX(**pass,past,neg**)	auxiliary, passive, past, negative	Rome *wasn't* built in a day
AUX(**pass,pres**)	auxiliary, passive, present	I *am* trapped
AUX(**pass,pres,encl**)	auxiliary, passive, present, enclitic	He*'s* often driven to school
AUX(**pass,pres,neg**)	auxiliary, passive, present, negative	It *isn't* considered first-class
AUX(**pass,subjun**)	auxiliary, passive, subjunctive	if it *were* mishandled
AUX(**pass,subjun,neg**)	auxiliary, passive, subjunctive, negative	if Tom *weren't* granted his wish
AUX(**perf,infin**)	auxiliary, perfect, infinitive	It's good to *have* met you
AUX(**perf,infin,encl**)	auxiliary, perfect, infinitive, enclitic	I would*'ve* liked to support it
AUX(**perf,ingp**)	auxiliary, perfect, *-ing* participle	*Having* said that, I still love you
AUX(**perf,past**)	auxiliary, perfect, past	I *had* finished my dinner by then
AUX(**perf,past,encl**)	auxiliary, perfect, past, enclitic	I would have got it if I*'d* known it
AUX(**perf,past,neg**)	auxiliary, perfect, past, negative	I *hadn't* felt that way before
AUX(**perf,pres**)	auxiliary, perfect, present	*Have* you been to Paris?
AUX(**perf,pres,encl**)	auxiliary, perfect, present, enclitic	I*'ve* finished it
AUX(**perf,pres,neg**)	auxiliary, perfect, present, negative	She *hasn't* come home yet
AUX(**prog,edp**)	auxiliary, progressive, *-ed* participle	I've *been* watching you
AUX(**prog,infin**)	auxiliary, progressive, infinitive	Will I *be* seeing you soon?
AUX(**prog,ingp**)	auxiliary, progressive, *-ing* participle	It's been *being* occurring to me for some time

102

TAG	EXPLANATION OF TAG	EXAMPLE
AUX(prog,past)	auxiliary, progressive, past	She *was* always drinking
AUX(prog,past,neg)	auxiliary, progressive, past, negative	I *wasn't* looking for you
AUX(prog,pres)	auxiliary, progressive, present	I *am* key-punching
AUX(prog,pres,encl)	auxiliary, progressive, present, enclitic	He*'s* cooking tonight
AUX(prog,pres,neg)	auxiliary, progressive, present, negative	*Isn't* he helping you?
AUX(prog,subjun)	auxiliary, progressive, subjunctive	If he *were* harassing you
AUX(semi,edp)	semi-auxiliary, *-ed* participle	He has *started to* talk
AUX(semi,edp,disc)	semi-auxiliary, *-ed* participle, discontinuous	they've *come* perhaps *to* fear the neighbours
AUX(semi,ellipt)	semi-auxiliary, elliptical	those *going* to protest
AUX(semi,ellipt,disc)	semi-auxiliary, elliptical, discontinuous	She's expecting a child, *due* perhaps *to* be born in April
AUX(semi,imp)	semi-auxiliary, imperative	*Be sure to* get my essay!
AUX(semi,imp,disc)	semi-auxiliary, imperative, discontinuous	*Continue* however *to* take the lead
AUX(semi,infin)	semi-auxiliary, infinitive	You can begin *to* plan it
AUX(semi,infin,disc)	semi-auxiliary, infinitive, discontinuous	She'll *start* perhaps *to* write
AUX(semi,ingp)	semi-auxiliary, *-ing* participle	They're *having to* rebuild the hut
AUX(semi,ingp,disc)	semi-auxiliary, *-ing* participle, discontinuous	They're *having* perhaps *to* restart
AUX(semi,past)	semi-auxiliary, past	It *appeared to* be true
AUX(semi,past,disc)	semi-auxiliary, past, discontinuous	Sue *was* now *going to* try
AUX(semi,past,ellipt)	semi-auxiliary, past, elliptical	Sam wasn't actually going to sue you, *was* he?
AUX(semi,past,encl)	semi-auxiliary, past, enclitic	The case*'d better* be dropped
AUX(semi,past,encl,disc)	semi-auxiliary, past, enclitic, discontinuous	You*'d* really *better* act fast
AUX(semi,past,neg)	semi-auxiliary, past, negative	I *wasn't going* to kill him
AUX(semi,past,neg,disc)	semi-auxiliary, past, negative, discontinuous	Liz *wasn't* actually *going to* resign
AUX(semi,past,neg,ellipt)	semi-auxiliary, past, negative, elliptical	Jim was going to cook for us, *wasn't* he?
AUX(semi,pres)	semi-auxiliary, present	I *have to* go
AUX(semi,pres,disc)	semi-auxiliary, present, discontinuous	He *is* perhaps *due to* retire soon

TAG	EXPLANATION OF TAG	EXAMPLE
AUX(**semi,pres,ellipt**)	semi-auxiliary, present, elliptical	Jim isn't due to come, *is* he?
AUX(**semi,pres,encl**)	semi-auxiliary, present, enclitic	He*'s bound to* phone
AUX(**semi,pres,encl,disc**)	semi-auxiliary, present, enclitic, discontinuous	You*'re* not *going to* win
AUX(**semi,pres,neg**)	semi-auxiliary, present, negative	She *isn't likely to* be there
AUX(**semi,pres,neg,disc**)	semi-auxiliary, present, negative, discontinuous	Peter *isn't* actually *going to* cook
AUX(**semi,pres,neg,ellipt**)	semi-auxiliary, present, negative, elliptical	Nick's due to come, *isn't* he?
AUX(**semi,procl**)	semi-auxiliary, proclitic	Spain is how things *used t'*be
AUX(**semi,subjun**)	semi-auxiliary, subjunctive	If I *were to* marry you
AUX(**semi,subjun,neg**)	semi-auxiliary, subjunctive, negative	If I *weren't* to stay
AUX(**semip,edp**)	semi-auxiliary, *-ed* participle	He has *continued* disobeying my instructions,
AUX(**semip,edp,disc**)	semi-auxiliary, *-ed* participle, discontinuous	He's *kept* perhaps *on* working just for me
AUX(**semip,imp**)	semi-auxiliary, imperative	*Keep* writing
AUX(**semip,imp,disc**)	semi-auxiliary, imperative, discontinuous	*Carry* uhm *on* writing
AUX(**semip,infin**)	semi-auxiliary, infinitive	I'll *begin* working
AUX(**semip,infin,disc**)	semi-auxiliary, infinitive, discontinuous	I'll *keep* perhaps *on* working for another hour
AUX(**semip,ingp**)	semi-auxiliary, *-ing* participle	They were *carrying on* singing
AUX(**semip,ingp,disc**)	semi-auxiliary, *-ing* participle, discontinuous	they were *going* uhm *on* shouting
AUX(**semip,past**)	semi-auxiliary, past	We *stopped* trying
AUX(**semip,past,disc**)	semi-auxiliary, past, discontinuous	I *went* uhm *on* trying
AUX(**semip,pres**)	semi-auxiliary, present	He *keeps* complaining
AUX(**semip,pres,disc**)	semi-auxiliary, present, discontinuous	The workers *go* uhm *on* talking
AUX(**semip,subjun**)	semi-auxiliary, subjunctive	It's essential that he *begin* writing his thesis
CONJUNC(**coord**)	conjunction, co-ordinating	Henry *and* June
CONJUNC(**subord**)	conjunction, subordinating	Stay *if* you like
CONJUNC(**subord,disc**)	conjunction, subordinating, discontinuous	*Provided* however *that* there's time
CONJUNC(**subord,ellipt**)	conjunction, subordinating, elliptical	Provided that you're happy and *that* I'm happy
CONNEC(**appos**)	connective, appositive	*for example*
CONNEC(**appos,disc**)	connective, appositive, discontinuous	*that is* perhaps *to say*

TAG	EXPLANATION OF TAG	EXAMPLE
CONNEC(ge)	connective, general	*as a result*
CONNEC(ge,disc)	connective, general, discontinuous	*as* perhaps *a consequence*
EXTHERE	existential *there*	*There* is a rat in the garden
FRM	formulaic expression	*I see*, thanks
GENM	genitive marker	Tom*'s* cat
INTERJEC	interjection	*shooh*
N(com,plu)	noun, common, plural	*dogs*
N(com,sing)	noun, common, singular	water
N(prop,plu)	noun, proper, plural	*Americans*
N(prop,sing)	noun, proper, singular	*England*
NADJ(comp,plu)	nominal adjective, comparative, plural	Take care of the *weaker*
NADJ(comp,sing)	nominal adjective, comparative, singular	for *better* or for *worse*
NADJ(edp,plu)	nominal adjective, *-ed* participle, plural	the *exploited*
NADJ(edp,sing)	nominal adjective, *-ed* participle, singular	Look at the *enclosed*
NADJ(ingp,plu)	nominal adjective, -ing participle, plural	the *discerning*
NADJ(plu)	nominal adjective, plural	the *rich*
NADJ(prop,plu)	nominal adjective, proper, plural	the *Chinese*
NADJ(prop,sing)	nominal adjective, proper, singular	Refer to God as the *Divine*
NADJ(sing)	nominal adjective, singular	in *public*
NADJ(sup,plu)	nominal adjective, superlative, plural	the *cleverest* in the class
NADJ(sup,sing)	nominal adjective, superlative, singular	do your *best*
NUM(card,plu)	numeral, cardinal, plural	*1990s*
NUM(card,sing)	numeral, cardinal, singular	*two*
NUM(frac,plu)	numeral, fraction, plural	*three-fifths*
NUM(frac,sing)	numeral, fraction, singular	*one-fifth*
NUM(hyph)	numeral, hyphenated number	*1990–91*
NUM(mult)	numeral, multiplier	*twice* as much
NUM(ord)	numeral, ordinal	*second* chance
NUM(ord,plu)	numeral, ordinal, plural	all the *others*
NUM(ord,sing)	numeral, ordinal, singular	*another* apple
PREP(ge)	preposition, general	*at* noon
PREP(ge,disc)	preposition, general, discontinuous	*as* probably *a consequence of*
PREP(ge,ellipt)	preposition, general, elliptical	in relation to X and *to* Y
PREP(inter)	preposition, interrogative	*What about* John?

TAG	EXPLANATION OF TAG	EXAMPLE
PREP(phras)	preposition, phrasal	Look *at* me
PROFM(conjoin)	proform, conjoin	a week or *so*
PROFM(so)	proform, *so*	I hope *so*
PRON(antit)	pronoun, anticipatory *it*	*It* is pleasant to be here
PRON(antit, procl)	pronoun, anticipatory *it*, proclitic	*'T* is easy to see that
PRON(ass)	pronoun, assertive	*some* books
PRON(ass,sing)	pronoun, assertive, singular	*something* nice
PRON(cleftit)	pronoun, cleft *it*	*It* was Kathy who made the noise
PRON(cleftit, procl)	pronoun, cleft *it*, proclitic	*'T* was Judith that I spoke to
PRON(dem)	pronoun, demonstrative	*such* things will happen to anyone
PRON(dem,plu)	pronoun, demonstrative, plural	*those* chairs
PRON(dem,sing)	pronoun, demonstrative, singular	*this* cup
PRON(neg)	pronoun, negative	*none*
PRON(neg,sing)	pronoun, negative, singular	*nobody*
PRON(nonass)	pronoun, nonassertive	*any* mistake
PRON(nonass,sing)	pronoun, nonassertive, singular	*anything* edible
PRON(one,plu)	pronoun, *one*, plural	These *ones* are not mine
PRON(one,sing)	pronoun, *one*, singular	I want the big *one*
PRON(pers)	pronoun, personal	*you*
PRON(pers,plu)	pronoun, personal, plural	*we*
PRON(pers,plu,encl)	pronoun, personal, plural, enclitic	Let*'s* do it
PRON(pers,procl)	pronoun, personal, proclitic	*y'*know
PRON(pers,sing)	pronoun, personal, singular	*she*
PRON(pers,sing,procl)	pronoun, personal, proclitic	I thought it was their dog but *'t*was mine
PRON(poss)	pronoun, possessive	*your*
PRON(poss,plu)	pronoun, possessive, plural	*ours*
PRON(poss,sing)	pronoun, possessive, singular	*his*
PRON(quant)	pronoun, quantifying	*enough* food
PRON(quant,plu)	pronoun, quantifying, plural	*few* buildings
PRON(quant,sing)	pronoun, quantifying, singular	*little* money
PRON(recip)	pronoun, reciprocal	*each other*
PRON(ref,plu)	pronoun, reflexive, plural	*yourselves*
PRON(ref,sing)	pronoun, reflexive, singular	*yourself*
PRON(rel)	pronoun, relative	Pick those *which* you like
PRON(rel,poss)	pronoun, relative, possessive	the neighbours *whose* party I went to

TAG	EXPLANATION OF TAG	EXAMPLE
PRON(univ)	pronoun, universal	*all* my friends
PRON(univ,plu)	pronoun, universal, plural	*both* my parents
PRON(univ,sing)	pronoun, universal, singular	*each* child
PRON(wh)	pronoun, *wh*	*What* are you up to?
PRTCL(for)	particle *for*	something *for* you to do
PRTCL(to)	particle *to*	Do we want *to* eat?
PRTCL(to,disc)	particle *to*, discontinuous	*in order* not *to* lose
PRTCL(with)	particle *with*	*with* Justin guarding the door
REACT	reaction signal	*yes*
v(cop,edp)	verb, copular, *-ed* participle	I have *been* sick
v(cop,edp,disc)	verb, copular, *-ed* participle, discontinuous	He's *served* briefly *as* her assistant
v(cop,imp)	verb, copular, imperative	*Be* good
v(cop,imp,disc)	verb, copular, imperative, discontinuous	*Act* temporarily *as* my agent
v(cop,infin)	verb, copular, infinitive	I'd love to *be* there
v(cop,infin,disc)	verb, copular, infinitive, discontinuous	He *posed* for a time *as* a poet
v(cop,ingp)	verb, copular, *-ing* participle	You are *being* naughty
v(cop,ingp,disc)	verb, copular, *-ing* participle, discontinuous	I am *acting* temporarily *as* your spokesperson
v(cop,past)	verb, copular, past	I *was* in London
v(cop,past,disc)	verb, copular, past, discontinuous	He *functioned* occasionally *as* her advisor
v(cop,past,neg)	verb, copular, past, negative	I *wasn't* in despair
v(cop,pres)	verb, copular, present	I *am* confident of victory
v(cop,pres,disc)	verb, copular, present, discontinuous	She *serves* only as an advisor
v(cop,pres,encl)	verb, copular, present, enclitic	He*'s* unlucky
v(cop,pres,neg)	verb, copular, present, negative	Fiona *isn't* at home
v(cop,pres,procl)	verb, copular, present, proclitic	*S'*okay
v(cop,subjun)	verb, copular, subjunctive	If I *were* you
v(cop,subjun,disc)	verb, copular, subjunctive, discontinuous	It's imperative that he *count* now *as* your agent
v(cop,subjun,neg)	verb, copular, subjunctive, negative	If he *weren't* here
v(cxtr,edp)	verb, complex-transitive, *-ed* participle	Have you *kept* him busy?
v(cxtr,imp)	verb, complex-transitive, imperative	*Keep* him warm!
v(cxtr,infin)	verb, complex-transitive, infinitive	They'll *get* the meal ready
v(cxtr,ingp)	verb, complex-transitive, *-ing* participle	Are you *putting* it in the bank?

TAG	EXPLANATION OF TAG	EXAMPLE
v(cxtr,past)	verb, complex-transitive, past	We *made* them happy
v(cxtr,past,encl)	verb, complex-transitive, past, enclitic	I*'d* a tooth out yesterday
v(cxtr,past,neg)	verb, complex-transitive, past, negative	She *hadn't* them in for the party
v(cxtr,pres)	verb, complex-transitive, present	She *considers* us her friends
v(cxtr,pres,encl)	verb, complex-transitive, present, enclitic	I*'ve* nobody in mind at the moment
v(cxtr,pres,neg)	verb, complex-transitive, present, negative	I *haven't* anybody in mind then
v(cxtr,subjun)	verb, complex-transitive, subjunctive	The doctor advised Mary that she *keep* the child warm
v(dimontr,edp)	verb, dimonotransitive, *-ed* participle	As I have *warned* you
v(dimontr,imp)	verb, dimonotransitive, imperative	*Show* me
v(dimontr,infin)	verb, dimonotransitive, infinitive	Do *tell* me
v(dimontr,ingp)	verb, dimonotransitive, *-ing* participle	I'm *asking* you
v(dimontr,past)	verb, dimonotransitive, past	I *told* you before
v(dimontr,pres)	verb, dimonotransitive, present	I *promise* you
v(dimontr,subjun)	verb, dimonotransitive, subjunctive	I insist that Tom *write* me weekly
v(ditr,edp)	verb, ditransitive, *-ed* participle	I've *written* you five letters
v(ditr,imp)	verb, ditransitive, imperative	*Drop* me a line!
v(ditr,infin)	verb, ditransitive, infinitive	I might *do* you two days a week
v(ditr,ingp)	verb, ditransitive, *-ing* participle	I'm *sending* you a parcel
v(ditr,past)	verb, ditransitive, past	He *booked* me two suites
v(ditr,pres)	verb, ditransitive, present	I *owe* you ten pounds
v(ditr,subjun)	verb, ditransitive, subjunctive	It's imperative that Tom *fax* us his progress report
v(intr,edp)	verb, intransitive, *-ed* participle	I've *eaten*
v(intr,imp)	verb, intransitive, imperative	*Stand* up!
v(intr,infin)	verb, intransitive, infinitive	I don't *care*
v(intr,ingp)	verb, intransitive, *-ing* participle	I'm *listening*

TAG	EXPLANATION OF TAG	EXAMPLE
v(intr,past)	verb, intransitive, past	She *nodded*
v(intr,past,neg)	verb, intransitive, past, negative	There *wasn't* anybody in the room
v(intr,pres)	verb, intransitive, present	Cats *miaou* and dogs *bark*
v(intr,pres,encl)	verb, intransitive, present, enclitic	There*'s* somebody at the door
v(intr,pres,neg)	verb, intransitive, present, negative	There *isn't* anybody in the room
v(intr,subjun)	verb, intransitive, subjunctive	I demand that Tom *leave*
v(intr,subjun,neg)	verb, intransitive, subjunctive, negative	If there *weren't* a God
v(montr,edp)	verb, monotransitive, *-ed* participle	Have you *seen* the book?
v(montr,imp)	verb, monotransitive, imperative	*Look* the word up in the dictionary!
v(montr,infin)	verb, monotransitive, infinitive	John is likely to *beat* Tom
v(montr,ingp)	verb, monotransitive, *-ing* participle	I'm *learning* Chinese
v(montr,past)	verb, monotransitive, past	Tom *planted* a tree
v(montr,past,neg)	verb, monotransitive, past, negative	They *hadn't* any money
v(montr,pres)	verb, monotransitive, present	I *eat* fish every day
v(montr,pres,encl)	verb, monotransitive, present, enclitic	I*'ve* no complaint
v(montr,pres,neg)	verb, monotransitive, present, negative	They *haven't* any children
v(montr,subjun)	verb, monotransitive, subjunctive	I insist that Tom *finish* his meal
v(trans,edp)	verb, transitive, *-ed* participle	I've *asked* him to go
v(trans,imp)	verb, transitive, imperative	*Allow* me to help you
v(trans,infin)	verb, transitive, infinitive	I'll *ask* John to tell you this
v(trans,ingp)	verb, transitive, *-ing* participle	I'm *telling* you to stop
v(trans,past)	verb, transitive, past	I *heard* him talking
v(trans,past,neg)	verb, transitive, past, negative	She *hadn't* her eyes closed then
v(trans,pres)	verb, transitive, present	Sue *wants* her sheets changed
v(trans,subjun)	verb, transitive, subjunctive	It's essential that Tom *help* the workers unload the truck

9

AUTASYS: Grammatical Tagging and Cross-Tagset Mapping

ALEX CHENGYU FANG

1. INTRODUCTION

Ever since the advent of the first computer linguistic corpus in the 1960s, linguists and computer programmers have been working on the annotation of material thus stored. Word-class tagging, the assignment of an unambiguous indication of the grammatical word class to each word in a text, has been in great demand, not only in lexicographical and grammatical studies, but also in natural language processing (NLP), an area where the corpus-based, or more specifically, probabilistic approach is becoming increasingly popular. Taggers have flourished and the past twenty years or so have witnessed TAGGIT (Greene and Rubin, 1971), CLAWS (Marshall, 1983; Garside *et al.*, 1987), FALSUNGA (DeRose, 1988), AGTS (Huang, 1991), and TOSCA (Oostdijk, 1991), to name just a few. Tagsets different in various aspects have also come into being, with Brown (Francis, 1980), LOB (Johansson *et al.*, 1986), and Lund (Svartvik, 1987) as the best known. Most recently, a tagset has been designed at the Survey of English Usage (SEU), University College London (Greenbaum and Ni, 1994; Greenbaum, 1995), which has been used to annotate the one-million-word British component of the International Corpus of English (ICE-GB, cf. Greenbaum, 1992).

This has created an intriguing situation in corpus annotation. On the one hand, compilers of corpora vary in what they intend as the primary uses of their corpora. Grammarians, lexicographers, language teachers, and NLP researchers naturally want different information from corpus annotation: grammatical, morphological, discoursal, statistical, semantic, pragmatic, or prosodic. On the other hand, unfortunately, we have not seen any single annotation scheme that meets all these requirements. Corpora thus differently annotated according to different schemes have become 'isolated islands', rendering cross-corpora studies virtually impossible. Consequently, it is desirable that either a standard annotation scheme be agreed upon in this field, or flexible systems be designed that can readily adapt themselves to different annotation schemes.

The tagger described in this chapter, AUTASYS, was designed by Alex Chengyu

Fang and Chen Xiaoli at the Guangzhou Institute of Foreign Languages, China (Fang, 1992). It assigns not only LOB tags, but also ICE and SKELETON tags to the words in the input text, a feature not yet available with other taggers. The input text can be 'clean' and unedited, or it can be pre-processed with the Standard Generalised Markup Language (SGML). Using the well-developed stochastic approach, AUTASYS has an accuracy rate of 96 per cent. It is also fast, able to process 10,000 words per minute on 486 IBM PC compatibles. So far, it has tagged the one-million-word SEU Corpus (Fang and Nelson, 1994) and nine million words of the Wall Street Journal available on CD ROM.

In what follows, I shall present some of the main features of AUTASYS, and then describe its major tag selection stages, which include tag assignment, tag selection, and measures taken to control the quality. Finally, I shall address some major issues in mapping LOB tags to ICE tags, a technique used in AUTASYS whereby ICE tags can be arrived at from LOB tags.

2. FEATURES OF AUTASYS

There are eight headings in the menu of AUTASYS, which are as follows:

Spell	Checks the word forms in the text to be tagged and adds them, if necessary, to the dictionary.
Assign	Assigns all possible tags to every word in the input text.
Tag	Disambiguates multiple tags that have been assigned to one word.
Lemmatise	Lemmatizes texts that have been tagged.
Edit	Edits texts.
Dictionary	Modifies dictionary entries, updates the dictionary, and gives information about the dictionaries used in the system.
Options	Tells the tagger which tagset(s) to use, in what format, etc.
Quit	Exits to DOS.

I shall describe only Options, as it best represents the performance and features of AUTASYS. Its main features are described in the following sections.

2.1. *Tagsets*

In the present version, AUTASYS uses three tagsets, namely, LOB, ICE, and SKELETON. The LOB Tagset has 132 tags altogether, and is the same set that was used to tag the LOB Corpus (cf. Johansson *et al.*, 1986). The ICE Tagset notes twenty-two general word classes and seventy-two features, resulting in 270 possible lexical tags (Greenbaum and Ni, 1994: 5). The differences between the two tagsets will be discussed in Section 4. The SKELETON tagset is directly derived from the ICE Tagset. It covers the twenty-two word classes noted in ICE but does not contain the features. AUTASYS also allows the user to annotate a text with both LOB and ICE tagsets.

2.2. *Compounds and Formulaic Expressions*

AUTASYS tags some fossilized or fixed expressions as 'ditto tags'. For instance, *because of* is treated as a complex preposition, and *so that* as a compound conjunction. AUTASYS also allows the tagging of compound nouns: *Mrs Mary Jones* can be tagged as a compound noun, instead of one titular noun plus two proper nouns as in LOB tagging. Ditto tags are similarly applied to such formulaic expressions as *Thank you, Goodbye, How do you do*. For some studies, especially those concerned with discourse analysis in speech, it is uninformative to tag those expressions at face value. To suit this need, AUTASYS can be instructed to tag them as formulaic expressions. Of course, they can also be tagged individually if the user is only concerned with lexical studies.

2.3. *SGML-Marked Texts*

AUTASYS tags both 'clean' unedited texts and those that have been pre-processed with SGML. At present, it recognizes markup schemes used in the SEU and ICE Corpora and the Wall Street Journals. They are illustrated in the following extracts.

A Sample from the SEU Corpus

```
<#4> <$A\> <]_> @ : m <]/> which is <%{> quite <%RF> right
<close^> but I <%{> mean <,,,,,,> that's <%{> defEAting
the whole <%'> point of the <%F:> Exercise it <%'> strikes
<%R> me <close^> I <%{> mean that <%:> is a <%'> mEAning
of <%'> <%R> mAmpAula <close^> that is <%{> not in <%'>
Any <%F:> dIctionary <close^> <,,>
<#5> <$a\> yes <,,> it's hard to know how seriously it
was taken by the person who <,,> wrote the column <,,,,,,>
I suppose what she <,,> thought was that everybody <,,>
really knows what mam mam paula really means you see so
<,,> <{_> <[_> it's <[/> all right to use it in this <,>
<{_> <[_> rather <[/> snide way and everybody will know
it's snide and no one will take it seriously <,>
```

A Sample from the ICE Corpus

```
<#32:2:B> <sent> And so <}> <-> I had </-> <=> I had </
=> </}> the feeling that here were people learning to use
their bodies learning to develop a physical language <,>
uhm <,> and yet that language was being channelled into
a very narrow <,> field and <,,> <}> <-> the the </-> <,>
<=> the </=> </}> opportunity <}> <-> <.> tha </.> </->
<=> that </=> </}> has arisen through the group that <}>
<-> <w> we 're </w> <.> w </.> </-> <=> <w> we're </w>
```

</=> </}> working with now is that those <,> movement
skills <}> <--> are </-> <,> uhm <=> are </=> </}> allowed
to be used to communicate <,> rather than to develop <}>
<--> a </-> <=> a </=> </}> narrow band of activity that
only certain people can be involved in <,>
<#33:2:B> <sent> Uhm <,,> the movement language <w> that's
</w> being developed is one which involves different people
with different skills to talk to each other <,>

A Sample from the Wall Street Journal

<DOC>
<DOCNO> 880729-0045 </DOCNO>
<HL> Interco Receives Bid From Rales Group For Takeover
Valued at $2.26 Billion </HL>
<AUTHOR> Francine Schwadel (WSJ Staff) </AUTHOR>
<SO> </SO>
<CO> ISS </CO>
<IN> TNM RET </IN>
<TXT>
<p>

2.4. Output Format

A text can be tagged in two formats: vertical or horizontal. In the vertical format,
each line of text contains one lexical item, with its tag aligned to the right. To the
left of the word are two serial numbers indicating the word's location in the original
text so that the tagged text can be easily restored to the original state, as is shown
in the following sample text from a BBC broadcast tagged by AUTASYS with both
LOB and ICE tags.

0000	001	(	PUNC(obrack)	(
0000	002	ZZ	UNTAG	c
0000	003	)	PUNC(cbrack)	)
0000	004	NP	N(prop,sing)	BBC
0001	005	CD-CD	NUM(hyph)	11-06-1991
0002	006	CD	NUM(card,sing)	1
0002	007	*-	PUNC(dash)	-
0002	008	NN	N(com,sing)	PATTEN
0002	009	VBZ	V(trans,pres)	TELLS
0002	010	NNPS	N(prop,plu)	TORIES
0002	011	TO	PRTCL(to)	TO
0002	012	VB	V(cop,infin)	KEEP
0003	013	JJ	ADJ	COOL

113

```
0004 014 NNP*    N(prop,sing):1/4          Tory
0004 015 NN*     N(prop,sing):2/4          chairman
0004 016 NP*     N(prop,sing):3/4          Chris
0004 017 NNP*    N(prop,sing):4/4          Patten
0004 018 HVZ     AUX(perf,pres)            has
0004 019 VBN     V(trans,edp)              told
0004 020 PP$     PRON(poss,sing)           his
0004 021 NN      N(com,sing)               party
0004 022 XNOT    ADV(ge)                   not
0004 023 TO      PRTCL(to)                 to
0004 024 VB      V(intr,infin)             panic
0004 025 CC      CONJUNC(coord)            but
0004 026 VB      V(intr,infin)             wait
0005 027 IN      PRTCL(for)                for
0005 028 JJ      ADJ                       economic
0005 029 NN      N(com,sing)               recovery
0005 030 TO      PRTCL(to)                 to
0005 031 VB      V(montr,infin)            revive
0005 032 PP$     PRON(poss,sing)           its
0005 033 NNS     N(com,plu)                fortunes
0005 034 IN      PREP(ge)                  in
0005 035 NN      N(com,sing)               time
0005 036 TO      PRTCL(to)                 to
0005 037 VB      V(montr,infin)            win
0005 038 AT      ART(indef)                an
0005 039 NN      N(com,sing)               election
0005 040 .       PUNC(per)                 .
---- --- ------- -------------------------- 0001
```

In the horizontal format, lexical items, immediately followed by their tags, are written consecutively one after another, as shown in the following sample from the Wall Street Journal, tagged with ICE tags in the horizontal format.

<p> <#1> <s> Velda <tag N(prop,sing)> Sue <tag N(prop,sing)> is <tag V(cop,pres)> a <tag ART(indef)> lady <tag N(com, sing)> that <tag PRON(rel)> small-business <tag ADJ> owners <tag N(com,plu)> would <tag AUX(modal,past)> like <tag V(montr,infin)> to <tag PRTCL(to)> meet <tag V(intr,infin)> . <tag PUNC(per)> </s> <#2> <s> She <tag PRON(pers,sing)> is <tag V(cop,pres,encl)> rich <tag ADJ> , <tag PUNC(com)> and <tag CONJUNC(coord)> she <tag PRON(pers,sing)> likes <tag V(montr,pres)> to <tag

```
PRTCL(to)> raise <tag V(montr,infin)> money <tag N(com,sing)>
for <tag PREP(ge)> budding <tag V(montr,ingp)> capital-
ists <tag N(com,plu)> . <tag PUNC(per)> </s> <#3> <s>
Unfortunately <tag ADV(ge)> for <tag PREP(ge)> cash-starved
<tag ADJ> entrepreneurs <tag N(com,plu)> , <tag PUNC(com)>
Velda <tag ADJ> Sue <tag N(prop,sing)> so <tag ADV(inten)>
far <tag ADV(inten)> exists <tag V(intr,pres)> only <tag
ADV(excl)> on <tag PREP(ge)> paper <tag N(com,sing)> ,
<tag PUNC(com)> some <tag PRON(ass)> 90 <tag NUM(card,sing)>
pages <tag N(com,plu)> of <tag PREP(ge)> controversial
<tag ADJ> federal <tag ADJ> legislation <tag N(com,sing)>
that <tag PRON(rel)> Congress <tag N(prop,sing)> will
<tag AUX(modal,pres)> be <tag AUX(pass,infin)> asked <tag
V(montr,edp)> to <tag PRTCL(to)> consider <tag
V(montr,infin)> this <tag PRON(dem,sing)> fall <tag
N(com,sing)> . <tag PUNC(per)> </s> </p>
```

3. The Tagging Procedures

Generally speaking, AUTASYS is a probabilistic tagger that employs stochastic information to disambiguate multiple tags assigned to the same lexical item. In this
respect, it is the same as other taggers that are currently being used at different
research centres—CLAWS and TOSCA, for instance. However, there are differences
in the various tagging stages. The main tagging stages in AUTASYS are assignment,
disambiguation, and refinement.

3.1. *Assignment*

At this initial stage, all words in the input text are assigned all the possible word-
class grammatical tags, only one of which is to be selected at the next stage,
disambiguation. CLAWS at Lancaster uses mainly prefixes and suffixes to predict the
potential tags that can be associated with a word form. For instance, all words
ending in *-tion* are very likely nouns. Exceptions such as *mention* and *position*,
which can also be verbs, are listed in a separate 'exception list'.

AUTASYS does not try to predict or guess at a word's possible tags. Instead, it
uses a lexicon of about 80,000 word forms, which carry with them all the tags they
are likely to be used with. When a word form is not found in the lexicon, it will
then be subjected to a set of morphological rules which decide its possible word

class. When a word form fails all the morphological rules, it will be arbitrarily assigned as a noun and an adjective. This double security check keeps error rate at a minimal level.

3.2. *Disambiguation*

AUTASYS employs the same probabilistic disambiguating algorithm as that fully described in Garside *et al.* (1987), which, however, has been greatly simplified in AUTASYS. In CLAWS, all possible paths created by a span of ambiguous words are examined and evaluated, a very expensive procedure in terms of computer resources (cf. DeRose, 1988). AUTASYS keeps a very small 'window' that examines only three words, or a triplet, at a time, the first of which is invariably unambiguous. The word to be disambiguated is 'focused' between the previous, unambiguous word and the following one, which may have more than one tag. Then the procedure examines and evaluates all the possible paths by calculating the corresponding collocational probabilities. The most likely sequence decides the tag for the word in focus. The newly disambiguated word then serves as the first in the next triplet, with which the system proceeds to disambiguate the following word if it is ambiguous. The whole process can best be demonstrated with the following example.

After the initial assignment of all the possible tags, the sentence *The man still saw her* can be represented as the following:

Word	Potential Tags		
The	ATI		
man	NN	VB	
still	JJ	RB	VB%
saw	NN%	VBD	
her	PP	PPO	
.	.		

In this sentence, all but two items receive an initial assignment of more than one tag. *Still*, for instance, has at least three potential tags: JJ (adjective), RB (adverb) and VB (verb). In common with CLAWS, the % sign indicates rare use that should be down-weighted.

AUTASYS looks at the first three words: The-man-still. In this triplet, the focus is on *man*, and the following paths are yielded by the span:

Paths	Likelihood
ATI-NN-JJ	$4918 \times 62 = 304916$
ATI-NN-VB	$4918 \times 37 = 181966$
ATI-NN-RB	$4918 \times 148 = 727864$

ATI-VB-JJ	$0 \times 305 =$	0
ATI-VB-VB	$0 \times 17 =$	0
ATI-VB-RB	$0 \times 322 =$	0

The numbers used to calculate the likelihood are drawn from a transitional matrix, which represents degrees of probability that any two tags co-occur. In this example, 4918 indicates a very strong link between ATI (definite article) and NN (singular noun). The zero indicates that it is so rare for the definite article to precede a base form verb (ATI-VB) that this sequence was not encountered in the training data from which the matrix was derived. The sequence yielding the largest value, ATI-NN-RB, thus chooses NN for *man*, which in turn serves as the first in the next triplet man-still-saw, where the word under focus is now *still*:

Paths	Likelihood
NN-JJ-NN%	$62 \times 4476 = 277512 \times .0001 = 27.7512$
NN-JJ-VBD	$62 \times 2 = 124$
NN-VB-NN%	$37 \times 386 = 14282 \times .0001 = 1.4282$
NN-VB-VBD	$37 \times 1 = 37$
NN-RB-NN%	$37 \times 1 = 37$
NN-RB-VBD	$148 \times 398 = 58904$

Note that .0001 is used to down-weight any tags that have the rarity sign %. The best of the above paths indicates that RB (adverb) should be chosen as the preferred tag for *still*. The procedure will go on to take the final triplet saw-her-. and disambiguate *her* in the same manner. (Note that punctuation marks are treated as unambiguous items.) This simplified disambiguation algorithm is by no means the best but it certainly enjoys simplicity and, as a result, speed.

3.3. *Refinement*

Several measures have been taken to control the tagging quality. The most important one is the set of 200 context-frame rules that check obvious tagging errors and those typical of the stochastic tagger. Those rules take the forms of:

$$X ? Y \rightarrow A$$

$$X ? Y \rightarrow !A$$

The first rule says that in the context of X and Y, the word in question (?) must be A. The second rule says that in this context, the word in question cannot be A. For example, the three-word sequence *the tagging of* receives the tag sequence ATI-VBG-IN (definite article + *-ing* verb + preposition). When subjected to the rules

$$AT ? IN \rightarrow !VB$$

$$AT ? IN \rightarrow NN$$

VBG in the original assignment will be retagged as VBG+N, indicating that it is a noun in the *-ing* form. Similarly, when *-ing* verbs are used adjectivally, for instance, a *running* horse, the following rule can be used:

$$\text{AT ? NN} \rightarrow \text{!VB}$$

Accordingly, *running* is tagged as VBG+J, a present participle used in an attributive position. Incidentally, there is another type of *-ing* verb that needs special attention. This is the gerundial use in the attributive position, for example, a *banking* company, a *gardening* glove, a *sleeping* car, etc. This is where a special lexicon comes into use, which was constructed by extracting from tagged material all the noun phrases that have a gerund in the modifying position. Gerunds thus detected are tagged as VBG+N, indicating that they are gerundial uses of *-ing* verbs. (The +J and +N signs are not used in LOB but are a feature in AUTASYS).

Another important measure is the use of a lexicon of 3,000 transitive verb forms that are always used transitively. This lexicon was specially constructed to cope with one of the commonest tagging mistakes, where VBN (past participial verb) is wrongly tagged as a simple past tense verb VBD (DeRose, 1989: 107). The mistakes arise from the fact that the context of the disambiguating algorithm is very limited (two adjacent words in AUTASYS). The solution involves global analysis. Take the following sentence as an example:

> This problem can be very easily *solved*.

The word *solved* is ambiguous, since it can be both VBD and VBN. When selecting tags for the sequence easily-solved-., the stochastic procedure would choose RB-VBD-. instead of RB-VBN-., as the likelihood of the former tag sequence is greater than that of the latter. With a lexicon of transitive verbs, however, the tagger 'knows' that *solved* is transitive and thus expects an NN following it. If such an NN is not found, the tagger readjusts its decision and tags the verb as VBN. Results show that such a lexicon greatly reduces the number of errors.

4. MAPPING LOB TO ICE

Existing annotation schemes require a tagger that is able to tag texts with different tagsets in order to meet different needs. Tagsets do share similarities in terms of general word classes. They all cover, for instance, nouns, verbs, adjectives, adverbs, prepositions. What makes them differ from each other are features of annotation designed to reflect different levels or areas of analysis. Very often these features are research-specific, having been decided by the nature of the study to be based on the annotated corpus. Some are related to detailed sub-categorizations of word classes to bear out their syntactic characteristics; for instance, the detailed notation of verb transitivity types and certain prepositions in ICE tagging go beyond the scope of the word into phrases and sometimes clauses (Fang, 1994). Some features are concerned with detailed indications of word forms, such as the tagging of third person singular verbs in LOB. Others are designed to bring out discourse features in speech. The TESS project at Lund notes detailed discourse items which are categorized as appositions, expletives, greetings, hesitators, softeners, etc. These differences, however diverse in nature, can be dealt with satisfactorily either through inferences based on morphological and grammatical rules or by means of special lexicons and lists. At the Survey of English Usage, an endeavour was made to modify AUTASYS so that the LOB tags can be 'translated' or 'mapped' to ICE tags (cf. Fang and Nelson, 1994). The text is first of all tagged with LOB tags, which are then transformed into ICE tags. The attempt proved to be successful and the texts thus tagged with the mapped ICE tags retain the same accuracy rate. In what follows, I shall discuss and exemplify the various stages involved and the methods used in mapping LOB tags to ICE tags.

4.1. *Comparisons and Analyses of the Two Tagsets*

Obviously, the initial stage is the comparison of the two tagsets, to see how much they have in common. Generally speaking, the two sets are similar in terms of general word classes. The LOB tagset notes the following twenty-three main base tags (cf. Johansson *et al.*, 1986):

A . . .	determiner/pronoun	**N** . . .	noun
BE . . .	*be* (lexical verb or aux)	**OD** . . .	ordinal numeral
CC	co-ordinating conjunction	**P** . . .	pronoun
CD . . .	cardinal numeral	**QL** . . .	qualifier
CS	subordinating conjunction	**R** . . .	adverb
DO . . .	*do* (lexical verb or auxiliary)	**TO**	infinitival *to*
DT . . .	determiner/pronoun	**UH**	interjection
EX	existential *there*	**VB** . . .	lexical verb
HV . . .	*have* (lexical verb or auxiliary)	**W** . . .	WH-word
IN	preposition	**XNOT**	*not*
J . . .	adjective	**ZZ**	letter
MD	modal auxiliary		

The ICE tagset notes twenty-two base tags (cf. Greenbaum, 1995):

ADJ	adjective	**INTERJEC**	interjection
ADV	adverb	**NADJ**	nominal adjective
ANTIT	anticipatory *it*	**N**	noun
ART	article	**NUM**	numeral
AUX	auxiliary	**PRTCL**	particle
CLEFTIT	cleft *it*	**PREP**	preposition
CONJUNC	conjunction	**PROFM**	proform
CONNEC	connective	**PRON**	pronoun

119

EXTHERE	existential *there*	**PROPIT**	prop *it*
FRM	formulaic expression	**REACT**	reaction signal
GENM	genitive marker	**V**	verb

This tagset has recently been modified. For a description of the most recent tagset, see Chapter 8. Both tagsets note such general classes as adjectives, adverbs, conjunctions (subordinating and co-ordinating), numerals, prepositions, verbs, etc. However, they do differ significantly in detailed features.

LOB and ICE differ most considerably in the tagging of verbs. LOB notes **BE** (*be*), **DO** (*do*), **HV** (*have*), and **VB** (other verbs). Their various inflections are indicated by **D** (past tense), **N** (past participial), and **G** (-*ing* form). **Z** is used when the verb is third person singular and has a distinct form. Take the verb *have* as an example. It has the following potential tags:

[1] **HV**   *a.* The guests *have* just arrived.
             b. It is vital to *have* him in the project.
             c. Have some tea.

[2] **HVD**   *a.* When I looked up, he *had* already gone.
             b. She *had to* copy the word a hundred times as a punishment.

[3] **HVN**   He's just *had* his breakfast.

[4] **HVG**   *a. Having* finished his coffee, he hurried to the office.
             b. We are *having* a house warming-up party tomorrow.

[5] **HVZ**   *a.* The little girl *has* bright eyes.
             b. My brother *has* been quite successful.

The LOB tags are more concerned with form and tense distinctions than syntactic features; for example, it does not distinguish the lexical and auxiliary uses of *have*. Also, when the verb is in the base form as in (1a), it is not indicated whether the verb is finite or infinitive.

The ICE tagset is a feature system; that is, it has a general head tag indicating word class, with features listed within brackets, giving more detailed information. A typical ICE tag takes the form **WordClass(feature1,feature2,feature3)**, where **feature1** notes the sub-category of the word class, **feature2** word form, and **feature3** other information.

Accordingly, the above examples of *have* are tagged quite differently in ICE:

[6] **AUX(perf,pres)**   *a.* The guests *have* just arrived.
    V(cxtr,infin)   *b.* It is vital to *have* him in the project.
    V(montr,imp)   *c. Have* some tea.

[7] **AUX(perf,past)**   *a.* When I looked up, he *had* already gone.
    AUX(semi,past)   *b.* She *had to* copy the word a hundred times as a punishment.

[8] **V(montr,edp)**   He's just *had* his breakfast.

[9] `AUX(perf,ingp)`   *a.* *Having* finished his coffee, he hurried to the office.
     `V(montr,ingp)`   *b.* We are *having* a house warming-up party tomorrow.

[10] `V(montr,pres)`   *a.* The little girl *has* bright eyes.
     `AUX(perf,pres)`   *b.* My brother *has* been quite successful in his career.

`AUX` = auxiliary	`cxtr` = complex transitive	`edp` = past participle
`imp` = imperative	`infin` = infinitive	`ingp` = *-ing* form
`montr` = monotransitive	`past` = past tense	`perf` = perfect aspect
`pres` = present tense	`semi` = semi-auxiliary	`V` = lexical verb

The first important different treatment of *have* is that its auxiliary and lexical uses are distinguished. In the auxiliary use, *have* may be used as a perfect auxiliary in (6*a*), or as a semi-auxiliary in (7*b*), where *have to* is taken as a unit and receives a ditto tag. The second important treatment of lexical verbs in ICE is the differentiation of transitivity features. In all, ICE notes eight complementation types. As a lexical verb, *have* is tagged as a complex transitive in (6*b*), and a monotransitive in (6*c*), (8), (9*b*) and (10*a*). Unlike LOB, ICE further distinguishes between finite verbs in the base form and the infinitive. Thus, (6*a*) is tagged as present tense, (6*c*) as imperative, and (6*b*) as infinitive.

4.2. *Solutions*

In our example of *have*, the first task in this LOB-ICE translation is to separate the lexical use from the auxiliary one. If the various auxiliary uses can be recognized, all the rest can be straightforwardly assigned to the lexical use, which is then further subcategorized as monotransitive and complex transitive.

4.2.1. *Auxiliary vs. lexical*

To recognize *have* as a perfect auxiliary, the apparent solution is to see if it is followed by a past participle. However, adverbials may occur between the auxiliary and the main verb:

[11] He has *hardly* done anything today.

[12] We have, *in the meantime*, managed to fulfil the task.

Thus, the tagger has to by-pass *hardly* in (11) in order to find the following past participle. (12) poses a more difficult task since what comes between the auxiliary and the participle is a prepositional phrase functioning as an adverbial. This means that some minimal phrase structure rules also have to be built into the tagger. In this case, AUTASYS has been programmed to overlook adverbs and prepositional phrases. To recognize *have to* as a semi-auxiliary, one solution is to designate it as such in a special lexicon.

4.2.2. *Monotransitive vs. complex transitive*

The next but more difficult task is to subcategorize the lexical uses of *have*. In examples (6)–(10), lexical *have* has two different transitivity features, complex transitive and monotransitive. Monotransitives can be quite easily dealt with by looking for a following NP. In the case of a preposed object (the zero relative) as in

[13] This is the most wonderful evening I've ever *had*.

the lexicon of transitive verbs described in Section 3.3 has to be utilized.

The detection of complex transitives is more problematic, as the tagging of this type involves judgements of semantic interpretation more than of structural considerations. Consider

[14] *a*. He *read* the book in the room.

b. He *left* the book in the room.

In (14*a*), *read* is tagged as monotransitive but *left* as complex transitive in (14*b*). Though different in the transitivity types of their verbs, the two sentences in (14) do not show any structural difference. Thus, this type of verb cannot be dealt with by any syntactic rules that are appropriate for the computer. An empirical examination of the tagged British ICE Corpus revealed that complex transitive verbs typically have the following structures:

[15] *a*. She always calls me *Ginge*.

b. He parked the car right *in front of the gate*.

c. The busy traffic outside the window makes him *nervous*.

The examples in (15) show that complex transitives typically take NP, PP, and ADJP as their second complements. Based on this observation, AUTASYS tags as complex transitive any non-ditransitive verbs complemented by a second NP and those complemented by an NP which precedes an ADJP. To cope with those that take PP as the second complement, another special lexicon was constructed, which contains all such complex transitives together with the complementing PP head found in the British ICE Corpus. *Have* complemented by *in* PP in (6*b*) is thus recognized by checking in the lexicon. This approach, though not always correct, proves to be fairly successful in the actual tagging.

4.2.3. *Finite vs. nonfinite*

This issue involves the tagging of the present and past tenses, infinitives and imperatives. Present participles have distinct forms and thus can be easily differentiated. The distinction of past tense and past participles was described in Section 3.3. So in this section, I shall discuss mainly verbs in their base forms using the example of *have*.

In mapping LOB to ICE, it was found that to cope with base-form verbs properly, three properties have to be considered or registered by the tagger. They are: (1) sentence-initial NPs, (2) auxiliaries involving the use of infinitives, and (3) the infinitive marker *to*. Sentence-initial NPs are presumed to be the sentence subject.

When sentence-initial NPs, auxiliaries, and the infinitive marker *to* are all missing, the tagger searches for a question mark at the end of the sentence, which decides whether the base-form verb should be tagged as an imperative or a finite present tense verb. This procedure tags (6c) as imperative and (16) as finite present tense.

[16] *Have* you seen the film Schindler's List?

This solution, however, works only in writing. Unless question marks are put in manually, spoken material cannot be dealt with sufficiently. But since the perfect aspect is almost never used imperatively, the tagger can be instructed to tag as present tense any construction like (16). With sentence-initial NPs present, the tagging decision is made according to whether auxiliaries or the infinitive marker *to* have been registered. This ensures that correct tags are assigned to (6a), (6b), and (7b). However, those two properties are valid only within a certain scope or boundary. Consider

[17] *a.* The job *has to* be finished before they *arrive.*

b. To put it briefly, we *have* very little time left.

In (17a), *has to* is effective only in the main clause. In (17b), the infinitive marker is restricted to the infinitive clause. AUTASYS does not including parsing, but it deregisters auxiliaries and the infinitive marker *to* after conjunctions and a certain number of NPs, in order to tag the above sentences correctly.

4.3. *Summary*

As evidenced by mapping LOB to ICE in AUTASYS, tagsets can be directly translated or mapped in terms of general word classes. Detailed sub-categorizations and research-specific codings, such as the transitivity features and formulaic expressions noted in ICE, can be satisfactorily dealt with by means of constructing special lexicons of close sets. It is also desirable for mapping procedures to have minimal phrase structure rules and to register important syntactic properties like auxiliaries, the infinitive marker *to*, and clause or phrase boundaries.

5. CONCLUDING REMARKS

The emergence of different corpus annotation schemes will surely encourage the development of natural language processing systems that accommodate different needs and requirements. Studies based on corpora annotated by those systems will, in return, contribute to the quality of those systems. Like the well-developed tagging technologies available today, which have benefited much from annotated corpora, the demanding task of natural language parsing will certainly achieve a great leap forward with better and more detailed word-class tagging. Indeed, a parser is currently being developed at the Survey of English Usage that incorporates

AUTASYS as described in this chapter and uses the syntactically annotated ICE-GB corpus as its linguistic knowledge base (Fang, 1995). Its promising results at this stage demonstrate great potential applications of annotated corpora in natural language processing.

REFERENCES

DeRose, S. (1988), 'Grammatical Category Disambiguation by Statistical Optimization', in *Computational Linguistics*, 14:1: 31–9.

—— (1989), Stochastic Methods for Resolution of Grammatical Category Ambiguity in Inflected and Uninflected Languages, Ph.D. diss. (Brown University, Providence).

Fang, A. C. (1992), 'Tagging Words, Tackling Ambiguities', paper presented at a Seminar on Lexis, held at Hong Kong University of Science & Technology, June.

—— (1994), 'ICE: Applications and Possibilities in NLP', in *Proceedings of International Workshop on Directions of Lexical Research*, Beijing, 15–17 August, 23–44.

—— (1995), 'Parsing with the ICE Corpus as Syntactic Knowledge Base', paper presented at the ICAME Conference, Toronto, 24–8 May.

—— and Nelson, G. (1994), 'Tagging the Survey Corpus: A LOB to ICE Experiment Using AUTASYS', in *Literary and Linguistic Computing*, 9/2: 189–94.

Francis, W. N. (1980), 'A tagged Corpus—Problems and Prospects', in S. Greenbaum *et al.* (eds.), 193–209.

Garside, R., Leech, G., and Sampson, G. (1987) (eds.), *The Computational Analysis of English: A Corpus-Based Approach* (London: Longman).

Greenbaum, S. (1992), 'A New Corpus of English: ICE', in J. Svartvik (ed.), 171–9.

—— (1995), *The ICE Tagset Manual* (London: Survey of English Usage, University College London).

—— and Ni, Y. (1994), 'Tagging the British ICE Corpus: English Word Classes', in N. Oostdijk and P. de Haan (eds.), 33–45.

—— Leech, G., and Svartvik, J. (1980) (eds.), *Studies in English Linguistics: For Randolph Quirk* (London: Longman).

Greene, B. and Rubin, G. (1971), *Automated Grammatical Tagging of English*, MA thesis. (Brown University, Providence).

Huang, R. J. (1991), *A Technical Report of the JDEST Corpus Tagging Project* (Shanghai: Shanghai Jiao Tong University).

Johansson, J., Atwell, E., Garside, R., and Leech, G. (1986), *The Tagged LOB Corpus Users' Manual* (Bergen: Norwegian Computing Centre for the Humanities).

Marshall, I. (1983), 'Choice of Grammatical Word-Class without Global Syntactic Analysis: Tagging Words in the LOB Corpus', in *Computers in the Humanities*, 17: 139–50.

Meijs, W. (1987) (ed.), *Corpus Linguistics and Beyond* (Amsterdam: Rodopi).

Oostdijk, N. (1991), *Corpus Linguistics and the Automatic Analysis of English* (Amsterdam: Rodopi).

—— and de Haan, P. (1994) (eds.), *Corpus-Based Research into Language* (Amsterdam: Rodopi).

Svartvik, J. (1987), 'Taking a New Look at Word Class Tags', in W. Meijs (ed.), 33–43.

—— (1992) (ed.), *Directions in Corpus Linguistics: Proceedings of Nobel Symposium 82, Stockholm, 4–8 August 1991* (Berlin: Mouton de Gruyter).

10

An Outline of the Survey's ICE Parsing Scheme

JUSTIN BUCKLEY

1. INTRODUCTION

Another form of annotation applied to ICE-GB (the British component of the ICE corpus) was parsing, in which our aim was to analyse each of the utterances in the corpus according to their *form*, or *category*, and their *function*, and according to the relationships between their component parts. ICE-GB was initially parsed using the TOSCA automatic parser, which provided one or more analyses to be checked and selected manually. Most utterances were parsed in this way, but for those that could not be parsed by the TOSCA parser, a new parser was created at the Survey of English Usage (cf. Chapter 11). The Survey parser offers one analysis for each utterance, either a complete parse or a partial parse. ICETREE, a manual tree editor, was compiled at the Survey to cater for the analyses produced by the Survey parser. It is used to check and correct parses and to complete partial parses.

Manual tree editing has given us the opportunity to introduce new parsing terms that enable us to complete the analysis of problematic constructions, or of constructions hitherto not catered for. The new scheme also applies to the Survey parser. The Survey parsing scheme is based on the TOSCA system, but differs from it in many respects. What follows is a general overview of the Survey parsing scheme, which includes many of the new terms introduced into the ICE parsing hierarchy.

2. PARSING

Each word in the corpus is given a word-class tag to show what category of word it belongs to. Each word also performs a *function*. Groups of words are categorized, and they also perform functions. Every group of words, from the largest (a whole sentence, say) to the smallest (an individual word) performs a function and is described by a category. The process of parsing is the gradual narrowing of word groupings, and the identification of the function each grouping performs and its category. The result of such analysis is displayed as a labelled *tree*, as in Fig. 10.1.

125

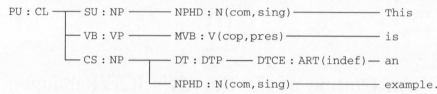

FIG. 10.1. The tree for the parsing unit *This is an example*

For the abbreviations used in the labels in Fig. 10.1 and elsewhere, see the Appendix. Information is shown on the trees at nodes. In Fig. 10.1, PU : CL and SU : NP are nodes, each made up of a function label, PU and SU, and a category label, CL and NP. At each node a narrowing of focus occurs, resulting in a new set of branches and a new set of nodes describing the function and category of the finer divisions that have been made.

In our parsing language, a function is said to be *realized* by a category at a node. That category is then *expressed* in terms of its functional constituents—functions at the next level of nodes, in turn realized by categories. In Fig. 10.1, the first node of the tree consists of the function (PU) realized by the category (CL). The clause is then expressed by the functions at the next level of nodes branching from it (SU, VB, CS). These functions are each realized by a category (NP, VP, NP). The focus of the tree eventually narrows down to the individual words, and each word is categorized by a word-class tag, the final categorizations on the tree. These final nodes are known as the *leaf-nodes*.

2.1. *The Highest Level of the Tree*

Each group of words subjected as a whole to parsing analysis is known as a *parsing unit* (PU on the tree), and this is the function label at the first node (root) of every parsed tree. A parsing unit can be realized by two main categories: *clause* or *non-clause*. A third realization of *parsing unit* is *disparate*, when two unlike elements are co-ordinated (see below).

2.2. *Clauses*

The traditional term *sentence* has been replaced with the label *clause*, which is used to refer to parsing units that are realized by either main clauses or dependent clauses. A main clause contains a verb phrase, or has had a verb phrase ellipted from it, and may stand on its own without reference to outside constructions.

[1] I hated him for that.

[2] You always ask the same thing.

[3] The best way I know is to go by bus.

126

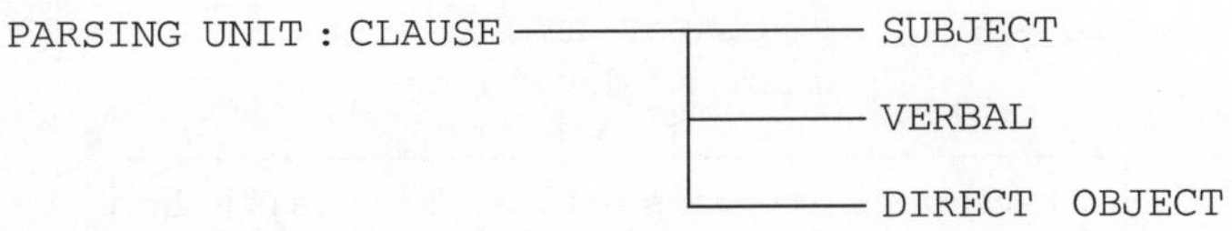

Outline of the Survey's ICE Parsing Scheme

```
PARSING UNIT : CLAUSE ─────────┬───── SUBJECT
                               ├───── VERBAL
                               └───── DIRECT OBJECT
```

FIG. 10.2. The root of a tree for a clause cluster, showing the highest level of the tree and the clausal top-level functions

A dependent clause is one that occurs within another clause or, if it stands alone, depends on a construction in another parsing unit.

[4] The best way *I know* is *to go by bus*.

[5] Because you asked me to.

The clause in [4] contains two dependent clauses: *I know* is a relative clause, and *to go by bus* is a complement. The clause in [5] consists simply of a dependent clause.

The category *clause* is expressed by its primary functional constituents known as clausal *top level* functions. These include functions such as *subject, verbal, direct object, subject complement*. The tree for a clause might therefore read from its root as in Fig. 10.2. The top level functions are in turn realized by the appropriate categories, which are expressed by function labels and so on, so that the full tree for a clause is drawn, as was seen in Fig. 10.1.

2.3. *Features of a Clause*

The clause is further specified by a list of features attached to the clause label itself, which are chosen according to the composition of the clause. A clause is specified according to its level: the clause *I always see him in there* is categorized as CL(main, ...); and the clause *Because I like him* is categorized as CL(depend, ...). Features are then added from various feature groups (cf. Fig. 10.3).[1]

If the clause is *main*, a feature for *main clause type* is added to *interrogative* and *exclamative* clauses, *declarative* being the default.

[6] He is walking the dog.   = CL(main, montr, pres ...)

[7] Is he walking the dog?   = CL(main, montr, pres, inter ...)

[8] How clever you are!   = CL(main, cop, pres, exclam ...)

If a clause is dependent, it must carry a feature for *dependent clause type*. Choose one from: *subordinate, relative, zero-subordinate*, or *independent relative*.

[9] Because I had to   = CL(depend, **sub** ...)

Note that a dependent clause may additionally carry the feature *interrogative*, although dependent clauses are not normally distinguished by this main clause type feature. Interrogative dependent clauses usually stand alone. For example:

127

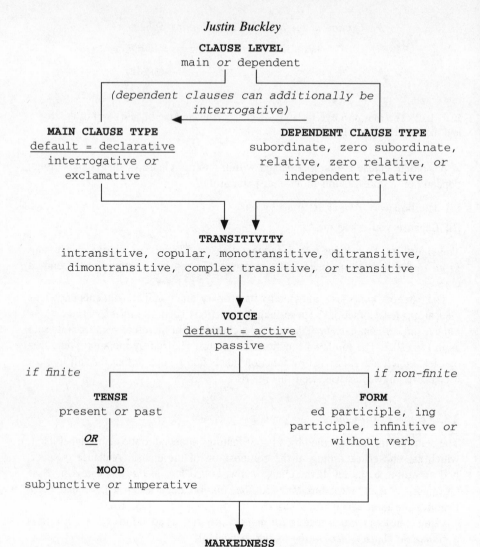

CLAUSE LEVEL
main *or* dependent

(dependent clauses can additionally be interrogative)

MAIN CLAUSE TYPE
default = declarative
interrogative *or*
exclamative

DEPENDENT CLAUSE TYPE
subordinate, zero subordinate,
relative, zero relative, *or*
independent relative

TRANSITIVITY
intransitive, copular, monotransitive, ditransitive,
dimontransitive, complex transitive, *or* transitive

VOICE
default = active
passive

if finite   *if non-finite*

TENSE
present *or* past

OR

MOOD
subjunctive *or* imperative

FORM
ed participle, ing
participle, infinitive *or*
without verb

MARKEDNESS
default = unmarked
inverted, preposed direct object, preposed indirect object,
preposed subject complement, preposed object complement,
preposed prepositional complement, preposed subject,
extraposed subject, extraposed object, existential,
cleft, *or* push-down

(ADDITIONAL FEATURES)
without subject, without operator, reduced,
incomplete, coordination

FIG. 10.3. Adding features for a clause

[10] What about going to the pictures?

[11] What if it's raining?

All clauses must carry features for *transitivity* (*intransitive, copular, monotransitive, ditransitive, dimonotransitive, complex transitive, complex ditransitive* or *transitive*[2]). A feature for *voice* is inserted only for a passive clause, active being the default. Both of these groups of features are based on the nature of the verb phrase that performs the function of *verbal* within the clause; the *verb phrase* label itself carries the same features. The *main verb* within the verb phrase (described by its word-class tag) determines the *transitivity* of the verb phrase/clause, and the presence or absence of a passive auxiliary (or a passive construction from which a passive auxiliary has been ellipted) determines the *voice*.

[12] They brutally beat him = CL(main, **montr** . . .)

[13] He was brutally beaten = CL(main, **montr, pass** . . .)

We now have to decide whether our clause is *finite* (containing a verb phrase that is marked for tense) or *non-finite* (containing a verb phrase where there is no *main verb* or *operator* marked for tense).[3] If the clause is *non-finite*, it carries a feature to show the *form* of the verb phrase, as does the *verb phrase* label itself: *ed-participle, ing-participle*, or *infinitive*.

[14] Walking the dog = CL(depend, zsub, montr, **ingp** . . .)

If the clause is *finite* it carries features for *tense* (based on the *main verb* or *operator* of the verb phrase—either *present* or *past*) or *mood* (based on the form of the verb phrase—*subjunctive* or *imperative*).

All clauses must carry a feature for *markedness*. Since unmarked word order is the norm in English, we only include a feature for the following marked word orders:

inverted (inv) e.g. Has he finished the paper?
preposed direct object (preod) e.g. What has he finished?
preposed indirect object (preoi) e.g. Who did you give the paper?
preposed subject complement (precs) e.g. Where is it?
preposed object complement (preco) e.g. What do you call him?
extraposed subject (extsu) e.g. It's great to be here.
extraposed direct object (extod) e.g. He made it acceptable to be unhappy.
cleft (cleft) e.g. It was my paper that he was talking about.

There are *additional features*—on/off features that are only added to the list when specific constructions occur. These include *without subject, without operator*, and *reduced*.

[15] Been to the doctor today. = CL(main, intr, -**su** -**op**)

[16] I don't want *to*   = CL(main, montr, pres, **red**)

In [16] *to* is a reduced clause, categorized as CL(depend, zsub, red).

Clauses exhibit the most exhaustive and complicated features lists. *Verb phrase*, *adjective phrase*, and *adverb phrase* labels must also carry features, while the *noun phrase* label carries the feature *genv* if it contains a genitive construction (such as *my friend's new car*), or takes one of a variety of features when it acts as a *detached function* (see Section 2.9).

2.4. *Nonclauses*

A parsing unit may alternatively be realized by a *nonclause*. These are utterances standing alone as an entire parsing unit that do not have a clausal structure: that is, they do not contain a *verb phrase*. A verb phrase standing alone is considered to be a clause. A *nonclause* has two possible expressions: *element* or *discourse marker* are assigned as functional expressions according to the type of expression that occurs as the nonclause. If a nonclause consists of a phrase standing alone as the entire parsing unit, then the nonclause is said to be expressed by an *element*, which is in turn realized by the phrase itself. A tree for, say, a *prepositional phrase* might be drawn as in Fig. 10.4.

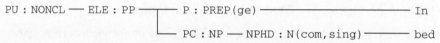

FIG. 10.4. The tree for a prepositional phrase standing alone as an entire parsing unit

If a nonclause consists of a stand-alone *interjection, reaction signal, formulaic expression*, or *connective* then it is said to be expressed by the function *discourse marker*, the function performed by such words within a clause. A tree for a *nonclause* expressed by a *discourse marker* is shown as Fig. 10.5.

FIG. 10.5. The tree for a non-clause expressed by a discourse marker

2.5. *Co-ordination*

Co-ordination can occur at practically any level of the tree, and a parsing unit can be realized directly by co-ordinated clauses or nonclauses, or by co-ordination of disparate elements. Co-ordination has proved to be a very important aspect of parsing as it has tested the parameters of the parsing hierarchy and terms, and has forced the addition of many new terms to the set of parsing labels.

Co-ordination may be *syndetic* (when a conjunction is present—*We need bread and milk*) or *asyndetic* (no conjunction is present—*We bought bread, milk, biscuits, tea*). Co-ordination can take place between any elements that perform the same function (*subject complement*, say, or *noun phrase head*). The function is then realized by a *co-ordination category*. If the co-ordinated elements are of the same category, the category that describes them is copied up to the preceding node, to become the *co-ordination category*. The label is, however, modified by the feature *coordn*. So a parsing unit might be realized by a co-ordinated *clause*, consisting of two or more clauses co-ordinated together. Fig. 10.6 shows how co-ordinated stand-alone *prepositional phrases* are analysed.

The co-ordination category is expressed by *conjoins*, the function performed within the co-ordination by the co-ordinated elements, and by *coordinators*, if present. *Adverbials* may also appear anywhere within the co-ordination. For example:

[17] I'm expecting Nick, *definitely* Jane, but *not* David.

In [17], the italicized *adverbials* appear at the top level of the co-ordination alongside the *conjoins* and the *coordinator*, as in Fig. 10.7.

If the elements that are co-ordinated are of different categories, then the co-ordination category that describes them cannot be constructed in the way described above. In such cases, the co-ordination category is *disparate* (cf. Fig. 10.8).

2.6. *Co-ordination of Predicates*

A *predicate element* is formed when a verb phrase and a verb complement[4] together form an element within co-ordination.

[18] He *shut the door* and *locked it*.

[19] They *told him* and *left*.

Example [18] above contains two predicate elements, both containing *direct objects* as verb complements. Example [19] also has two predicate elements and, while only the first has a complement (the *indirect object him*), both are labelled as *predicate element* for the sake of symmetry. Where predicate co-ordination occurs, the co-ordinated *predicate elements* are said to realize the function within the clause of *predicate group*. When the co-ordinated *predicate elements* contain verb phrases of different transitivity, tense or voice, the clause that contains them inherits such verbal features from the first element. This principle also applies when one element has a finite verb phrase and another a non-finite one, or when the verb phrases are of a different non-finite form (*infinitive, -ed participle*, etc.). The tree for example [18] above would appear as in Fig. 10.9.

An *adverbial* on its own does not constitute a verb complement. In the example *He tripped and fell to the ground*, we know that *to the ground* is semantically attached to the second co-ordinated element *fell*. Because the parser does not make semantic judgements, this adverbial is analysed in the same way as *quickly* in the

Fig. 10.6. The tree for coordinated stand-alone prepositional phrases

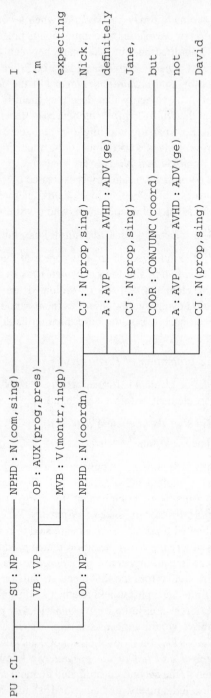

Fig. 10.7. A tree showing coordination modified by adverbials

example *He eats and drinks quickly.* The co-ordination takes places within the verb phrase as in Fig. 10.10.

Should an adverbial appear after any coordinated element except the last, it is attached to that element and then verb phrase and adverbial together form a *predicate element.*

2.7. *Phrases*

Generally speaking, the most significant word-groupings to identify within a parsing unit are phrases. There are seven different phrase categories within the ICE parsing scheme, consisting of a single word or a whole group with their own functions within the phrase:

adjective phrase	e.g. *good*; *very good at what he does*
adverb phrase	e.g. *quickly*; *much more quickly than that*
determiner phrase	e.g. *the*; *all the many*
noun phrase	e.g. *boy*; *the prettiest boy in the world*
prepositional phrase	e.g. *in time*; *just in time for the match*
subordinator phrase	e.g. *because*; *even if*
verb phrase	e.g. *stop*; *was about to be stopped*

Phrases have an internal structure and can contain other phrases. The category of, say, *noun phrase* can be expressed in terms of its functional constituents, which are each realized by the appropriate category as in Fig. 10.11.

Our noun phrase contains two further phrases, a *determiner phrase* and an *adjective phrase*, as well as a *clause*. All of these have their own internal structure, expressed in terms of their functional constituents, which will in turn be realized by the appropriate category labels. Some of the category labels will be given features according to their internal structure or type, so that the tree for the complete phrase will read as in Fig. 10.12.

2.8. *The Functions of Phrases*

Once a phrase has been identified and appropriately categorized, the analyser must decide its function. We have seen (Figs. 10.11 and 10.12) how the function labels within the phrase are realized by category labels. The label of *noun phrase* will similarly be the realization of a function. In [20], the noun phrase is performing the function of *subject* within a clause.

[20] *The best way I know* is to go by bus.

Alternatively, a phrase may stand alone as the whole parsing unit, in which case it performs the function of *element* within the category of *nonclause*.

[21] In the morning.

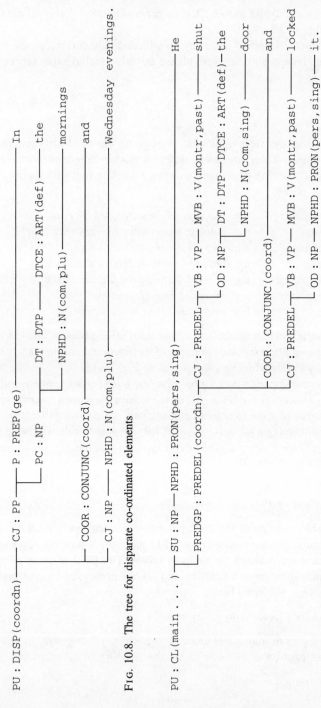

Fig. 10.8. The tree for disparate co-ordinated elements

Fig. 10.9. A tree containing a predicate group

A partial parse involves the categorization of phrases and the labelling of the functions and categories within the phrase but the function of the phrase within a larger structure might not be labelled. Such partial parses are produced automatically by the Survey parser, reducing the amount of work involved when manually creating a parsed tree.

2.9. *Constructions Outside the Clausal Syntax*

During the manual parse-editing we have encountered many problems with constructions that seem to operate either outside the clausal syntax or with a degree of independence from it. These constructions include parenthetical clauses, reported utterances in direct speech, vocatives, and bibliographical references within the text. We have had to introduce function and category labels to accommodate these constructions while keeping in mind the difficulties for the automatic parser in recognizing such constructions and the distinctions between them. We have introduced two function labels: *parataxis* for parenthetical main clauses and reported utterances in direct speech; and *detached function* for phrases and clauses that are to a greater or lesser extent independent of the clausal syntax.

Where a main clause appears inside another main clause as a parenthetical utterance, it is said to perform the function *parataxis*, which can appear either at the top level of the clause or at a lower level, inside a phrase, say. This is also the function performed by a clause or nonclause that is the reported part of a direct speech construction. The following examples all contain *parataxis,* italicized:

[22] This is *and I'm being quite frank here* an absolute shambles.

[23] I'm facing a *what's it called* dilemma.

[24] She said, '*I'm not coming tonight.*'

[25] '*In the cupboard,*' he shouted.

(Note that punctuation is not present in spoken material.)

Examples [22] and [23] above contain parenthetical main clauses performing the function *parataxis*. Examples [24] and [25] contain a main clause and a nonclause respectively; both perform the function of *parataxis*. The reported utterance is effectively removed from the clausal syntax and so the reporting verb (*said* and *shouted* above) is tagged as *intransitive*. A tree for Example [24] would be drawn as in Fig. 10.13.

The other function label used to deal with these semi-independent constructions is *detached function*. This function is performed typically by noun phrases, but also by dependent clauses, adjective phrases, or potentially any other phrase, when they are in the vocative, when they offer an aside comment, or when they are a bibliographical reference. Appositive constructions are also said to perform this function; an appositive noun phrase, for example, will therefore not have a direct connection

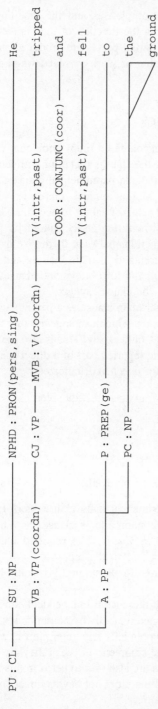

FIG. 10.10. A tree for coordination of verb phrases where coordination of predicates does not apply

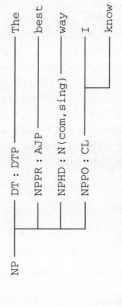

FIG. 10.11. A tree for a noun phrase with its primary functional constituents

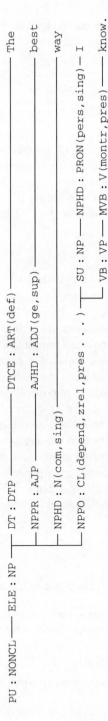

FIG. 10.12. The complete tree for a noun phrase

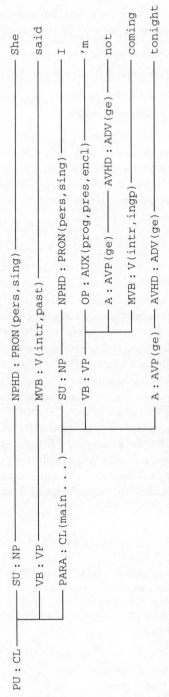

FIG. 10.13. Tree containing *parataxis*. Punctuation has been omitted

to its appositive mate since *detached function* appears at the top level of the clause. The following examples all contain a *detached function*, italicized:

[26] Come here, *whatever your name is*.

[27] They didn't check it all, *a terrible mistake*.

[28] All these factors have been well documented (*Brown, 1978*).

[29] That's Susan, *his girfriend*.

Example [26] above contains a vocative clause; example [27] contains a commenting noun phrase; example [28] contains a noun phrase as bibliographical reference; and example [29] contains an appositive noun phrase. The construction performing the function of *detached function* carries one of a variety of features to indicate its actual use, so that *whatever your name is* in example [26] is categorized as CL(depend, **voc** . . .).

3. COMPILING THE ICE PARSING SCHEME

When considering what to include in the ICE parsing scheme, we have had to strike a balance between sometimes conflicting requirements: the ability to complete an analysis, the importance of being able to retrieve constructions from a completed database, and conformity with the automatic parser that cannot make purely semantic decisions. Above all, we have tried to make the manual parsing and parse-editing as comfortable, obvious and user-friendly as possible, while still maintaining a link with the automated parsing process. We have found that the constructions that occur in the ICE corpus can never be entirely accounted for by a theoretical system. We are constantly modifying the ICE parsing scheme: for instance, the feature *incomplete* has been added to category labels since this paper was begun, to deal with interrupted or unfinished clauses, noun phrases, etc. We have found that the examples in the corpus test our parsing scheme and terms to their limits, and often stimulate major as well as minor changes.

NOTES

1. Fig. 10.3 is taken from TREEHELP, the help-system for the manual tree-builder and editor, ICETREE. See Chapter 6 in this volume.
2. *Transitive* is a term used for verbs followed by a noun phrase and a non-finite clause, where the noun phrase may either be an indirect object or the subject of the non-finite clause. For example:

We *saw* the man drive off in his car.

The verb *saw* is tagged as *transitive*, the verb phrase and clause in which it appears carrying a similar feature.

3. Although imperative and subjunctive verbs are not marked for tense, we treat them as finite. Cf. Quirk *et al.*, 1985: 3.52.
4. In the ICE parsing scheme, verb complements include objects, indirect objects, subject complements, object complements and transitive complements.

REFERENCE

QUIRK, R., GREENBAUM, S., LEECH, G., and SVARTVIK, J. (1985), *A Comprehensive Grammar of the English Language* (London: Longman).

APPENDIX

This appendix contains a list of the abbreviations for ICE terms used in this paper, together with their full forms. This is not a comprehensive list of the terms used in the Survey's ICE parsing scheme. Each term is marked as a function label, category label, word-class tag, feature for a category label or feature for a tag.

-op = without operator [*category feature*]

-su = without subject [*category feature*]

A = adverbial [*function label*]

ADV = adverb [*word-class tag*]

ADJ = adjective [*word-class tag*]

AJP = adjective phrase [*category label*]

AJHD = adjective phrase head [*function label*]

ART = article [*word-class tag*]

AUX = auxiliary [*word-class tag*]

AVHD = adverb phrase head [*function label*]

AVP = adverb phrase [*category label*]

CJ = conjoin [*function label*]

CL = clause [*category label*]

cleft = cleft [*category feature*]

com = common [*tag feature*]

CONJUNC = conjunction [*word-class tag*]

COOR = coordinator [*function label*]

coord = coordinating [*tag feature*]

coordn = coordinated [*category feature*]

cop = copular [*tag/category feature*]

CS = subject complement [*function label*]

def = definite [*tag feature*]

depend = dependent [*category feature*]

DISMK = discourse marker [*function label*]

DISP = disparate [*category label*]

DT = determiner [*function label*]

DTCE = central determiner [*function label*]

DTP = determiner phrase [*category label*]

ELE = element

encl = enclitic

exclam = exclamative [*tag/category feature*]

ge = general [*tag/category feature*]

genv = genitive [*category feature*]

indef = indefinite [*tag feature*]

ingp = -ing participle [*tag/category feature*]

inter = interrogative [*category feature*]

intr = intransitive [*tag/category feature*]

inv = inverted [*category feature*]

main = main [*category feature*]

montr = monotransitive [*tag/category feature*]

MVB = main verb [*function label*]

N = noun [*word-class tag*]

NONCL = nonclause [*category label*]

NP = noun phrase [*category label*]

NPHD = noun phrase head [*function label*]

NPPO = noun phrase postmodifier [*function label*]

NPPR = noun phrase premodifier [*function label*]

OD = direct object [*function label*]

OP = operator [*function label*]

P = prepositional [*function label*]

PARA = parataxis [*function label*]

pass = passive [*category feature*]

past = past [*tag/category feature*]

PC = prepositional complement [*function label*]

pers = personal [*tag feature*]

plu = plural [*tag/category feature*]

PP = prepositional phrase [*category label*]

PREDEL = predicate element [*category label*]

PREDGP = predicate group [*function label*]

preod = preposed direct object [*category feature*]

PREP = preposition [*word-class tag*]

pres = present [*tag/category feature*]

prog = progressive [*tag/category feature*]

PRON = pronoun [*word-class tag*]

prop = proper [*tag feature*]

PU = parsing unit [*function label*]

REACT = reaction signal [*word-class tag*]

red = reduced [*category feature*]

sing = singular [*tag feature*]

SU = subject [*function label*]

sub = subordinate [*category feature*]

sup = superlative [*tag/category feature*]

V = verb [*word-class tag*]

VB = verbal [*function label*]

voc = vocative [*category feature*]

VP = verb phrase [*category label*]

zrel = zero relative [*category feature*]

zsub = zero subordinate [*category feature*]

11

The Survey Parser: Design and Development

ALEX CHENGYU FANG

1. INTRODUCTION

Automatic parsing aims at the decomposition of a sentence into its syntactic constituent structures, so that the relations between words and groups of words are
clarified. It is a process deemed essential as a help in understanding the sentential
meaning. It is also the first step towards a reversed process whereby a natural
language sentence can be automatically constructed according to the specification
of abstract semantic meanings. The best example to demonstrate the application of
parsing is multi-lingual machine translation. A sentence in Language *A* is first of
all parsed to help to arrive at its semantics, which are then formalized and finally
represented as a corresponding sentence in Language *B*. Success in parsing will
represent a major breakthrough in natural language processing. Nearly all the major
universities around the world host research teams working on different approaches
to parsing. Britain alone boasts research teams in this area at Cambridge, Edinburgh,
Leeds, Nottingham, Sheffield, Sussex, and York.

Despite efforts in the past 50 years or so, however, 'the state of the art in parsing
general English by computer is but primitive' (Black *et al.*, 1993: 2). In 1990–2,
three experiments were carried out on eleven rule-based parsers, which subsequently
produced a success rate of only 33 per cent on naturally occurring sentences (cf.
Black *et al.*, 1993). The increasingly popular stochastic approach (Fujisaki, 1984;
Garside and Leech, 1985; Atwell, 1988; Briscoe and Carroll, 1991; Fujisaki *et al.*,
1991; Magerman, 1994), despite its advantage over the rule-based approach, suffers from incorrect analyses, especially in the attachment of constituent structures
(cf. Briscoe and Carroll, 1991). SPATTER, a probabilistic parser, achieved a 78 per
cent crossing-brackets score,[1] and yet only about 35 per cent of the parses exactly
matched the human annotations for those sentences (Magerman, 1994: v). Some
systems try to remedy these parsing problems through man-machine interactions,
but this usually proves too costly. The TOSCA Parser developed at the University of
Nijmegen, Holland, for instance, requires considerable manual pre-editing of the
input text in order to reduce parsing times and ambiguities.

This chapter describes the design and development of an automatic parser at the Survey that aims at remedying as many parsing problems as possible without any man-machine interaction. The approach adopted is characterized by the application of linguistic knowledge in the form of phrase structure rules that are automatically extracted from the syntactically analysed ICE-GB. This approach therefore addresses two important issues in information processing, i.e. the automatic extraction of syntactic knowledge from annotated corpora and the application of this knowledge to parse unannotated naturally occurring linguistic data. The following sections describe in detail the general design of the parser and present some initial results.

2. THE DESIGN OF THE SURVEY PARSER

Software for the grammatical annotation of ICE-GB has been provided by the TOSCA Research Group. Their parsing system has produced detailed analyses, providing information on the categories and functions at the level of sentence, clause, phrase, and word, and during the past year the analyses have proved their value for research. However, the parsing has involved much more manual effort than we had originally expected. A preliminary stage of manual marking was required for certain syntactic features including very frequently occurring constructions—such as all co-ordinations and all postmodifiers of nouns—so as to reduce the number of ambiguities in the parsing. The initial success rate of the parser was less than 50 per cent. Since it usually offered multiple analyses (sometimes in the hundreds and even occasionally in the thousands) it required manual selection of the correct analysis. Interactive parsing manipulation of the tags and syntactic markings was needed, followed by further applications of the parser, to add an additional 25–30 per cent of successful parses. We are now left with a residue of 20–25 per cent in terms of the number of text units, or a residue of 38 per cent in terms of the number of words.

Most of the ICE teams will neither be able to raise the funding nor be able to find skilled researchers for the enormous amount of manual work required by the TOSCA system. The primary design of the Survey parser is therefore a fully automatic system that will use the same grammatical annotation scheme—the same terminology and types of analyses—as that used for ICE-GB, providing the opportunities for valid grammatical comparisons across the ICE corpora. The system is fully automatic in the sense that there is no need for human intervention between the input of raw texts and the final output of syntactic analyses. When the parser cannot produce any global analysis for the sentence, the parser will try to come up with a 'partial parse', which is analysed at the phrase level but with some indeterminacies regarding syntactic functions.

The second and yet more ambitious consideration in the design of the Survey parser has been to add a new dimension to the possible future application of the

ICE corpora. Though ICE has been primarily designed for the linguistic study of varieties of English throughout the world, the annotated output of the project is by no means restricted to linguistic studies. The detailed annotations represent the linguistic knowledge that describes the various language phenomena manifested in the ICE corpora. The design of the Survey parser therefore also aims at testing the reusability of this knowledge by first of all extracting it and then incorporating it in a parser that in turn analyses new data with the same knowledge. The success of this attempt will prove that the syntactic analysis of the ICE corpora is not a study of the English language as such but a qualitative contribution to research in natural language processing (NLP), a major component in artificial intelligence.

Before a detailed description of the Survey approach to automatic parsing, I shall look at the ICE annotation schemes from a parsing point of view.

3. THE ICE ANNOTATION SCHEMES

The ICE annotation schemes include grammatical tagging and syntactic parsing for all the tokens in the corpus. As will be described in the following two sections, the ICE tagging scheme aims at providing not only word-class details for linguistic studies but also invaluable syntactic information for subsequent parsing. The output from the syntactic parsing in turn offers detailed descriptions of the hierarchical constituent structures in which lexical items are accommodated.

3.1. *The ICE Tagging Scheme*

Altogether there are twenty-two head tags and seventy-one features in the ICE word-class tagging scheme, resulting in about 270 grammatically possible combinations. The ICE tagging scheme has been modified; for a description of the most recent scheme, see Chapter 8.[2] The features of ICE cover all the major English word classes and provide morphological, grammatical, collocational, and semantic information. A typical ICE tag has two components: the head tag and its properties that bring out the grammatical features of the associated word. An ICE tag is represented as HeadTag(feature1,feature2). For instance, N(com,sing) means that the lexical item associated with this tag is a common (com) singular (sing) noun (N). V(montr,past) says that the word is a past tense (past) monotransitive (montr) verb (V). Some ICE tags note lexical items that involve a special phrasal, clausal, and even sentential analysis.

Tags that indicate phrasal collocations are PREP(phras) and ADV(phras), prepositions (as in [1]) and adverbs (as in [2]) that are frequently used in collocation with certain verbs and adjectives:

[1] W1A-017-68 Thus the dogs' behaviour had been changed because they associated the bell *with* the food.

[2] W2B-001-24 I had been filming The Paras at the time, and Brian had had to come *down* to Wales with the records.

Some tags, such as profm(so,cl) and prtcl(with), indicate the presence of a clause. *So* in [3] signals an abbreviated clause while *with* in [4] a non-finite clause as prepositional complement.

[3] If *so*, I'll come and meet you at the station.

[4] W1A-017-27 The number by the arrows represents the order of the pathway causing emotion, *with* the cortex lastly having the emotion.

Examples [5]–[7] illustrate tags that note special sentence structures. *There* in [5] is tagged as EXTHERE, existential *there* that indicates a marked sentence order. [6] is an example of the cleft sentence (which explicity marks the focus), where *it* is tagged as CLEFTIT. [7] exemplifies anticipatory *it*, which is tagged as ANTIT.

[5] W2B-001-35 *There* were two reasons for the secrecy.

[6] W1A-001-19 *It* is from this point onwards that Roman Britain ceases to exist and the history of sub-Roman Britain begins.

[7] W1A-001-7 Before trying to answer the question *it* is worthwhile highlighting briefly some of the differences between current historians.

The verb class is divided into auxiliaries and lexical verbs. The auxiliary class notes modals, perfect, passive, and semi-auxiliaries. The lexical verbs are further annotated according to their complementation types. There are altogether eight types: complex-transitive, complex-ditransitive, copular, dimonotransitive, ditransitive, intransitive, monotransitive, and trans as shown by Fig. 11.1.

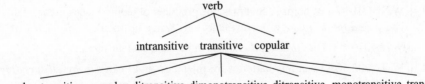

FIG. 11.1. Verb transitivity types in the ICE tagging scheme

Syntactically, these types can be represented as:

a. complex-transitive (V + Direct Object + Object Complement)

[8] W2B-001-30 If television was going to be bloody-minded, radio would *keep* me busy.

b. complex-ditransitive (V + Indirect Object + Direct Object + Object Complement)

[9] I sold him my car secondhand.

c. copular (V + Subject Complement)

[10] W2B-001-7 Of all my broadcasting, the Monday morning spot *was* perhaps the best fun.

d. dimonotransitive (V + Indirect Object)

[11] W1B-007-149 The pen though, as Shakespeare will *tell* you is more Mighty than the sword.

e. ditransitive (V + Indirect Object + Direct Object)

[12] W1A-017-95 His parents were then recommended to stop comforting him as they were *giving* him positive reinforcement for undesirable behaviour.

f. intransitive (V)

[13] W2B-001-4 As an actor, I had *appeared* in innumerable schools broadcasts, in Saturday Night Theatre and in The Dales.

g. monotransitive (V + Direct Object)

[14] W2B-001-9 The programme *had* a biggish audience (in radio terms) because it *followed* the Today programme, and because people listened to it in their cars on the way to work.

h. trans (V + Clause, V + Direct Object + Object Complement)

The notation trans here is used in the ICE project to tag transitive verbs followed by a noun phrase that may be the subject of the following nonfinite clause. They are so tagged in order to avoid making a decision on their transitivity types[3] (cf. Greenbaum, 1993). This verb type is best demonstrated by the following sentences:

[15] W2B-001-97 Just before Christmas, the producer of Going Places, Irene Mallis, had *asked me to make* a documentary on 'warm-up men'.

[16] W1A-010-53 They *make others feel* guilty and isolate them . . .

[17] W1B-002-135 I can buy batteries for the tape—but I can *see myself spending* a fortune!

[18] W1B-011-91 The person who booked me in *had his eyebrows shaved & replaced* by straight black painted lines and he had earrings, not only in his ears but through his nose and lip!

In examples [15]–[17], *asked, make, see,* and *had* are all complemented by non-finite clauses with overt subjects, the main verbs of these non-finite clauses being infinitive, present participle and past participle.

As illustrated by examples [1]–[17], the ICE tagging scheme has indeed gone beyond the wordclass to provide some syntactic information and has thus proved itself to be an expressive and powerful means of pre-processing for subsequent parsing.

3.2. *The ICE Parsing Scheme*

The ICE parsing scheme recognizes five basic syntactic phrases. They are adjective phrase (AJP), adverb phrase (AVP), noun phrase (NP), prepositional phrase (PP), and verb phrase (VP). Their major sentential syntactic functions are captured in the list in the Appendix.

Each tree in the ICE parsing scheme is represented as a functionally labelled hierarchy, with features describing the characteristics of phrases, clauses, and the sentence.[4] Each line contains information about the function and the category of a certain node. Features are listed between brackets to give detailed descriptions about a particular category. All terminal symbols are ICE tags. All leaf-nodes (nodes immediately associated with lexical items) are represented as

Function HeadTag(feature1,feature2) {Lexical Item}

and all the other nodes are represented as

Function Category(feature1,feature2, . . .)

To illustrate, the sentence

[19] W2B-009-39 Hannah is not a putative feminist like Hervey who wants equal opportunities with men.

is represented as the following tree structure:

```
PU CL(main,act,decl,indic,cop,pres,unm)
 A CONNEC(ge) {But}
 SU NP()
  NPHD N(prop,sing) {Hannah}
 V VP(act,indic,cop,pres)
  MVB V(cop,pres) {is}
 A AVP(gen)
  AVHD ADV(ge) {not}
 CS NP()
  DT DTP()
   DTCE ART(indef) {a}
  NPPR AJP(attru)
   AJHD ADJ {putative}
  NPHD N(com,sing) {feminist}
  NPPO PP()
   P PREP(ge) {like}
   PC NP()
    NPHD N(prop,sing) {Hervey}
    NPPO CL(depend,act,indic,montr,pres,rel,unm)
     SU NP()
      NPHD PRON(rel) {who}
```

```
    V VP(act,indic,montr,pres)
     MVB V(montr,pres) {wants}
    OD NP()
     NPPR AJP(attru)
      AJHD ADJ {equal}
     NPHD N(com,plu) {opportunities}
     NPPO PP()
      P PREP(ge) {with}
      PC NP()
       NPHD N(com,plu) {men}
PUNC PUNC(per) {.}
```

From this tree, we know that [19] is a parsing unit (PU) realized by a clause (CL) which has the following features:

main	main clause
act	active voice
decl	declarative
indic	indicative
cop	copula
pres	present tense
unm	unmarked word order (SVO)

Hannah in [19] is labelled as **SU NP()**, indicating that it is a noun phrase **(NP())** as the subject **(SU)**. Within this NP, the word form is enclosed between curly brackets, with the indication that it is a singular proper noun **(N(prop,sing))** and that it is the head of the **NP (NPHD)**. The relative clause in [19] is explicitly indicated by **NPPO CL**, which means that this clause functions as an NP postmodifier, with features such as montr (monotransitive), rel (relative), etc.

4. THE APPROACH OF THE SURVEY PARSER

Central to the Survey approach to parsing is the application of the syntactically annotated ICE-GB, most of which was parsed using the TOSCA parser. This corpus embodies the syntactic knowledge used to annotate its 78,000 sentences. Since its texts were carefully selected to represent British English, we have every reason to believe that this corpus (by far the largest annotated collection in such detail) represents a repertoire of phrasal as well as clausal structures. Heavily annotated at lexical, phrasal, clausal, and sentential levels, this corpus has been turned into a linguistic knowledge base, where one can query all the possible syntactic functions of, say, infinitival clauses. This type of query proceeds in a top-down manner, from the specification of a higher level node to the retrieval of all the constituent structures including the lexical items. This process is described by Fig. 11.2.

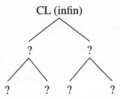

CL (infin)

FIG. 11.2. Top-down retrieval for the constituents in an infinitival clause

Indeed, a retrieving system (TQuery) has been developed at the Survey to carry out exactly this task. More relevant to parsing, this corpus can be made to automatically generate phrase structure (PS) rules which derive from and describe authentic data. Further, given a sentence as a cluster of PSs, this corpus can deduce how many and what sentential analyses there are for this cluster and what the most common analysis is. If such a cluster is not found in the knowledge base, an optimally similar structure can be retrieved to assist parsing decisions. This parsing approach can be seen as a two-stage reversed process of TQuery that proceeds in a bottom-up manner (see Fig. 11.3). That is, the constituent structure is retrieved according to the sequence of terminal symbols.

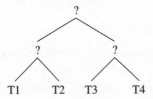

FIG. 11.3. Bottom-up retrieval for the governing node of specified items

The first stage includes the application of PS rules that are directly linked to subtrees anchored to a sequence of wordclass tags, a process that groups words into phrases. The second stage is the application of phrase structure cluster (PSC) rules that are directly linked to sentential trees anchored to PSs. The rules used in these two stages are automatically generated from the syntactically analysed ICE-GB.

4.1. *Automatic extraction of PS rules*

As described in Section 3.2, we recognize five major phrases: noun phrase (NP), verb phrase (VP), prepositional phrase (PP), adjective phrase (AJP), and adverb phrase (AVP). Rules describing these phrases up to the head (or the tail, in the case of PP) will be extracted from ICE-GB, but excluding postmodification or complementation. When extracted, these PS rules constitute two separate databases: (1) PS rules represented as sequences of ICE wordclass tags, and (2) PS rules represented as bracketed and functionally labelled tree structures. These two databases

149

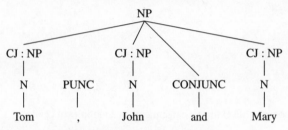

FIG. 11.4. A graphic tree representation of *Tom, John, and Mary*

are integrated in such a manner that given a sequence of word-class tags, its tree structure can be conveniently retrieved. The syntactic unit associated with each rule in such a database is a tree structure where each node is labelled with both a syntactic function and a syntactic category.[5] The category is usually further defined by a list of properties that describe its syntactic features. This rule structure is very close to that of the Lexicalised Tree Adjoining Grammar (LTAG. cf. Joshi *et al.*, 1975; Abeille *et al.*, 1990; Schabes and Joshi, 1991; Doran *et al.*, 1994*a* and 1994*b*; Evans *et al.*, 1995) except that each tree is anchored to an ICE word-class tag rather than a lexical item as in LTAG.[6]

For instance, the noun PS rule to describe *Tom, John and Mary* has the following two forms:

(1) wordclass tag sequence:[7]

```
N(prop,sing) PUNC(com) N(prop,sing) CONJUNC(coord)
                    N(prop,sing)
```

(2) bracketed and functionally labelled tree structure:[8]

```
CJ NP()
NPHD N(prop,sing) {John}
PUNC PUNC(com) {,}
CJ NP()
NPHD N(prop,sing) {Tom}
COOR CONJUNC(coord) {and}
CJ NP()
NPHD N(prop,sing) {Mary}
```

(1) and (2) combine to say that any three singular proper names in the form of (1) will be analysed as three coordinated NP conjoins as in (2). The implied graphic tree is shown in Fig. 11.4. So far, PS rules for 1,649 NPs, 1,047 VPs, and 58 AJPs have been automatically extracted and duly incorporated into the parser.

The PSC rules contain sequences of PSs. In most of the cases, these clusters correspond to the sentence (SVA: NP+VP+AVP; SVO: NP+VP+NP). They functionally label the PSs to produce the final global structure. This process also results in two databases: (1) the PSC as a sequence of PSs, and (2) the PSC as a bracketed and functionally labelled tree structure. Again, these two databases are integrated

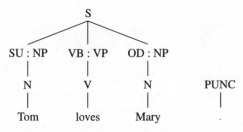

FIG. 11.5. A graphic tree representation of *Tom loves Mary*

in such a manner that given a sequence of PSs, its tree structure can be conveniently retrieved.

For instance, *Tom loves Mary* is represented as

(1) PSC:[9]

`NP V:montr NP PUNC(per)`

(2) bracketed and functionally labelled tree structure:[10]

```
PU CL(main,act,decl,indic,montr,pres,unm)
 SU NP()
  NPHD N(prop,sing) {Tom}
 VB VP(act,indic,montr,pres)
  MVB V(montr,pres) {loves}
 OD NP()
  NPHD N(prop,sing) {Mary}
PUNC PUNC(per) {.}
```

(1) and (2) in the above example specify that (2) should be retrieved as the global analysis for any two NPs with an interposed VP whose main verb is monotransitive. Note the detailed properties attached to the clause (CL) and the verb phrase (VP) to bring out their syntactic features. Graphically, (2) can be represented as Fig. 11.5. So far, 43,063 PSC rules have been automatically generated, together with their corresponding tree structures.

It has been planned that some extra information will be provided alongside these PS and PSC rules. Frequencies and text sources of occurrence, for instance, will be useful in that we can choose the most common analysis in the case of multiple parses for a single PSC or tag sequence, and also in that we can make sound judgements about whether a particular rule is exclusively used in a particular sublanguage. We envisage a rule management system that can add, delete, or select any subset of rules to suit the need of different parsing tasks. For instance, the parsing of formal English probably means the exclusion of a certain set of rules observed only in the spoken genre. This rule management system should also be able to update the knowledge base so that it is possible to 'teach' new rules to the database by incorporating manually parsed examples.

4.2. *Parsing with PS Rules*

Subsequent parsing has three stages: (1) assigning a word-class tag to each item in the input string, (2) chunking the tags into a PSC, and (3) querying in the knowledge base the possible analyses for this PSC.

We have already developed a probabilistic tagging system (AUTASYS) that assigns ICE tags to words in the input string (Fang and Nelson, 1994; Chapter 9 in this volume). Fast in speed, this system processes 10,000 words per minute, at an accuracy rate of 96 per cent. The Survey parser incorporates AUTASYS to annotate the input at word-class level.

The input string, as a sequence of word-class tags, is then processed at the phrase level according to the PS rules, which are applied deterministically, though we might find it necessary to apply these rules recursively, depending on results. In our experience, the deterministic application of NP and VP rules is surprisingly successful. When applied, these PS rules chunk the input string into a cluster of PSs, with feature information about the head.

Finally, the input string, now as a PSC, is presented to the set of PSC rules in the database, to query if an exact or similar cluster exists. If it does, then the corresponding tree structure is retrieved to determine the global syntactic structure of the input string. In the case of multiple analyses, the frequency of PSC rules as observed in the ICE-GB corpus will be used, in connection with feature constraints, to decide on the most common analysis. When the query fails, the input string is subjected to a process described in Section 3.4 and then the process described in this section. If a global analysis still cannot be achieved after that, the parser will offer a partial analysis whose internal structures are determined at the phrase level.

4.3. *An Example*

In this section, I shall illustrate the various parsing stages through an example.

[20] He found the book very interesting.

[20] is first of all tagged by AUTASYS for wordclass information:

```
He            PRON(pers,sing)
found         v(cxtr,past)
the           ART(def)
book          N(com,sing)
very          ADV(inten)
interesting   ADJ(ingp)
.             PUNC(per)
```

And then the input string, now as a sequence of word-class tags, is subjected to the PS rules, which in due course chunk and analyse the input string into the following phrases:

```
NP()
 NPHD PRON(pers,sing) {He}
VP(act,cxtr,indic,past)
 MVB V(cxtr,past) {found}
NP()
 DT DTP()
  DTCE ART(def) {the}
 NPHD N(com,sing) {book}
AJP(prd)
 AJPR AVP(int)
  AVHD ADV(inten) {very}
 AJHD ADJ(ingp) {interesting}
```

Analysed at the phrase level, the input string is now represented as a sequence of syntactic phrases:

NP VP:cxtr NP AJP

which is then subjected to the PSC rules. The appropriate rule produces the final analysis:

```
PU CL(main,act,cxtr,decl,indic,past,unm)
 SU NP()
  NPHD PRON(pers,sing) {He}
 VB VP(act,cxtr,indic,past)
  MVB V(cxtr,past) {found}
 OD NP()
  DT DTP()
   DTCE ART(def) {the}
  NPHD N(com,sing) {book}
 CO AJP(prd)
  AJPR AVP(int)
   AVHD ADV(inten) {very}
  AJHD ADJ(ingp) {interesting}
 PUNC PUNC(per) {.}
```

Fig. 11.6 is the graphic tree of [20].

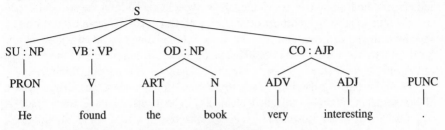

FIG. 11.6. The graphic representation of example [20]

Alex Chengyu Fang

5. INITIAL RESULTS

So far, the experimental model has been tested on a few different sets of data. In this section, I present the results of one experiment, which compared the Survey parser with the Alvey Natural Language Tools (ANLT). The test data consisted of a list of noun phrases which are used as definitions in the Longman Dictionary of Contemporary English (LDOCE).

This list consists of 117 noun definitions automatically extracted from LDOCE and was used in the experiment on a probabilistic parsing model at Cambridge Computer Laboratory (Briscoe and Carroll, 1991). This data contains two sets. The first set (63) is part of the data used to train the probabilistic parser. The second set has 54 definitions and was not used as training data. The parser produced an average of 7.17 parses per string. 95 (81.2 per cent) received one or more analyses, and probability of rule associations was used to choose the best parse. Among the 95 analyses chosen by the stochastic algorithm, 78 were successfully picked out as the correct parse, which means that 82 per cent of the analyses were correct, with an overall performance of 66.6 per cent accuracy rate.

This list of noun phrases was also fed into the Survey parser. Of the 117 noun phrases, 84 received only one analysis, with 77 correctly parsed. This means that 91.7 per cent of the analyses proposed by the parser were correct and the overall accuracy rate was 65.8 per cent. More interestingly, if the list is split into the training set and the unseen set, we see that the Survey parser is very close to the ANLT parser for the training set and out-performs the ANLT parser with the unseen set. With both sets, significantly, the Survey parser demonstrated consistently higher success rates (93.8 per cent and 88.9 per cent) of the proposed analysis being the correct one.

This comparison is summarized in Tables 11.1 to 11.3.

6. FURTHER RESEARCH

While their internal structure remains more or less stable and predictable, phrases and clauses can be immensely complex because of such non-obligatory elements as PP and relative or adverbial clauses. Syntactically ambiguous constructions, PP, and clauses, both finite and non-finite, are active and versatile in the sentential syntax, and able to take up a number of potential attachments. They can occur virtually anywhere in the sentence and can be easily compounded as many times as the speaker or writer wants them to be. This fact adds to the complexity of the sentence and is one of the major reasons for multiple analyses and parsing failures.

This understanding naturally leads to the need for the automatic determination of the syntactic functions of such elements. Indeed, efforts have been made in this area, for instance, to disambiguate PP attachment (Hindle and Rooth, 1993; Brill and Resnik, 1994; Ratnaparkhi and Roukos, 1994). At the Survey we have

TABLE 11.1. *Training data (63 noun phrases)*

	NPs analysed		Correct analyses		Overall(%)
	No.	%	No.	%	
ANLT	58	92.1	47	81	74.6
AUTASYS	48	76.2	45	93.8	71.4

TABLE 11.2. *Unseen data (54 noun phrases)*

	NPs analysed		Correct analyses		Overall(%)
	No.	%	No.	%	
ANLT	37	68.5	31	83.8	57.4
AUTASYS	36	66.7	32	88.9	59.3

TABLE 11.3. *Overall performance (117 noun phrases)*

	NPs analysed		Correct analyses		Overall(%)
	No.	%	No.	%	
ANLT	95	81.2	78	82.1	66.6
AUTASYS	84	71.8	77	91.7	65.8

also carried out similar investigations to disambiguate the attachment of PP (Fang, 1994). The experiment on PP used *with* as a prototypical preposition, examined its morpho-syntactic relations with the antecedent NP, and reported a disambiguation rate of 80 per cent, a figure similar to those reported by the others. We believe that a similar figure can be achieved with other prepositions through the same approach and that work on clauses will yield a similar result.

To achieve this end, we plan to investigate the following areas:

- *Collocation.* This will include the more or less prefabricated but common collocations such as verb-preposition, noun-preposition, adjective-preposition.
- *Morphological derivations.* The database will have a mechanism such that given a lexical form, its morphological derivations can be cross-referred. This information is needed because of the strong parallel between verb-preposition collocations and their nominal derivations (cf. Gazdar *et al.*, 1985), e.g.,

He *argued with* his brother   vs.   His *argument with* his brother

- *Syntactico-semantics.* We are concerned with only those syntactico-semantic properties that trigger a different syntactic structure. For instance, when the *with* phrase is used in connection with an action verb, this prepositional phrase is very likely an adverbial of instrument. On the other hand, a relational verb (cf. Quirk *et al.*, 1972 and Schlesinger, 1995) seldom requires an adverbial realized by a prepositional phrase.

If the above procedures can solve the attachment problem fairly successfully, it means that those non-obligatory elements do not need to take part in global parsing. Thus the sentence complexity will be greatly reduced and the input string (as a PSC) is more likely to be described by the rules.

7. CONCLUSION

In this chapter, I have described the design and development of a parser at the Survey. Its design not only reflects the need of the ICE project, and indeed other similar projects, but also the potential application of syntactically annotated corpora in NLP. The fact that the present model of the Survey parser was developed within only five months has already demonstrated the great benefit ICE offers to the development of NLP application systems.

NOTES

1. According to Magerman (1994: 94 ff.), the crossing-brackets score was introduced during the PARSEVAL workshop on parser evaluation at the University of Pennsylvania in 1990, where participants reached a consensus that the constituent-based measures of crossing-brackets rate, precision, and recall sufficiently represented the performance of their parsers in comparison to a skeletal treebank. A single crossing-bracket error is a constituent in a parse tree which contains parts of two different constituents from a treebank analysis without completely containing either. For instance, if [[AB][CD][EF]G] is the correct analysis, then the parse tree [[ABC]D[EFG]] is an instance of crossing-brackets violation. In fact, only [ABC] is considered as a violation, not [EFG].
2. For more detailed descriptions of the ICE tagging scheme, see Chapters 8 and 9 in this volume.
3. This type of verb can be analysed differently according to various tests into, for instance, monotransitives, ditransitives, and complex transitives (cf. Quirk *et al.*, 1972, 1985: ch. 15; Mair, 1990). Accordingly, to avoid arbitrary decisions, the complementing non-finite clause is assigned a catch-all term 'transitive complement' in parsing.
4. For a brief description of the ICE parsing scheme, see Chapter 10 in this volume.
5. The root of the tree, however, is not described in terms of its function, which is to be decided in the sentential tree (see sect. 4.2).
6. Actually, grammars of non-trivial size like XTAG (cf. Doran *et al.*, 1994a, 1994b) have given rise to questions of efficient representation. Since lexical entries in LTAG are associated with families that group together related trees, it has been suggested to use an inheritance hierarchy to define abstract trees that describe, for instance, various verb

transitivity types (cf. Briscoe *et al.*, 1993; Evans *et al.*, 1995). It is in this sense that strictly speaking LTAG trees are anchored to a finite set of feature-based word-class tags.

7. **N(prop,sing)** = singular proper noun; **PUNC(com)** = comma; **CONJUNC(coord)** = coordinating conjunction.

8. **CJ** = conjoin; **NP** = noun phrase; **NPHD** = NP head; **PUNC** = punctuation; **COOR** = coordinator.

9. **V:montr** = monotransitive verb.

10. **PU** = parsing unit; **CL** = clause; **act** = active; **decl** = declarative; **indic** = indicative; **montr** = monotransitive; **pres** = present tense; **unm** = unmarked word order; **SU** = subject; **VB** = verb; **VP** = verb phrase; **MVB** = main verb; **V**(montr,pres) = present tense monotransitive verb; **OD** = direct object.

References

ABEILLE, A., BISHOP, K., COTE, S., and SCHABES, Y. (1990), 'A Lexicalized Tree Adjoining Grammar for English', *Technical Report MS-CIS-90-24* (Department of Computer and Information Science, University of Pennsylvania).

ATWELL, E. (1988), 'Grammatical Analysis of English by Statistical Pattern Recognition', in J. KITTLER (ed.), 626–35.

BLACK, E., GARSIDE, R., and LEECH, G. (1993), *Statistically-Driven Computer Grammars of English: The IBM/Lancaster Approach* (Amsterdam: Rodopi).

BRILL, E. and RESNIK, P. (1994), 'A Rule-Based Approach to Prepositional Phrase Attachment Disambiguation', *Proceedings of COLING 1994*, Kyoto.

BRISCOE, T. and CARROLL, J. (1991), 'Generalised Probabilistic LR Parsing of Natural Language (Corpora) with Unification-Based Grammars', *Technical Report No. 224* (Cambridge: University of Cambridge).

—— DE PAIVA, V., and COPESTAKE, A. (1993), *Inheritance, Defaults, and the Lexicon* (Cambridge: Cambridge University Press).

DORAN, C., EGEDI, D., HOCKEY, B. A., and SRINIVAS, B. (1994*a*), 'Status of the XTAG System', in *Proceedings of the Third International Workshop on Tree Adjoining Grammars*, 20–3.

—— —— —— —— and ZAIDEL, M. (1994*b*), 'XTAG System—A Wide Coverage Grammar for English', in *Proceedings of COLING 1994*, Kyoto, 922–8.

EVANS, R., GAZDAR, G., and WEIR, D. (1995), 'Encoding Lexicalized Tree Adjoining Grammar with a Nonmonotonic Inheritance Hierarchy', in *Proceedings ACL 1995* (San Francisco: Morgan Kaufmann).

FANG, A. C. (1994), 'ICE: Applications and Possibilities in NLP', *Proceedings of International Workshop on Directions of Lexical Research*, 15–17 August 1994, 23–44, Beijing.

—— and NELSON, G. (1994), 'Tagging the Survey Corpus: A LOB to ICE Experiment Using AUTASYS', *ALLC Literary and Linguistic Computing*, 9/2: 189–94.

FUJISAKI, T. (1984), 'A Stochastic Approach to Sentence Parsing', in *Proceedings of COLING 1984*, 16–19.

—— JELINEK, F., COCKE, J., BLACK, E., and NISHINO, T. (1991), 'A Probabilistic Parsing Method for Sentence Disambiguation', in M. TOMITA (ed.), 139–52.

GARSIDE, R. and LEECH, F. (1985), 'A Probabilistic Parser', in *ACL Proceedings, Second European Conference*, 166–70.

GAZDAR, G., KLEIN, E., PULLUM, G., and SAG, I. (1985), *Generalized Phrase Structure Grammar* (Oxford: Basil Blackwell).

GREENBAUM, S. (1993), 'The Tagset for the International Corpus of English', in C. SOUTER and E. ATWELL (eds.), 11–24.

HINDLE, D. and ROOTH, M. (1991), 'Structural Ambiguity and Lexical Relations', in *Proceedings of the 29th Annual Meeting of the Association for Computational Linguistics*, Berkeley, Calif.

JOSHI, A., LEVY, L., and TAKAHASHI, M. (1975), 'Tree Adjunct Grammars', in *Journal of Computer System Science*, 10/1: 136–63.

KITTLER, J. (1988) (ed.), *Pattern Recognition: Proceedings of the 4th International Conference, Cambridge* (Berlin: Springer Verlag).

MAGERMAN, D. (1994), 'Natural Language Parsing as Statistical Pattern Recognition', Ph.D. thesis (Stanford).

MAIR, C. (1990), *Infinitival Complement Clauses in English* (Cambrige: Cambridge University Press).

QUIRK, R., GREENBAUM, S., LEECH, G., and SVARTVIK, J. (1972), *A Grammar of Contemporary English* (London: Longman).

————————— (1985), *A Comprehensive Grammar of the English Language* (London: Longman).

RATNAPARKHI, A. and ROUKOS, S. (1994), 'A Maximum Entropy Model for Prepositional Phrase Attachment', in *Proceedings of the ARPA Workshop on Human Language Technology, Plainsboro, NJ*, March 1994.

SCHABES, Y. and JOSHI, A. (1991), 'Parsing with Lexicalized Tree Adjoining Grammar', in M. TOMITA (ed.), 25–47.

SCHLESINGER, I. (1995), *Cognitive Space and Linguistic Case: Semantic and Syntactic Categories in English* (Cambridge: Cambridge University Press).

SOUTER, C. and ATWELL, E. (1993) (eds.), *Corpus-based Computational Linguistics* (Amsterdam: Rodopi).

TOMITA, M. (1991) (ed.), *Current Issues in Parsing Technology* (Boston: Kluwer Academic Publishers).

Appendix

A	adverbial
AJHD	adjective phrase head
AJPO	adjective phrase postmodifier
AJPR	adjective phrase premodifier
APPOS	appositive
AVB	auxiliary verb
AVHD	adverb phrase head
AVPO	adverb phrase postmodifier
AVPR	adverb phrase premodifier
CF	focus complement
CJ	conjoin
CLOP	cleft operator
CO	object complement
COAP	appositive connector
COOR	coordinator
CS	subject complement
CT	transitive complement
DT	determiner
DTCE	central determiner
DTDE	deferred determiner
DTPE	predeterminer
DTPO	determiner phrase postmodifier
DTPR	determiner phrase premodifier
DTPS	postdeterminer
EXOP	existential operator
FLAP	floating appositive
FNPPO	floating noun phrase postmodifier
FOC	focus
GENF	genitive function
IMPOP	imperative operator
INTOP	interrogative operator
INVOP	inversion operator
MVB	main verb
NOOD	notional direct object
NOSU	notional subject
NPHD	noun phrase head
NPPO	noun phrase postmodifier
NPPR	noun phrase premodifier
OD	direct object
OI	indirect object
P	prepositional
PC	prepositional complement
PMOD	prepositional modifier

PROD	provisional direct object
PRSU	provisional subject
PS	stranded prepositional
PU	parsing unit
PUNC	punctuation
SA	subject attribute
SBHD	subordinator phrase head
SBMO	subordinator phrase modifier
SU	subject
SUB	subordinator
TO	*to* infinitive marker
VB	verb

PART III

Problems of Implementation

12

The New Zealand Spoken Component of ICE: Some Methodological Challenges[1]

JANET HOLMES

New Zealand linguists have been involved over the last eight years in planning and collecting data for a number of different written and spoken corpora of New Zealand English. These include the Wellington Corpus of New Zealand English (WCNZE) with its one million word written and one million word spoken components, and the New Zealand contributions to the International Corpus of English (ICE) Project, which involved a total of one million words composed of representative extracts of written and spoken New Zealand English.[2] This paper describes some of the methodological problems encountered in collecting material for a spoken corpus of New Zealand English, including the issue of who counts as a speaker of New Zealand English, the problems of collecting data in particular categories, and the procedures put in place to process collected data.

The idea of collecting a Corpus of New Zealand English had been discussed by New Zealand linguists since the mid-1980s. A number of New Zealand linguists had been using corpora in their research into vocabulary (Kennedy, 1991; Bauer and Nation, 1993), and the expression of speech functions such as quantity (Kennedy, 1987), causation (Kennedy and Fang, 1992) and certainty (Holmes, 1982, 1983). They were very aware of the valuable resources which had been made available by the Brown Corpus of American English in the early 1960s, the LOB Corpus of British written English in 1987, and the LUND Corpus of British spoken English in 1980. In 1987, after much debate about design and methodology, linguists at Victoria University began collecting data for the Wellington Corpus of Written and Spoken New Zealand English. Hence, when Sidney Greenbaum proposed that an International Corpus of English should be gathered (1988), it seemed sensible to ensure that New Zealand linguists also collected material suitable for inclusion in that corpus.

1. CONTRIBUTIONS TO THE STRUCTURE AND COMPOSITION OF ICE

The parameters of the International Corpus were debated and finally decided at international gatherings where it was not always possible for New Zealand linguists to be present. Nevertheless, we felt that our written contributions to the discussion were taken into account, and reflected in the large proportion of conversational data which it was finally agreed should be included in the sample design, as well as in the exclusion of broadcast short stories from the spoken component of ICE. Informal conversational interaction is the most pervasive, unmarked, daily expression of a language variety, and it therefore seemed very important that this text category be well represented in any corpus. Short stories, on the other hand, are essentially written rather than spoken data, and thus belonged more appropriately in the written section of ICE. Though we had some reservations about the precise proportions of different text categories in the finally agreed composition of the ICE spoken component, we felt that overall it represented a satisfactory design.

Another area where experience collecting data for the Wellington Corpus of Spoken New Zealand English (WCSNZE) proved valuable was in anticipating the problems raised for the notion of a standardized size of excerpt by the wide disparity in the normal length of different text categories. Taking account of the integrity of different text categories means that they will inevitably vary in natural length: a news broadcast, a judge's summing up, a transaction in a shop, and a television discussion vary considerably in the number of words they involve. In constructing the WCSNZE we had decided that while an 'excerpt' size of 2,000 words (as used by the Brown and LOB corpora) constituted a useful target for many speech samples, in general the discourse type should be allowed to dictate the appropriate length for any particular speech sample. This inevitably led to the need for (*a*) composite texts made up of a number of sub-texts packaged together for ease of use by researchers; (*b*) the selection of appropriate 'samples' from larger texts with beginnings and endings at structurally justifiable points in the discourse. Both these solutions were also adopted by those working on the ICE Corpus.

2. Whose Speech Should be Included in the Spoken Corpus?

2.1. *Who counts as a New Zealander?*

One of the most fundamental issues addressed by the New Zealand spoken corpus research group[3] was the problem of defining who counted as a New Zealander. Who should be allowed to contribute to the corpus? This problem is one which has presumably faced all those involved in corpus collection, but it has received little explicit attention. It is a particularly vexatious problem for colonial societies where large sections of the community are immigrants. At what point does an immigrant become a New Zealander?[4]

We rejected the notion of selecting people who 'sounded like' New Zealanders, since this would have self-evidently pre-judged an issue which the corpus data was intended to illuminate—namely what constitutes New Zealand English. Similarly, non-linguistic criteria such as citizenship or residency are fraught with problems, since those who hold such qualifications may be very recent arrivals from else-where. Even longer-term residents cannot be expected to have acquired features which distinguish New Zealand speech from other varieties if they have arrived in the country after puberty. Consequently, we adopted a criterion which has been regarded by others as very stringent, but which we felt confident would ensure the integrity of the New Zealand samples included in the corpus.

A speaker of New Zealand English is defined as someone who has lived in New Zealand since before the age of 10.

A certain amount of overseas experience was regarded as normal within New Zealand, but, again for reasons relating to the need to establish the distinctive fea-tures of a New Zealand variety of English, people who had spent extensive periods of time overseas were excluded. More than ten years or over half their lifetime (whichever was the greater) was considered an 'extensive period of time', and this rendered people ineligible for inclusion in the spoken corpus. Also excluded were people who had returned from an overseas trip within the last year.

2.2. *Ethnic and Gender Representation*

People of any ethnicity (e.g. Dutch, Samoan, Greek, Tongan) were considered eli-gible for inclusion in the spoken corpus provided they satisfied the criterion for eligibility as a New Zealander. No attempt was made to include representative samples from particular ethnic groups other than Maori. It was considered import-ant to include an appropriate proportion of the speech of the indigenous Maori people, and while this was not possible within each sub-category, it was recog-nized as a reasonable aim for the corpus as a whole. Hence we adopted a goal that approximately 12 per cent of the transcribed participants should be Maori, with the remaining 88 per cent non-Maori. Our current estimates suggest this goal will be achieved.

Some degree of gender balance was also considered desirable, with an ideal overall goal of 50 per cent female speech and 50 per cent male speech within the 600,000 word sample. By making very deliberate efforts to include as many women speakers as possible, this goal has been achieved.

2.3. *Other Social Factors*

Recognizing that it would be unrealistic to attempt to collect a representative sample which took account of additional social variables such as social class, re-gional origin, level of education, and occupation, no attempt has been made to pre-determine such categories. However, as agreed by ICE participants (Greenbaum, 1990), every speech sample collected is described as fully as possible in these respects for each speaker contributing to the corpus.

3. Collecting the Spoken Data

3.1. *No Surreptitious Recording*

A firm decision was taken at the start of the project that all contributors would know that they were being recorded. There was to be no surreptitious taping. Some comment is useful, however, on the ways this requirement was met in relation to particular categories of data.

Ideally, linguists wish to observe how people interact in the most natural possible manner. The observer's paradox, as Labov has called it, means that we face the impossible conundrum of collecting data on how people speak when they are not being observed: 'the aim of linguistic research in the community must be to find out how people talk when they are not being systematically observed; yet we can only obtain this data by systematic observation' (Labov, 1972: 181). And it is clearly unacceptable to tape-record people without their knowledge.

It is undoubtedly true that people talk differently when they are aware of the presence of the tape-recorder. One interesting example of this is the pressure to 'feed the machine'. People who are not being tape-recorded often tolerate long pauses. When they are being recorded people are initially very aware of the tape-recorder, though they may forget it as they become absorbed in the topic. This tends to happen in many recordings after about five minutes or so. However, if a natural lull in the conversation occurred, the silence often revives people's awareness of the tape-recorder and they then begin to talk again, presumably in order to avoid leaving long silences on the tape. It seems unlikely, then, that patterns of pauses are 'natural' in non-surreptitious recordings. Nevertheless, despite such possible disadvantages, as a general principle surreptitious recording was proscribed.

It was sometimes possible to collect recordings without the person recorded being aware that they were being recorded on that particular occasion. This involved the data collector asking the person in advance if they would agree to be recorded at some future date without necessarily being informed at the specific time of the recording. They would be told afterwards and would have the right to veto the use of the tape. This strategy was used for a small number of telephone conversations and some face-to-face conversations. But it is worth noting that the quality of surreptitious recordings is often dubious, since the microphone cannot always be placed in the best position for collecting the data (cf. Labov, 1984).

Our general practice was to ask people recording conversations to collect at least 30 minutes of conversation. This allowed us to take a sample from a point at which it seemed likely that they had forgotten the tape-recorder. In general this proved a very successful technique, and the majority of recorded conversations are reasonably 'natural' as a result of selecting samples which begin well into the recorded material.

4. Operationalizing the Categories

The New Zealand data collection was a collaborative effort drawing on the good-will and generosity of many volunteers as well as a team of paid research assistants. The first step in actually collecting the data was to translate the list of ICE text categories into small manageable data-collection tasks which were consistent with the overall guidelines. Each text category was treated as a project, and strategies were developed for collecting suitable data. A small selection of categories will be used to illustrate the kinds of problems encountered and remedial strategies adopted: lectures and tutorials, transactions, telephone conversations, and casual conversations.

4.1. *Collecting Lectures and Tutorials*

In order to collect suitable lecture and tutorial material a number of steps were necessary. Most of this data was collected at Victoria University of Wellington, for obvious practical reasons. Using departmental secretaries as sources of information, the first step was to establish which members of the university staff were eligible contributors. A large proportion of New Zealand university staff are recruited from overseas, so the number of eligible contributors was relatively small.

The second step involved selecting, from those who proved eligible, a sample to represent a range of disciplines and to provide appropriate Maori and gender representation. Data was recorded from lecturers and tutors in arts, sciences, and the professional areas (law, commerce, architecture), and the sample included equal numbers of female and male teachers, as well as four Maori lecturers and two Maori tutors.

The third step, the actual recording, proved relatively painless for lectures, since all the staff involved were very co-operative. The range of lecturing styles, however, proved to be a further variable which we did not attempt to control, but which was noted. Some staff used a relatively formal style, staying close to their notes and to the lectern; others moved around much more and invited participation from the class. While the former were easier to record, it seemed important to include a representative range of styles rather than to select those who provided the fewest methodological problems.

The process of recording interactions in tutorials proved much more difficult. Indeed our first attempts proved totally untranscribable. First, the tutorials often involved several small groups talking at once, and the contributions simply could not be heard clearly. Secondly, it was often impossible to tell from the tapes who was contributing at any particular point.

The second attempt to collect tutorial data involved videoing the tutorials so that speakers could be identified. This proved a complex exercise. We first needed to persuade teachers to allow us to videotape their tutorials. Since they had often spent a great deal of time getting a group to relax and interact effectively, we expected that the intrusion of two extra people and a video camera might not be greeted with enthusiasm. Research assistants were trained to use the camera as unobtrusively as possible. One assistant made the recording; the other noted who was saying what, so that each contributor's background information could be matched to their transcribed contribution. Fortunately, staff and students were extremely co-operative during this complex process. And it was also fortunate that 90 per cent of the students turned out to be New Zealanders as defined by our criteria.

4.2. *Collecting Transactions*

Our original conception of a 'transaction' was a canonical business transaction in which goods or services were exchanged. The corpus research group generated many ideas for collecting business transactions, but the reality regularly defeated us. It was impossible to obtain consent from many potential venues (e.g. travel agents, estate agents, information desks) because the management feared clients would be inhibited by the tape-recorder and this would adversely affect their business. Many people felt it would be an intrusion on clients' privacy (e.g. student loans desk, banks). A number of shops were investigated, but they frequently proved too noisy and the management often had reservations about recording interactions at the complaints or order desk. At the other extreme, the library provided many interactions which were totally non-verbal and thus inappropriate for a speech corpus.

We did finally collect a reasonable range of business transactions, but many involved a huge amount of work and planning for very small returns. Transactions in shops, for instance, required a great deal of setting up, including notices to customers that they were being recorded, and the end result was generally a very short exchange often of very unclear quality. Transactions where our aims had been discussed with the customer in advance were much more successful. In some cases friends agreed to allow us to record a transaction in which they were involved: e.g. planning a holiday, ordering photographs, buying dress material. Transactions in travel agents and at the hairdressers were particularly useful, since they tended to be naturally more extended. Longer transactions, such as those involving administrators advising students at enrolment, were also more worthwhile in terms of quality and return for effort. Contact with the ICE project personnel about these problems indicated they were having similar experiences, and they had decided to include formal meetings as examples of transactions. We therefore collected data from a range of different types of meetings, from school staff meetings through university committee meetings, to the meetings of recreational clubs. With this modification, the goal of 20,000 words for this category became feasible.

Thus, our final definition of a transaction identified two crucial criteria: 'a transaction consists of an interaction between two or more people (i) where the participants are acting predominantly in role (e.g. customer-shop-keeper, client-lawyer, student-adviser) or (ii) where the structure of the interaction is mainly determined by an agreed agenda'.

168

4.3. *Collecting Telephone Conversations*

Collecting sufficient telephone conversations also proved extremely difficult. First, it required special equipment and the first few 'telephone pick-up' microphones used were not satisfactory. The microphone finally used (an Olympus Pearlcorder TP3) required one speaker to place it in an ear, and this picked up both ends of the conversation well. Secondly, the requirement that people inform their addressees that they were being recorded severely inhibited the data collection. Some found this so difficult that (as mentioned above) they arranged to record 'in advance', so they did not need to inform addressees at the beginning of the call on the specific occasion when they actually recorded it.

We explored the possibility of using a variety of established HELP services (e.g. the student hotline at enrolment, police enquiries), but none were willing to assist because they feared that recording would discourage users. Another strategy which finally proved not worth the cost or effort involved was a free phone service (with a toll bar!) provided during the university enrolment period. This was set up in a room where students could phone their friends free of charge provided they were willing to record the conversation. Follow-up was then necessary to collect background information from the people phoned in order to eliminate any who were ineligible. This ultimately proved an expensive way of collecting telephone conversations when account was taken of the cost of a research assistant to monitor the equipment, the cost of the calls, and the cost of the follow-up in terms of time and stamped addressed envelopes.

4.4. *Collecting 'Natural' Conversations*

The most difficult data to collect was undoubtedly natural relaxed conversations between people who knew each other reasonably well. We were determined to ensure that this category was included, since we judged it the most important in representing current usage in New Zealand English. On the one hand, many linguistic changes, and especially sound changes, begin in people's vernacular style, and this style is therefore crucial in any attempt to identify current changes in progress in a particular speech variety. On the other hand, even changes with their origins in a prestige style or borrowings from an admired out-group, will not be considered established until they can be heard in the vernacular speech of a range of speakers. Strategies for collecting vernacular speech were therefore given some attention.

Previous experience had demonstrated that artificially constructed groups were a waste of time if one wanted relaxed colloquial speech. We decided to concentrate on naturally occurring talk situations and naturally occurring groupings of participants: e.g. people talking in their own homes or people in their work-places chatting at a coffee break. After a great deal of experimenting, it became clear that the most effective method of collecting conversational data involved the following steps.

First, it was very important that the person collecting the data thoroughly understood and sympathized with the project's aims; otherwise, the data collected was consistently too formal and self-conscious, and often of unsatisfactory quality. In order to avoid such problems, we used colleagues and friends, or friends of friends (the 'network' method described in Milroy, 1987), who agreed to record themselves or their families and friends talking to friends and family, with no outsiders present. This was the situation most conducive to people relaxing and forgetting the tape-recorder.

Secondly, the management of the equipment required some thought. Good quality recording involves paying attention to details such as the placement of the microphone, remembering to turn the microphone and recorder on, checking the sound quality before starting, making sure all relevant batteries are charged, and so on. A trained research assistant is the best person to check on such technicalities, but she will inevitably inhibit the relaxedness of the conversation being recorded. We adopted two alternative solutions to this problem. In some cases it was possible for a trained person to set up the equipment in someone's home or work-place and then to disappear, leaving them alone with instructions about how to turn over the tape if necessary. This was very effective in ensuring good quality recording. Alternatively, we provided the equipment to a sympathetic volunteer who was given both verbal and written instructions on how to use it (see Appendix 1 to this chapter). On the whole this worked well, though inevitably there were the usual raft of predictable disasters: e.g. a TV or stereo drowning out the speech, a small child occupying large proportions of the tape, the tape-recorder being switched off inadvertently during recording, the microphone getting dislocated, etc. One such story involved a friend who was recording a conversation with her father who had dropped in for a cup of tea. Both were sitting at the table when her oven timer buzzer went off. She jumped up to switch off the buzzer and in doing so disconnected the microphone. They then 'recorded' an hour of family gossip which we never got to hear!

Another aspect of recording which required some explanation was the criteria for inclusion in the Corpus. We told people we needed only New Zealanders, but the finer points of our criteria were not always absorbed. So some friends kindly collected data from people too young for the Corpus; others recorded people just back from an overseas trip; still others recorded people without realizing they had arrived in New Zealand after the age of 10. Our background information sheets were thus crucial in enabling us to sift out those who did not qualify as New Zealanders. These friends' efforts have not been wasted, however, since all good quality tapes are catalogued and stored in a separate archive where they may be used for linguistic projects where status as a New Zealander is not a relevant criterion.

As will be clear from this account, our targets were finally reached as the result of co-operation from many friends and colleagues, as well as from a large number of students who collected data voluntarily, or sometimes as part of an assignment for credit. We pushed all our networks to their limits in order to collect data from as wide a socio-economic spread of people as possible. And our Maori friends and colleagues were especially patient and responsive in assisting us reach targets for ethnic representation.

5. BACKGROUND INFORMATION SHEETS

It was essential to collect a certain amount of personal information from every contributor to the corpus for two reasons (*a*) to ensure that they were eligible for inclusion in the corpus: i.e. they qualified as New Zealanders (as discussed above); (*b*) to provide information for researchers regarding social characteristics of speakers.

The background information (BI) sheet is attached as Appendix 2 to this chapter. The first page refers to the contributor; the second page gathers information on the context of data collection. In the light of experience a number of weaknesses were identified which others may find it useful to take into account.[5]

1. The BI sheet asks people to state whether they have spent time out of New Zealand, and if so for how long. It does not ask them where they have spent that time. In retrospect, it would clearly be useful to know whether people had spent a little time in many countries, or a larger amount of time in one place. It would also be useful to know whether those places had been English-speaking or not.

2. Questions intended to elicit information on regional origins could usefully be more specific. The BI sheet asks only for place of birth. Questions asking where people had grown up or where they had lived for more than *x* years would have been more informative.

3. The questions on language background provided only minimal information. Information on any language regularly used, not just on first language, could usefully be elicited.

4. Any question on ethnicity should indicate that respondents may circle more than one ethnic group if appropriate.

5. The question asking for highest educational qualifications caused embarrassment to some contributors. Rewording could avoid this.

6. Questions on employment need to be worded to distinguish between students and non-students employed in similar part-time jobs: e.g. in pubs, restaurants, unskilled manual labour, etc.

The task of obtaining accurate background information from all of those whose speech was collected turned out to be one of the most problematic aspects of the whole project. One very obvious rule was to ensure participants completed BI sheets at the time of the recording, and that they filled them in with as much detail as possible. A check at the time by the data collector saved hours of inconvenience later, when attempting to collect information which had been inadvertantly omitted.

This worked well for most of the non-broadcast data, but obtaining background information from those who had been recorded from radio and TV was an on-going problem throughout the project.

In some cases interviewees on recorded radio programmes proved impossible to identify. Though their interviewers were often remarkably helpful, there were always some who proved untraceable. So, for instance, some wonderful examples of New Zealand speech were recorded at a motor-bike rally and a country fair, but it was simply not possible to locate the contributors. Moreover, in some cases the excerpts from different contributors included in the broadcast programme were too short to justify the huge amount of effort which would have been involved in identifying them and obtaining their consent to use their speech.

The best advice in the light of experience in this area is that BI sheets be sent out with stamped addressed envelopes as soon as possible after a programme has been recorded. Intensive follow-up by telephone and fax can be reasonably effect-ive, especially if sympathetic and helpful administrators within the broadcasting network can be located. Indeed, good relations with broadcasters proved essential for a number of reasons, since their assistance was so important in tracing contrib-utors and obtaining copyright permission (see below).

It is also obviously important to conserve resources by not transcribing any material until BI sheets establishing the eligibility of contributors for inclusion have been obtained for all contributors involved.

6. TRANSCRIPTION

The problems of transcription are well known and have been widely discussed (e.g. Ochs, 1979; Crystal and Davy, 1975; Stubbs, 1983; Coulthard, 1985; Poplack, 1989; Du Bois *et al.*, 1992, 1993). Even where orthographic rather than phono-logical transcription is the goal, the time and effort involved is formidable. Ochs (1979) points out the theoretical implications of decisions about how to write down speech, and Poplack (1989: 435) describes transcription as 'the most arduous and time-consuming aspect of the corpus construction'. Every transcription system is shaped by the goals of the particular project of which it is a part, or, to put it another way, it is necessary to develop transcription conventions which are appro-priate for the data being transcribed. While accuracy is paramount, there are many decisions to be made about the degree of detail to record. The conflicting demands of adequate detail and a readable relatively transparent system must be resolved to produce a transcript which is machine-readable and which can be analysed with appropriate concordance tools. In this section, I will draw attention to just a few points which emerged in developing adequate transcription conventions for the New Zealand spoken component of the ICE project.

We made a basic decision to use the minimum amount of punctuation because of the assumptions that punctuation conveys about grammar and phonology. It was agreed that it was best for analysts to consult the tape to resolve any ambiguities.[6] Pseudonyms were used to label speakers unless their names were a matter of public record. Pseudonyms were selected to reflect accurately the gender of the participant and to have the same phonological structure as the real name so far as possible (e.g. number of syllables, stress pattern).

Decisions were made about how to transcribe overlapping speech, laughter by one or more participants, co-ocurring conversations, non-standard usages, contractions, hesitations, and so on. So, for example, our general principle was to transcribe non-standard speech in the standard orthographic form closest to the full morpheme, in order to facilitate the accuracy of word frequency counts. So *he* rather than *'e* even though the speaker pronounced it without the initial /h/ (see Poplack, 1989: 431–2). The only exceptions were a small number of frequently occurring, commonly accepted variant forms which were specified in our transcription manual: e.g. *yeah* and *yep* as variants of *yes* where appropriate, *'cause* for *because*, *gonna* for *going to*. Mispronunciations were dealt with by inserting a comment in square brackets: e.g. 'trench warfare [pronounced as warfore]', 'brought [pronounced as bought]' etc.

Our stringent criteria for classification as a New Zealander made the data collection task considerably more difficult. In any discussion, for example, or tutorial, or court trial, there were inevitably some participants who did not qualify for inclusion in the Corpus. Indeed it was almost impossible to find television discussions involving four or more people where all participants qualified as New Zealanders. In such cases, the contributions of all speakers were generally transcribed in order to respect the integrity of the discussion, but contributions from non-New Zealanders were clearly identified in the transcript (as XX), and were not included in the total word count.

A third issue which is distinctive to the New Zealand component of ICE was that of how to deal with the occurrence of Maori words and phrases in our data. We made a decision to include without any special designation or typeface all Maori place-names and a few very commonly occurring words which are considered part of standard New Zealand English. These words are familiar to all New Zealanders and can be found in any dictionary of New Zealand English: e.g. Maori, Pakeha (a non-Maori New Zealander usually of European origin), marae (the traditional Maori meeting house and its surrounding area), Aotearoa (the Maori name for New Zealand). Less familar or less frequently occurring words were signalled in the text by a preceding phrase in square brackets: [in Maori], for example:

they want the [in Maori] wairua maaori.

In such phrases long vowels are marked when they occur by doubling the vowel. A gloss is provided for such words and phrases at the beginning of the transcription. Some of our older Maori informants tended to code-switch extensively when talking to another Maori person. In these cases we decided to transcribe switches involving isolated words or short phrases, but—since we were collecting a corpus of New Zealand *English*—we decided not to transcribe extensive sections of Maori talk. Where these occurred they were omitted and a brief English summary of the Maori content was provided in order to assist in following the discourse.

When words or phrases from other languages occurred in the data, they were marked only where it was judged that they were not part of standard New Zealand English: e.g. *au fait* was transcribed without comment, but *wunderbar* was transcribed as '[in German] wunderbar'.

Ideally, in undertaking to transcribe a corpus of the size of the New Zealand component of ICE, one would use a very few highly trained transcribers. Unfortunately, our resources were very limited and so transcription was spread over a considerable period, resulting in a much higher turn-over of transcribers than was desirable. In order to ensure standardization it was necessary to hold regular meetings of transcribers to discuss problems and agree on solutions which were recorded in a transcribers' training manual. On the other hand, our transcribers also served as data collectors, and this meant we had not only a renewable resource with a diverse range of contacts, but also that they were often able to transcribe tapes collected by their friends and family. This was a decided advantage. Since they knew the participants' voices, they could reliably assign speech to particular speakers and were often able to decode speech which might have been untranscribable by others.

7. CONFIDENTIALITY AND COPYRIGHT

7.1. *Guaranteeing Anonymity*

The BI sheets ask contributors to sign their name to a clause giving permission to use the recording for linguistic research. However, we promised people who contributed to the corpus that their identity would be protected. Consequently, when transcribing material, names were changed to names of equivalent length and phonological structure to protect the identity of people referred to. Moreover, the tapes will not be released to anyone other than bona fide researchers who need them for phonetic or phonological analysis. Speakers were given an ID number and after relevant social information was entered on the database, their BI sheet was filed with the individual's ID number on it. Thereafter, there is no direct connection between the BI sheet and the relevant tape. Information on tape sleeves and cover sheets of transcripts was checked to ensure that the identity of private contributors is protected.

7.2. *Copyright*

Discussion with Gerry Knowles and Geoffrey Leech, corpus researchers at Lancaster University, indicated that, in the light of their experience, great care should be taken to obtain copyright clearance for all recorded broadcast material. Though this did not appear likely to be a problem in New Zealand at the time recording began, it turned out in retrospect to be very valuable advice.

I wrote to and subsequently talked to appropriate representatives of the television and radio corporations from whom we wished to record material. They were extremely co-operative and all agreed that we could use any broadcast material, on condition that it was recorded primarily for bona fide research purposes, and would not be used for commercial gain. Following the Lancaster University researchers' advice, I obtained this agreement in writing.

A large expansion in the privatization of broadcasting took place during the period of data collection, and consequently the copyright situation changed dramatically in New Zealand. At a late stage in the project we were required to produce our copyright permission by the director of a private arm of the government broadcasting company—an arm which had been established in order to sell broadcast material. It seems likely that the cost of obtaining copyright permission at the later stage could have been prohibitive.

8. PROCEDURES FOR PROCESSING RECORDED MATERIAL

Finally it may be useful to provide a brief outline of the procedures put in place to ensure material was treated consistently from collection through to final editing.

Step 1: Checking Usability of Recorded Samples
When tapes arrived from collectors, they were checked for quality of recording: i.e. general audibility throughout the tape and whether it was usable for phonetic transcription. This information was noted on the cover of the tape box.

Step 2: Coding and Cataloguing
Every usable tape was given a code, reflecting its text category, and a number. Tapes provided by voluntary collectors often included a range of material which fitted different categories: e.g. news, weather, interviews. These were sorted out, and then classified and copied separately.

Tapes were then catalogued on two separate files: one relating to the tape (the extracts file), the other to the contributing speakers (the actor file).

1. The EXTRACTS file records information such as the following:

eligibility of speakers	speakers (type)	transcriber
duration of sample	speakers (number)	proofreader
quality check	data collector	
date recorded	location of tape	
source	topic	

2. The ACTOR file records information on participants taken from BI sheets.

Step 3: Copying

All tapes were copied and labelled ORIGINAL or COPY as appropriate. The copies were stored separately from the originals.

Step 4: Processing BI Sheets

1. BI sheets which came in with the tapes were processed as follows.

BIs were matched to the recorded sample and the tape code number was written on the BI sheet. Information from BI sheets was entered in summary in the EXTRACTS file and in detail in the ACTOR file.

2. For BIs which did not come in with the tapes, the BI follow-up procedure was adopted: (i) find names, telephone numbers, and addresses of contributors (ii) phone and explain need for BI (iii) post BI sheet and stamped addressed envelope (iv) phone/fax to remind if no BI sheet after one week (v) repeat (iv) as often as necessary.

Step 5: Transcribing

Because transcribing is so time-consuming, tapes were not transcribed until eligibility and quality had been checked and BI sheets obtained. A cover sheet was created for every transcription; it included the following information.

Tape catalogue number	Length transcribed: x words
Recording date	Time transcribed: y minutes
Place of recording	Total length of recording
Discourse type:	
e.g. family conversation	
Collector's name/source	
Brief information on participants	
Transcriber's name	Date transcribed
Transcriber's comments on tape:	

   e.g. RT is speaking loudly for benefit of deaf grandmother

Step 6: Proof-Reading

Proof-reading was undertaken by a different person from the transcriber.

Step 7: Editing

The original transcriber edited the tape on the basis of the proof-reader's amendments.

Step 8: Printing and Filing

A final copy of the transcript was printed and filed.

New problems and challenges emerge continuously throughout a project designed to collect a large sample of a language variety, and others will doubtless have encountered many of those outlined in this paper. I hope, however, that this account of the processes devised for collecting the New Zealand component of ICE, and the strategies adopted for solving some of the many problems that arose, may be useful to others involved in data collection for large corpora.

NOTES

1. This paper is a considerably expanded version of a report to the ICE Newsletter. The collection and transcription of New Zealand material for ICE has been supported by Victoria University's Internal Grants Committee and by the New Zealand Foundation for Research, Science and Technology.
2. Where spoken material satisfied the criteria for both the WCNZE and ICE it was included in both corpora. The methodological problems outlined in this paper will make it clear why this economy in data collection was considered desirable.
3. This group consisted of a range of different people over the period including Laurie Bauer, Allan Bell, David Britain, Chris Lane, Graeme Kennedy, Miriam Meyerhoff, and Maria Stubbe. The list of those who have worked for the Corpus in various capacities over the years is too long to include here but their contributions are gratefully acknowledged.
4. This issue is explored more fully in Bauer (1991).
5. The points made in this section owe a great deal to a valuable critique of the BI sheets written by Jenny O'Brien and Shelley Robertson, who worked on the Corpus project for a number of years.
6. Detailed information on the transcription conventions used can be obtained by contacting Janet Holmes.

REFERENCES

AIJMER, K. and ALTENBERG, B. (1991), *English Corpus Linguistics: Studies in Honour of Jan Svartvik* (London: Longman).
BAUER, L. (1991), 'Who Speaks New Zealand English?', *ICE Newsletter*, 11.
—— and NATION, P. (1993), 'Word Families', *International Journal of Lexicography*, 6: 253–79.
BAUGH, J. and SHERZER, J. (1984) (eds.), *Language in Use: Readings in Sociolinguistics* (Englewood Cliffs, NJ: Prentice-Hall).
BRUMFIT, C. (1993) (ed.), *Learning and Teaching Languages for Communication: Applied Linguistic Perspectives* (London: Centre for Information on Language Teaching and Research).
COULTHARD, M. (1985), *An Introduction to Discourse Analysis*, 2nd edn. (London: Longman).
CRYSTAL, D. and DAVY, D. (1975), *Advanced Conversational English* (London: Longman).
DU BOIS, J., CUMMING, S., SCHUETZE-COBURN, S., and PAOLINO, D. (1992) (eds.), *Santa Barbara Papers in Linguistics*, iv. *Discourse Transcription* (Santa Barbara, California: Dept. of Linguistics).

Du Bois, J., Schuetze-Coburn, S., Paolino, D., and Cumming, S. (1993), 'Outline of Discourse Transcription', in J. Edwards and M. Lampert (eds.) (1993).

Edwards, J. and Lampert, M. (1993) (eds.), *Transcription and Coding Methods for Language Research* (Hillsdale, NJ: Lawrence Erlbaum).

Fasold, R. W. and Schiffren, D. (1979) (eds.), *Language Change and Variation* (Amsterdam/Philadelphia: John Benjamins).

Greenbaum, S. (1988), 'A Proposal for an International Computerized Corpus of English', *World Englishes*, 7: 315.

—— (1990), 'Standard English and the International Corpus of English', *World Englishes*, 9: 79–83.

Holmes, J. (1982), 'Expressing Doubt and Certainty in English', *RELC Journal*, 13/2: 9–28.

—— (1983), 'Speaking English with the Appropriate Degree of Conviction', in C. Brumfit (ed.) (1993), 100–13.

Kennedy, G. D. (1987), 'Quantification and the Use of English: A Case Study of One Aspect of the Learner's Task', *Applied Linguistics*, 8: 264–86.

—— (1991), '*Between* and *Through*: The Company they Keep and the Functions they Serve', in K. Aijmer and B. Altenberg (eds.), 95–110.

—— and Fang, X. (1992), 'Expressing Causation in Written English', *RELC Journal*, 23/2: 62–80.

Labov, W. (1972), 'The Study of Language in its Social Context', in J. B. Pride and J. Holmes (eds.), 180–202.

—— (1984), 'Field Methods of the Project on Linguistic Change and Variation', in J. Baugh and J. Sherzer (eds.), 28–53.

Milroy, L. (1987), *Observing and Analysing Natural Language* (Oxford: Blackwell).

Ochs, E. (1979), 'Transcription as Theory', in E. Ochs and B. Schieffelin (eds.), 43–71.

—— and Schieffelin, B. (1979) (eds.), *Developmental Pragmatics* (London: Academic Press).

Poplack, S. (1989), 'The Care and Handling of a Mega-Corpus: The Ottawa-Hull French Project', in R. W. Fasold and D. Schiffren (eds.), 411–47.

Pride, J. B. and Holmes, J. (1972) (eds.), *Sociolinguistics* (Harmondsworth: Penguin).

Stubbs, M. (1983), *Discourse Analysis* (Oxford: Blackwell).

Appendix 1: Recording Data for the Corpus of New Zealand English

Tamati

Thank you for offering to make a tape for us for the Corpus of New Zealand English. There is no other way we can get good 'natural' data so we greatly appreciate the time and effort you are giving us.

We would be very grateful if you could record at least one side of the 60 minute tape provided. If you were able to record more that would be a bonus for us.

We would like you to record a relaxed conversation in English between you and one or more friends or members of your family. You can talk about any topic you wish and that you would normally talk about (e.g. friends, work, family, holidays, sport, school, etc.). Don't worry if you use the odd Maori word and don't be concerned about colloquialisms or swear words. We've heard them all before and, as far as we are concerned, the more natural and relaxed your conversation the better.

The identity of people who contribute to the Corpus is protected in that we change all names when transcribing the data.

We have provided some background information sheets for you and your friends/family to fill in for us. I hope this is not too much trouble and once again let me say how much I appreciate your help.

Additional notes to help you and us

1. Please use the tape-recorder and microphone we have provided. These are high quality machines because we need high quality sound.
2. Try to avoid background noise which will reduce the recording quality such as motor mowers, canaries, children, radios and television sets.
3. It is **essential** never to record people without them knowing that they are being recorded. Always tell people in advance.
4. We need background information sheets for each speaker and for the interaction as a whole. We would be very grateful for any useful additional background information you can provide: e.g. regional background, iwi (tribal) affiliation, information about the relationship between the speakers (e.g. brothers, friends), information on any other people present, etc.

Although you provide all this information, the anonymity of the contributors to the Corpus is protected. We need the information for classification purposes only.

BEFORE you start

* Check the tape-recorder and microphone are working and that both are switched on.

Appendix 2: Background information on Corpus Contributors

Circle answer where appropriate
1. *a.* Were you born in New Zealand?   Yes   No
   b. Please specify town or region   _____

2. *If no*   *a.* where were you born?   _____
             b. at what age did you come to NZ?   _____

3. *a.* Have you spent more than 6 months total overseas   Yes   No
   in the last 6 years?
3. *b.* If yes, please state year(s) and time spent overseas in that(those) year(s) _____
                                                                                     _____

4. How long in total have you spent out of NZ during your life? _____

5. *a.* Which language did you speak first in your home?   _____
   b. Which language did your mother speak first at home? _____
   c. Which language did your father speak first at home? _____

6. Please *circle appropriate answer*
   a. Gender: Female   Male
   b. Age group   16–19 20–24 25–29 30–34
                    35–39 40–44 45–49 50–54
                    55–59 60–64 65–69 70–74
                    75–79 80–84 85–89 90 years and over
   c. Which ethnic group do you identify with?
        Maori
        Other Polynesian (specify)
        Pakeha/European (British ancestry)
        Other (specify)   _____

7. How old were you when you left school?   _____

8. What is the highest educational qualification you have obtained? _____

9. Are you working/in paid employment at present?   Yes   No
   If yes what is your current job?   _____
   If no have you ever had a paid job?   Yes   No
   If yes what was it?   _____

I give permission for the recording of my voice to be included in a corpus of New Zealand English to be used for linguistic research purposes.

Signed _____

180

New Zealand Spoken Component of ICE

Please note the following information for every recording

Date recorded:

Place recorded:

Number of people present:

(Fill in additional sheets providing background information on all contributors)

Private or public:

Audience or not (if so state approximate size):

Domain (e.g. home, business, school, TV):

Topic:

Distance (i.e. telephone) or direct (i.e. face-to-face)

Spontaneous or prepared (scripted)

Formal/Neutral/Informal:

Dialogue or Monologue:

Any other relevant information:

13

Second-Language Corpora[1]

JOSEF SCHMIED

1. Introduction

Although the number of corpus-linguistic publications has increased dramatically in the last few years (e.g. Svartvik, 1992), the special problems and the potential of second-language corpora have not been given adequate systematic treatment. In sociolinguistic textbooks or in overviews of English as a world language the distinction between English as a Native Language (ENL), English as a Second Language (ESL), English as an International Language (EIL), and English as a Foreign Language (EFL) has been widely recognized as one of the special assets of English (cf. Asher, 1994 s.v.), but the implications of this have not penetrated to the heart of corpus linguistics.

Corpus linguistics began in the ENL context. The Survey of English Usage Corpus, the Lancaster–Oslo/Bergen (LOB) Corpus, and the Brown Corpus were the pioneering models of the first generation, combining a strong empirical data-based approach with a sensitivity for systematic (socio-)stylistic contextualism and variationism. In the EFL context (and its modern expansion the EIL context) the database approach has been used since the heyday of error and contrastive analyses in the 1960s. The International Corpus of Learner English (ICLE, cf. Ch. 2 this volume) is a logical continuation of these approaches, providing a more systematic account than individual collections by schoolteachers or publishers. ENL and EFL corpora are linked rather closely: in the development of ENL corpora the direct applications in target-language grammars (such as the *Oxford English Grammar*, 1996) and dictionaries (such as the COBUILD *Dictionary*, 1987) have played a driving role, as EFL texts are measured against these models.

The aim of this paper is to show that the expansion of corpus-linguistic work into ESL contexts can raise new challenges and provide new opportunities for corpus linguistics. Data collection on ESL varieties has previously been limited to salient features, 'deviations' from (near-)native-speaker intuition. But long lists of anecdotal evidence must remain unsatisfactory linguistically, as they leave open questions about the consistency, systematicity, and interrelatedness of linguistic features.

A major feature of the ICE philosophy is that it embraces ESL countries systematically in addition to ENL countries, to which many modern standard descriptions of English still restrict themselves because of the lack of empirical data (e.g. Burchfield, 1994*a*: 4). Even within the ESL nations there are differences: the ICE framework includes on the one hand prototypical ESL countries like India, Nigeria, and East Africa (Kenya, Tanzania, and Malawi), and on the other the city-states of Singapore and Hong Kong. The difference between these two types is not only in size but also in terms of their urban character and their integration into the world market. Linguistically, the prototypical ESL nations (cf. Schmied, 1991: sect. 2.3) are multilingual nations in the sense that several indigenous languages are used by different ethnic groups as first languages and English comes in as an additional language because it is ethnically neutral and internationally advantageous; Hong Kong is bilingual in that although it has Chinese (Cantonese) as a common first language it will find it convenient to maintain English even after the reintegration into China after 1997, because of its international values. Despite the economic parallels with Hong Kong, the linguistic complexity of Singapore is similar to that of larger ESL nations. This paper concentrates on characteristics of the multilingual nationwide type that can be found in the ICE countries in South Asia and Africa.

Even this ESL type is not homogeneous, however: whereas Tanzania as an ESL country leans towards EIL (Schmied, 1990), South Africa combines ENL and ESL characteristics (Schmied, forthcoming). On the one hand it has a sizeable number of inhabitants who use English as their first language, on the other it is mostly used as a second language. Interestingly, some of the special multilingual features of the ESL situations are shared by some ENL nations, e.g. in the Caribbean, where English is used in a bidialectal setting, Standard English as the official language and a related (pidgin or) creole form as a home language.

Even if not all prototypical features of second-language corpora occur in all countries, the common problems and challenges justify their description as a special corpus-linguistic type. In this description I will pay special attention to:

• the necessary variation of corpus-linguistic work in the ESL context and
• some specific challenges and concrete examples from recent work on ESL corpora.

2. THEORETICAL IMPLICATIONS AND BACKGROUND

Since it is impossible to record the totality of the language used in a community, samples have to be selected. If the aim of a corpus is to constitute 'a representative collection of texts', we have to ask ourselves: representative of what?[2]

Corpora usually contain samples from the production repertoire of a certain speech community. The reception is often markedly different (cf. Clear, 1992: 24 f.). In ESL countries, for instance, a large proportion of the language heard and read comes from ENL speakers. In many countries (e.g. in Swaziland) large portions of the TV broadcasting programmes are taken over from CNN directly, films from Hollywood (but also from India) dominate the market. This passive exposure to variation (in contrast to big EFL countries such as France or Germany, where English programmes are usually subtitled or even dubbed), influences the active usage in the community. But English in Nigeria, Zambia, Pakistan, Sri Lanka, etc., is not the same as English by Nigerians, Zambians, Pakistani, Lankans, etc.—and corpora usually record the latter only.

ESL varieties are used in a specific multilingual context and are influenced by the other language spoken by the polyglot speakers in the community. In these ESL countries English is the high (H) variety in a diglossic (or triglossic) framework, the low (L) variety being more local, indigenous languages and more regional lingua francas.[3] Thus in Northern Malawi, Tumbuka might be used as the home language, Chewa as the national language, and English as the educated and international language. In Madras most oral business would be conducted in Tamil, most written communication in English. The natural contexts in which English is used is therefore biased towards the written mode and restricted to certain domains and topics, such as education, trade, modernization, and development work. The educational importance of English can be seen in Asian and African newspapers, which compared to other countries serve educational purposes more than other media do.

ESL varieties derive from the superimposition of English on African or Asian languages during the colonial era. English was taught and learnt under the guidance and to the advantage of the colonial élite. This has had and still has important consequences for attitudes to English and to the indigenous languages as well as to specific forms of English.

The tendency to look towards the British model persists in all matters of 'standard', in language as in others (cf. Jeffery, 1993). Thus the English Academy of South Africa has recently proposed that British Standard English should be the official language for the New South Africa (cf. the submission to CODESA reprinted in Young, 1993: 186 f.). The balance between national or regional authenticity (African-ness or Indianness, for instance) and international conformity (Standard English) is often tipped surprisingly towards the latter. Although the fear of losing international intelligibility is real, subjective impressionistic views often seem oversensitive towards 'deviations', underestimating the common core of English. The impression of falling standards is usually not backed by evidence, because no really comparative language data have been available. Good English is still seen as equivalent to good education so that using English implies all positive educational, technological, and modernistic values.

Most colonized nations have become the developing countries of the Third World and this has technological and political consequences. The corpus boom is (partly) due to technical innovations of the First World (mainly computer storage and retrieval), which affect all stages of corpus-linguistic work, compilation, analysis, and interpretation and application. The compilation of newspaper texts, for instance, is easy in technologically advanced communities, where modern text-processing and desk-top publishing are used; in the Third World these technologies are just becoming available so the compiler tends to skew his sample towards the easily accessible or to postpone this category until the necessary software is more widespread. In Tanzania, for example, the old and influential *Daily News* may be neglected in favour of the more modern *Business Times*. For South Africa it is even possible to find samples from the *Weekly Mail and Guardian* on the internet or via gopher; this is not possible for the small new black papers, but too much from white establishment ENL language would skew the sample importantly.

Politically, the Westminster model of democracy was soon given up in many African and Asian countries and new forms of government developed. Although multi-party democracy is currently being introduced in many parts of the continent, old habits often prevail. The general political sensitivity in Africa and Asia is not favourable to empirical research in general and corpus compilation in particular. The 'harmless drudge' image (propagated by Dr Johnson's dictionary) may be associated with the 'fruitless exercise'—resulting in insufficient support from official quarters. Potentially more dangerous is the justifiable attempt by developing countries to channel research towards more urgent needs, which can lead to the restriction of research to politically opportune and/or economically advantageous areas, so that more basic and not directly profitable work is neglected.

3. COMPILATION

Despite intensive discussions (cf. Schmied, 1990 and Leitner, 1992) the ICE design is not geared towards ESL corpora primarily, but it can be used as a convenient framework—provided that some special, sociolinguistic issues in corpus compilation are taken into consideration.

3.1. *Natural English Language Situations in the Multilingual Context*

A corpus is a compilation of language produced by its natural speakers in natural language situations. However, locating naturally produced English is more difficult in ESL contexts. Whereas in an ENL context almost any utterance qualifies for entry into the corpus, in an ESL environment large portions are excluded, such as foreign TV and radio broadcasts. In many African or Asian ESL communities it is difficult to find a sufficient number of texts in certain categories.

In ESL communities English is normally used in domains related to the upper part of the formal spectrum. It may therefore be difficult to find texts for the spoken private categories, because other languages are preferred in conversations among family members and friends. In Tanzania, for instance, it would sound very strange if grandparents were addressed in English (even if they understood the language, which is unlikely). As the transmission of traditional cultural values, a major function of grandparent–grandchildren interaction, is firmly linked to first languages, English is highly inappropriate in such contexts. The vast majority of the direct conversations in ICE-GB would simply not be conducted in English: all the family conversations (e.g. S1A-007) and mealtime conversations (e.g. S1A-056) in the British corpus would be too exceptional to be included in an African or Asian corpus of English. In most ESL cultures the use of English would be considered rude in such contexts, as the older members of the family might be excluded because of their lack of language skills. A South African respondent emphasized that English is a language for the work environment, not for private matters. De Kadt (1993: 317) reports: 'It is bad to speak English at home—because there are people who are not educated. It is an embarrassment. It looks as if one is hiding something.' Even conversations between flatmates (e.g. S1A-030) and 'friends recorded in a pub' (S1A-015) could elicit hostile reactions, as Scotton (1978: 79) relates in an anecdote from Uganda:

At a beer party near my home two boys broke into talk in English. The reaction from the old men was bitter and they said, 'Who are those speaking in English? Are they backbiting us? They are proud. Push them out!' Although the boys had not been addressing the beer party as such but had been talking only to each other, this use of English was regarded as an insult.

Similarly, private letters are not written in English very often and certainly not as much as in Europe. Although English in Africa and Asia tends to be a public and written language, even texts with these features may be difficult to find. English may be used together with other languages in the same utterance. Much faithfully recorded language data in ESL nations includes instances of code-mixing and code-switching, because they stem from a multilingual repertoire and context. As ICE only records English we cannot include utterances that have more than a few expressions and phrases, which can be interpreted as loans. Where there are English-related pidgins and creoles, as in West Africa and the Caribbean, the task of distinguishing English from creole words can be much harder (cf. Mair, 1992).

3.2. *Natural Educated Second-Language English in Context*

Even in the limited spectrum where English is habitually used, recording natural speech is not easy. The positive attitudes associated with English cause the famous sociolinguistic paradox: corpus linguists need to record natural speech in context, but as soon as they come as outsiders to compile data within a speech community, the conversation tends to become less natural and 'distorted' towards more formal and prestigious forms. Thus all recordings of natural speech have to be made by in-group members. Although this problem occurs equally in ENL varieties in a bidialectal setting or with strong style variation, it is aggravated in ESL environments. Language is a much more important group marker in many ESL countries, because not only the use of a language as such but also the quality of the language can be interpreted as a socioeducational quality label much more clearly, as a second language is transmitted mainly through the formal education sector.

What is unique to EFL and ESL communities is the problem of learner languages, which affects the basic parameters age and education, because in a sociolinguistic context where English is learnt only as a second (or third, etc.) language it is difficult to determine where an interlanguage ends and educated English starts. ICE only collects texts from adults over 18 years of age, but the ESL corpora must be sure to include (if at all possible) only speakers who have received their formal education through the medium of English. In Asia secondary education is usually available in Asian languages as well as in English, in 'anglophone' Africa it is available in English only. The minimum length of English-medium education depends on the educational system in the respective country. In Africa, Tanzania has the shortest length, as it uses Swahili as a medium throughout primary education. That is why at least six years of English-medium secondary school count as the minimum requirement for 'educated English' in the ICE framework. Since the official medium of instruction cannot always be used in the first years of secondary (sometimes even of tertiary) education, learner language can even be recorded from university students. In India even universities teach in the national languages such as Tamil, Telugu, or Hindi.

Apart from interference from other languages there is also interference from native-speaker English. Since as yet there is no ESL norm, ENL norms are adhered to and this seems best ensured by filtering natural second-language English through an ENL intuition. The borderline between intravariety and intervariety stylistic improvement is very difficult to assess, particularly when ENL influence is constant and pervasive in certain contexts.

I had a striking experience during a visit to a leading Kenyan newspaper in Nairobi, where the chief editor turned out to be an Irishman, who was very interested in our corpus project—but also surprised us by introducing the newspaper's training editor, another Irishman, who not only undertook individual 'supervision' but issued a circular 'Let's Get it Right' with examples of 'what I got and what it should be like'. These issues were not only concerned with 'grammar problems' but also with reader-friendly style. The fact however that he was an Irishman raises of course questions about African English in newspapers, where the reporters give their names to their articles but the form is greatly influenced by English native speakers. The financial constraints and availability of qualified experts nowadays make such cases extremely rare in Africa and India (except in South Africa). The reaction of African colleagues is revealing, since they were always most grateful for the improvements added to their work (though this may also be culture-specific politeness to foreigners). As it is impossible to look behind every text's production history, one has to accept texts as African or Asian if they are associated with African or Asian names.

3.3. *Variation of Discourse in Language Situations: Culture-Specific Text Types*

Text categories may be quite different in different cultural contexts. What goes under the same name may not have the same weight or may have completely different content in non-native environments, as was pointed out by Shastri (1986: xiii) for the Kolhapur corpus:

The fact remains that the number of texts are matched only in the categories L [Mystery] and R [Humour]. In the case of K [General Fiction], we have double the number i.e. 58 in place of 29; science fiction only 2 as against 6; adventure only 15 in place of 29; and romance and love story only 18 in place of 29. Again, mystery and detective is for the West largely detective and mystery surrounding death, murder, etc. but for the Indian it includes other kinds of mystery in the sense of 'mysterious' or miraculous. Similarly in the case of adventure and Western fiction, there is simply nothing at all corresponding to 'western fiction' in India. So the subcategory is wholly composed of 'adventure'.

Since ICE text-types can usually be defined as a culture-specific combination of form and function, we have to ask whether the same functions are fulfilled by different text forms or whether the same forms have different functions. For instance, some of the entertainment functions as well as some of the educational functions of books have to be performed by newspapers and periodicals in ESL countries. The entire ICE category 'Printed: skills/hobbies' is problematic. This category (E 'skills, trades and hobbies' in the Brown/LOB/Kolhapur corpora) has been singled out before as containing very different types of discourse (Wikberg, 1992: 259 f.):

in the future we need to pay more attention to text theory when compiling corpora. For users of the Brown and LOB corpora, and possibly other machine-readable texts as well, it is also worth noting the multitype character of certain text categories. If you simply search the texts using various computer programs for retrieval of lexical and grammatical information, you may fail to see that there are important textual and organizational properties concealed in them.

This warning does not refer to culture-specific aspects, although it is obvious to the culture-sensitive reader that many of the concepts in this category are alien to many Third World cultures and the corresponding texts are imported from the First World. Africans seldom need to *Know about Tennis* (ICE-GB W2D-013) and when they do they import the book together with the other equipment needed for the game. Similarly, *The Complete Book of Video* would be taken over together with the video set from America or East Asia. What is Africa-specific in this context is that whereas watching videos is much more important in Africa, recording is much less frequent than in ENL countries—due to the poor production and broadcasting facilities in many African countries. Other skills such as most activities in the DIY area (e.g. the manual in ICE-GB W2D-012), a very culture-specific concept anyway, are not passed on in written form in Third World cultures. As 'reading', i.e. enjoying creative, imaginative writing, is also a hobby rooted in the Western leisure-oriented culture, the text category novel/short stories is also affected. English novels (and partly short stories) are related to education, so their popularity depends on whether or not they are set texts in the syllabus. Texts from related categories (e.g. school books) are more important than in ENL corpora.

The scarcity of books increases the multifunctionality and heterogeneity of newspapers. Thus the form category newspaper in Africa covers much more than news reports and editorials, it also serves for the distribution of 'Printed: informational: popular' as well as 'Printed: creative'. The borderline between newspapers and books is not the same in Africa as in Europe, due to economic constraints. Other discrepancies between ENL and ESL forms are related to cultural traditions. One example is the distinction between interviews and discussions in 'public dialogue'. In Radio Tanzania there is a broadcast 'discussion' (ICE-T: S1B-023) between academic staff and the visiting Minister of Education. Despite the intended discussion most of the time only the minister was talking, leaving pauses for questions, inviting his audience to express their discontent, as they had sent a complaint to the President, who in turn had sent the Minister because they might find it easier to talk to him. Unfortunately, nobody dared to say anything, except 'an anonymous personality' who did not want to give his name. Similarly, in 'Food for the future' (ICE-T: S1B-022) all 'discussants' have individual separate monologues, giving different perspectives of the same topic but not speaking interactively. On this formal level many ESL societies reveal more authoritative dialogue styles compared to the more interactive styles in ENL countries. The borderline between broadcast discussions and interviews may be blurred generally, but in ESL countries many programmes that are announced as discussions turn out to be interviews —at least when regarded through ENL eyes. It is felt that younger speakers should not argue with older ones nor socially lower with socially higher. Similarly in classroom lessons, forms of dialogue are less common between teachers and students than teacher monologues and instructions more than questions, etc. Since ICE guidelines suggest twenty discussions and ten interviews, if we aim at including the same content under a certain heading we have to regroup many dialogue texts as interview texts, and if we want to maintain a culture-specific proportion of text-types the two-to-one relationship between the two certainly has to be reversed.

Text-types are just one issue in the constant tension between global and local requirements. If global text types are maintained, their function in a certain society may be different or limited; if local text-types are chosen, the exotic nature of ESL varieties may be exaggerated. In either case the corpus runs the risk of becoming a reflection of prior assumptions about language usage rather than actual language usage itself.

3.4. *Compiling Texts in the Third World Context*

Economic and political factors may affect the practical availability of certain text types in the Third World. Thus it is not easy to compile sufficient samples for the published book categories. Even in a huge country like India there is only a 'limited number of publications in the second language situation as compared to that in a native language situation such as the American and British' (Shastri, 1986: v). In a small country like Malawi book production is so limited that it is difficult to collect enough samples when strict criteria are applied and all international editions or reprints are excluded. Under these circumstances excerpts from M.A. theses have to be included in the 'Printed: informational: learned' category. The discrepancy between the writing and the publishing dates is often great, affecting the corpus-linguistic ideal of collecting spoken and written data from the same time-period. 'Opposition books' that were published outside of the ESL, usually in ENL, countries were not included because of ENL editing. Political considerations in a very sensitive climate not only made publications difficult until very recently, but may still affect the willingness to provide texts. Even if they wanted to, parliaments might (think that they) have to wait for official approval or legislation before making tape recordings of parliamentary sessions available or possible (even though official versions are published in Hansard later).

Economic constraints may cause culture-specific traditions. Thus printed learned texts do not see the light of day, since academic traditions in Africa and Asia do not demand that research is printed, as access to international journals is limited and national journals are often only reproduced in mimeographed form. These publications do not have the same form as in Britain, but they fulfil basically the same functions and are thus suitable equivalents. Such issues also affect the systematicity of data collection that can be achieved.

Some distinctions of subcategories suggested, such as the one between distanced private dialogues over the telephone (ICE-GB: S1A-091 to 100) and face-to-face, are difficult from a theoretical as well as a practical point of view: they may be extremely difficult to record and they do not have the same importance in Third World societies (and thus do not have the same characteristic stylistic features).

Often practical and fundamental theoretical questions of corpus composition go hand in hand. The lower frequency of usage corresponds with the lower communicative and intracultural value of such text types including modern technologies. Does that mean that we should recompose the ESL corpora on the basis of the assessed relative importance of the genre or text-type? As this approach appears too radical and puts at risk the central goal of keeping all the ICE components compatible, the ICE-EA compilers decided to accept modifications wherever practical necessities suggested it and refrained from theoretically based changes. Whereas most other changes in ESL corpora compared to ENL corpora resulted in an underdifferentiation of categories (e.g. in many countries regional newspapers are much less important than in the USA), in some cases a closer look at the material seems to justify a finer subdivision. Whereas the persuasive newspaper category in ICE only collects editorials, the tradition of personal columns in many Third World countries makes a distinction between personal and institutional editorials appear useful. The former are usually more humorous and more localized in content and style and mixing the two would wipe out one of the most important features of newspapers in an ESL society (cf. Schmied and Hudson-Ettle, 1996). In any case, overdifferentiation does not restrict future analysis but rather provides material for additional studies.

The real issue is underdifferentiation. Many differentiations should be left open, so that ICE subcategories can be adapted to more community-specific texts, thus gaining, not losing in text information value.

4. ANALYSIS AND INTERPRETATION

4.1. *Tools for Analysis and Developmental Co-operation*

Scepticism towards corpus compilation in Third World countries is based on the fear that their understaffed and impoverished university departments may not be able to use the corpora adequately, even where national institutions have already provided a home for the data during the first stages of corpus work. The experience of previous research co-operation may contribute to this scepticism; sometimes data on certain local problems can only be found in international research centres and the local impact is almost non-existent. In addition, modern research methodologies, especially those tied to expensive equipment, may only become available at a later stage to developing departments in Africa (and sometimes in Asia). As long as potential researchers are not convinced that the necessary tools will be easily available to them and inexpensive, they rightly do not feel drawn towards new possibilities, however useful they may appear theoretically. In addition to all the general problems associated with sociolinguistic research collaboration in the Third World (Schmied, 1991: 208–10), the technological lag plays a decisive role.

The ICE framework, however, provides a unique chance to avoid many such problems, because the tools for corpus annotation and analysis (cf. Chapter 6 to 10 in this volume) will be developed within the framework of the lowest possible technological level (DOS-based, not UNIX-based, for instance) and made available to members in tailor-made form. This is a unique opportunity for methodological modernization and technology transfer, because global compatibility is the cornerstone of the ICE philosophy.

4.2. *Variables for Analysis and Standards*

All corpus-linguistic compilations serve a purpose and the main purpose of a corpus[4] is to assemble a database for variationist linguistic analysis. However, the parameters and variables of linguistic analysis are usually well-known for ENL communities but quite unknown for ESL communities. Of course, linguistic variables can be tried out, taking present-day changes in ENL varieties or developmental breaking points of native-speaker English as a starting-point. Thus the particularly unstable English vowel system, the fuzzy border between count and non-count nouns, or the expanding progressive form can be analysed in ESL varieties, hypothesizing either that the lack of feeling for clear boundaries might lead to progressive expansion further than in ENL varieties or that the lack of native-speaker confidence might not allow any experiments and might rather support conservative usage. Similarly, sociolinguistic parameters responsible for style variation have been investigated in ENL corpora in great detail, but for ESL corpora the relative importance of speaker relationship versus topic and of ethnic versus socioeconomic or socioeducational group is not yet fully established.

Unfortunately, there is at present no solution to all these problems, except that solutions should not be barred because possibly influential variables are left unspecified. Thus compilers have to be particularly careful with the definition of socioeducational and situational parameters, as it is impossible to say how important certain variables will turn out to be, and they must pay special attention to the central corpus-linguistic notions of consistency and context.

One solution to the issue of text categorization is to accept intuitively felt text types initially, as most text types are agglomerates anyway, and simply assume that it might be possible to isolate the parameters later by inductive comparisons. This illustrates a basic corpus-theoretical paradox (cf. Bungarten, 1979: 44): on the one hand, a corpus is more representative of language use in a community if its subdivisions reflect all the variables that determine language variation in that community; on the other, we need results from a representative corpus in order to determine these variables empirically. Thus whatever the compromise between local and global criteria, a first corpus must fall short of the ideal—but it is a starting-point. All the other doubtful, i.e. more or less culture-specific, texts can be included in a larger monitor corpus (cf. Leitner, 1992) and at a later stage different compositions of a corpus for different purposes can be devised. Culture-specific adaptations in multilingual situations are possible when all parameters are recorded faithfully and any interpretation is left for later.

Another way out of this dilemma is to rely on the intuitive knowledge of members of the speech community. Only they can assess internal variation and its sociosituational values. As far as external variation in the sense of deviation from Standard English is concerned, however, native-speaker intuition is also required, in particular when it comes to distinguishing the nice qualitative differences in idiomaticity and grammaticality and the consequent interpretation of qualitative and quantitative results. Thus both ENL and ESL characteristics are needed although they may be partly contradictory.

The main problem for corpus analysis in ESL communities is that the standard as a reference variety is not clear, because as *de facto* local norms of educated English are not codified and explicitly accepted by language institutions from examination boards to radio stations, language users are forced to have recourse to international standards (at least in prestige-related domains such as business and education) irrespective of their attitudes (cf. Shields, 1989).

As with the corpus-theoretical paradox above, the problem of analysis is that we need a corpus for the determination of variables on a purely descriptive level at the same time as we need a corpus as a reference variety. In very practical terms this means that if we include African academic writing even by third-year students in our corpus we include language structures that are not accepted by most English users. But students use this type of English at university and it is thus part of academic discourse, although it cannot serve as a model. Theoretically, we need a corpus application before a corpus analysis, and that is, of course, impossible.

4.3. *Assessing Grammaticality and Idiomaticity*

With all ESL data the problem of assessing the grammaticality of what are often called 'deviant' structures from a native-speaker point of view becomes pertinent. It is striking that although such deviations often cover some fairly central aspects of English grammar, where the flexibility of what is accepted as 'educated' is usually assumed to be fairly limited, logical, rational and in-system explanations seem to be possible (in contrast to the much quoted interference hypothesis). Inflectional endings of nouns and verbs and prepositions are such central structures besides patterns of complementation and idiomaticity (cf. Schmied, 1996). In many cases acceptability judgements vary even among native speakers and depend on the interpretation of stylistic values in context. As long as there is no codified standard within the ESL community such problems are difficult to solve.

In any comparison of closely related linguistic systems a distinction has to be attempted between the changing of English grammar rules, which is indicative of a different language system, and the neglect of (sub-)rules, which are often possible in the system but simply avoided in customary usage (because of prescriptive grammar?). In good descriptive corpus-linguistic tradition, the data from ESL corpora should speak for themselves.

5. Application

The limited attraction of corpus linguistics for ESL nations is also caused by a lack of understanding of its uses in an ESL community. Even linguists who know that practically all modern dictionaries and grammars are corpus-based tend to think that corpus application is something for big transnational publishers or theoreticians only. But ESL corpora can also be applied in areas that are central for many ESL specialists, such as English language teaching and literary analysis. For it is precisely in these fields that contextualized real-language texts can prove most useful. The possibilities of discussing realistic localized language usage with the help of newspapers has been demonstrated numerous times (e.g. Baumgardner, 1987). Because corpus texts cover a much wider spectrum of text types and communicative situations they are even more useful for teaching language variation. Even if real texts have to be adapted to various learner levels, a realistic starting-point for simplification and a final target level should help to make ELT more context-based, more situationally relevant, and thus more efficient. Even passive exercises of genre analysis may help to increase language awareness and finally active variation skills.

Furthermore, in ELT a good corpus can serve as a realistic basis for developing adapted syllabi and teaching materials. When a database with the specific needs of the learner in a specific ESL community is set up, community-specific attempts at assessing mistakes in national exams may be possible. The decisions of national examination boards (and even more so, those of international examination boards, such as Cambridge) are often based on reference books and impressionistic evidence from experience, and are often out of context and thus far from actual community-specific language practice and language needs. In other contexts the skill of assessing the realistic nature of language variation is a necessary prerequisite for assessing speaker or writer intentions. Thus the qualitative and quantitative analysis of style, especially literary style, is almost impossible for community outsiders. Only corpus analyses can provide the lexicographic basis for reference works that the general English reader from outside the community can use to find out the difference between the normal level of language variation in the speech community described (assuming the author has a good command of the English language and intends to reflect language reality in his writings) and the creative bending of language for literary effect (Hudson-Ettle and Schmied, 1992).

6. Conclusion

The problems of second-language corpora exemplified in this paper constitute a challenge for corpus-linguistic practice and theory, but they should also be considered as opportunities. In contrast to other 'hyphenated' branches of modern linguistics, corpus linguistics does not focus on a special section of language (like text linguistics) nor see it from a certain perspective (like sociolinguistics). Rather, it is a methodological basis for pursuing empirical linguistic research; it thus combines easily with other branches of linguistics—and second-language corpus research combines nicely with sociolinguistics and language change through language contact. Thus the expansion of the corpus-linguistic frame into second-language corpora is only the logical development of applying this new (but cf. Leech, 1992: 105) methodology that combined first with grammar and lexicography (Sinclair, 1987) and is slowly expanding into other areas of linguistics, such as error analysis (cf. Ch. 2 this volume) and translation studies (Schmied, 1994).

Notes

1. I wish to thank my colleagues in Africa and Germany, especially Kembo Sure and Eunice Nyamasyo (Kenya), Casmir Rubagumya (Tanzania), Teresa Chisanga (Zambia, now Swaziland), Moira Chimombo (Malawi), Alison Love (Zimbabwe), Chris Jeffery (South Africa), and Diana Hudson-Ettle (Bayreuth) for their co-operation in the project 'English in Africa', which has enabled me to do the data collection and analysis within the

framework of the Special Research Programme on Africa at the University of Bayreuth (Germany). I am grateful to the British ICE team (led by Sidney Greenbaum) for many years of fruitful co-operation and their willingness to share materials and data from the British ICE component.

2. The notion of representativeness has been challenged by Rieger (1979) and Mair (1990: 12–17), for instance, its application to the study of language is by no means clear (cf. Romaine, 1982).

3. The only area in the world where an English variety is not the H variety, but the L variety is in Caribbean Central America, where, for instance, around Bluefields (Nicaragua) a creolized variety is spoken with Spanish as the H variety. The consequences of such a situation are partly similar (colonial lag) and partly different (code-switching); in the world-wide context, however, they are clearly the exception. Unfortunately a Caribbean component could not be included in the ICE framework.

4. Additionally, corpus material can be used to provide illustrative examples, which can, however, also be achieved through any item-based sample collection (on the different approaches cf. Schmied, 1991: 202).

REFERENCES

ASHER, R. E. (1994) (ed.), *The Encyclopedia of Language and Linguistics* (Oxford: Pergamon).

BAUMGARDNER, R. (1987), 'Utilizing Pakistani Newspaper English to Teach Grammar', *World Englishes*, 6: 241–52.

BUNGARTEN, T. (1979), 'Das Korpus als empirische Grundlage in der Linguistik und Literaturwissenschaft', in H. BERGENHOLTZ and B. SCHAEDER (eds.), *Empirische Textwissenschaft: Aufbau und Auswertung von Textcorpora*, 28–51 (Königstein/T.: Sciptor).

BURCHFIELD, R. (1994a), 'Introduction', in Burchfield, 1–19.

—— (1994b) (ed.), *The Cambridge History of the English Language*, v. *English in Britain and Overseas: Origins and Development* (Cambridge: Cambridge University Press).

CLEAR, J. (1992), 'Corpus Sampling', in Leitner, 21–31.

HUDSON-ETTLE, D. and SCHMIED, J. (1992), 'Deviation and Language Awareness in Kenyan Popular Literature', in J. SCHMIED (ed.), *English in East and Central Africa 2*, Bayreuth African Studies Series, no. 24: 1–20 (Bayreuth University).

JEFFERY, C. (1993), 'Standards in South African English', *English Academy Review*, 10: 14–25.

DE KADT, E. (1993), 'Attitudes towards English in South Africa', *World Englishes*, 12: 311–24.

LEECH, G. (1992), 'Corpora and Theories of Linguistic Performance', in Svartvik, 105–22.

LEITNER, G. (1992a), 'The International Corpus of English: Corpus design—Problems and Suggested Solutions', in Leitner, 33–64.

—— (1992b) (ed.), *New Directions in English Language Corpora: Methodology, Results, Software Developments* (Berlin: Mouton de Gruyter).

MAIR, C. (1992), 'Problems in the Compilation of a Corpus of Standard Caribbean English: A Pilot Study', in Leitner, 75–96.

SCHMIED, J. (1990), 'Language Use. Attitudes. Performance and Sociolinguistic Background: A Study of English in Kenya, Tanzania and Zambia', *English World Wide*, 11: 217–38.

—— (1991), *English in Africa: An Introduction* (London and New York: Longman).

—— (1994), 'Translation and Cognitive Structures', *Hermes (Journal of Linguistics)*, 13: 169–81.

—— (1996), 'English in Zambia, Zimbabwe, and Malawi', in V. DE KLERK (ed.), *English in South Africa: Varieties of English around the World* (Amsterdam: Benjamins).

—— and HUDSON-ETTLE, D. (1996), 'Syntactic Complexity in Second-Language English: A Comparison of British, Kenyan and Tanzanian text types', *World Englishes*, 15.

SCOTTON, C. M. (1978), 'Language in East Africa: Linguistic Pattern and Political Ideologics', in J. FISHMAN (ed.), *Advances in the Study of Societal Multilingualism*, 719–59 (The Hague: Mouton).

SHASTRI, S. V. (1986), 'Manual of Information to Accompany the Kolhapur Corpus of Indian English, for Use with Digital Computers' (Kolhapur: Dept of English, Shivaji University).

—— (1988), 'The Kolhapur Corpus and Work Done on its Basis so Far', *ICAME Journal*, 12: 15–17.

SHIELDS, K. (1989), 'Standard English in Jamaica: A Case of Competing Models', *English World-Wide*, 10: 41–53.

SINCLAIR, J. M. (1987) (ed.), *Looking Up: An Account of the COBUILD Project in Lexical Computing* (London: Collins ELT).

SVARTVIK, J. (1992) (ed.), *Directions in Corpus Linguistics: Proceedings of the Nobel Symposium 82*, Stockholm, 4–8 August, 1991 (Berlin: Mouton de Gruyter).

WIKBERG, K. (1992), 'Discourse Category and Text Type Classification: Procedural Discourse in the Brown and the LOB Corpora', in Leitner, 247–61.

YOUNG, D. (1993) (ed.), *How Do We Ensure Access to English in a Post-Apartheid South Africa* (Cape Town: English Academy of Southern Africa and Language Education Centre, University of Cape Town).

14

The International Corpus of English in Hong Kong

PHILIP BOLT and KINGSLEY BOLTON

1. INTRODUCTION

The sociolinguistic realities of English in Hong Kong are unlike those of any other society in Asia, not least of all because Hong Kong is Britain's only surviving territorial colony of any economic or strategic significance. Although an estimated 97 per cent of the population is Chinese, and Cantonese is the principal local language, English has been an official language of government and law since 1841, and throughout the present century it has been accorded semi-official status as the major language in many secondary schools, colleges, and universities. In addition, English is also considered the dominant language of business in the larger companies.

Hong Kong is currently experiencing a period of transition in which the decolonialization of institutions from Britain is being given increasing priority. Partly as a result of this and of other economic and social forces, English and Chinese now have an increasingly complex coexistence in government, public administration, law, education, the business sector and the mass media. On 1 July 1997 Hong Kong will become a Special Administrative Region of the People's Republic of China. It is likely that after this date the *de facto* and *de jure* status of English will be changed, and that either Cantonese or Putonghua (Mandarin) will assume a greater proportion of some of the roles previously held by English.[1]

Considering the historical presence of English (of a quasi 'ESL' variety) and its public and official status, our motivations for undertaking the ICE work in Hong Kong were twofold. First, we were motivated by the opportunity to identify and analyse characteristics in the English used in the local setting across a broad range of contexts and text types. As such, it was anticipated that the ICE project would provide an excellent opportunity to carry out comparisons between the local data and data both from native-language countries on the one hand and from other ESL countries on the other. Secondly, our involvement in the ICE project was also motivated by the intention to consider the sociolinguistic background and context of English in use in Hong Kong, particularly as the local language situation has characteristics that distinguish it from other ESL settings, even in the Asian context; see, for example, Bacon-Shone and Bolton, 1995; Bolton and Kwok, 1990; Fu, 1987; Lord and Cheung, 1987; Luke and Richards, 1982; Richards and Luke, 1982; and So, 1987, 1992. In fact, over the four-year research period our focus on these two concerns has tended to be reversed, in that we have been obliged, from the outset, to consider the sociolinguistic context of the data collection, the functions of English and the participant roles of English language users as much as the nature of the language used.

In Bolt (1994: 23) it was noted that 'Having now collected a substantial amount of data we will soon be embarking on its analysis with a fairly confident target of 75% to 80% completion of the ICE total of 1,000,000 words.' This prognosis was set against a brief description of the principal issues that we had confronted, although not necessarily resolved: who could be counted as a Hong Kong person, the uses of English and Chinese in Hong Kong, their relative distribution and quantity, the linguistic background to the education system, and the features of the range of English encountered. At the 1993 ICAME conference we were happy to endorse the decision to extend the data-collection period until the end of 1994. Indeed, we have had to use 1995 as well and will only finish collecting the last few collectable texts in early 1996. A positive result, however, of this lengthened collection period is that we will probably achieve almost 90 per cent of the ICE total: some 445 texts (although a small proportion will not have complete biographical data). Below we present and discuss the issues noted above in the context of our experience of identifying and collecting texts within the ICE categories. Section 2 considers the sociolinguistic context, language proficiency, and language use. Section 3 considers the experience of applying the ICE categories, essentially issues of sourcing and text inclusion. Section 4 offers a brief prognosis for the next stages of the project—tagging and parsing written text.

2. The Sociolinguistic Context and the Quantification of Language Use

When we considered the ICE objective of collecting English language data and comparing the use of English in Hong Kong with its use in other societies, one basic assumption was that the particular range and quality of the Hong Kong data would be affected by a matrix of sociolinguistic relationships. These relationships include those between the ethnic and linguistic background; between the local educational system and the linguistic profile of the community; and between the linguistic backgrounds of local English speakers and salient features of the type of English found in Hong Kong. These relationships are by no means totally deterministic. Coming from a particular ethnic and linguistic background and attending a certain type of school do not, for example, necessarily define the nature of the language used by a particular individual. However, it is felt that the parameters outlined above should serve to distinguish our data from that collected in, for example, India, Singapore, and the Philippines.

Members of the population that we are interested in have three characteristics. First, they have a Hong Kong Chinese background (possibly from the People's Republic of China but increasingly they have been born in Hong Kong). Secondly, their first language is Cantonese, or they would normally use Cantonese outside their home environment. Thirdly they have had the majority of their primary and secondary education in Hong Kong. These characteristics reflect the pattern of immigration into Hong Kong since 1945, the continued existence and use of minority Chinese dialects other than Cantonese (Bacon-Shone and Bolton, 1995), and the fact that, until relatively recently, the provision of tertiary education locally was very limited (a proportion of local people still go overseas for their education at all levels). The criteria for inclusion in the ICE-HK corpus exclude the local Hong Kong Indian community, the temporary Vietnamese community, the Philippine community, and expatriates from Europe, the United States, and other countries. We have endeavoured to keep to a minimum the number of those who have had secondary education in an English-speaking country, because such an experience is likely to affect the nature of the language they use. The impact of the educational system must be emphasized, as English is almost entirely a 'learnt' language in Hong Kong and the main context of such language learning is the public school system. The proportion of people who have contributed to the ICE collection and who fit centrally into this framework is over 95 per cent (a few biodata forms have yet to be returned and some will not be provided).

In Bolt (1994: 16) it was noted that two assumptions were made when work was begun. The first of these was 'given the use of English in Government, public administration, large business corporations, the judicial system, the media and communications industries and education, we assumed that there must exist a genuinely widespread use and comprehension of English.' Naturally, it was felt that the status, quantity, and quality of the English used within a population would help or hinder data collection and the resulting collection would reflect these factors.

In an ESL/EFL society such as Hong Kong, there is a range of complex and vexed issues relating to who 'knows' English, and knows to what degree of proficiency, and who uses English, for what purpose(s) and under what circumstances. Estimates based on various surveys conducted during the ICE period vary from 56.7 per cent (Bacon-Shone and Bolton, 1995), to 29.4 per cent (*Hong Kong Population Census*, 1991) to 20–30 per cent (Language Proficiency Perception Survey, 1994), to 12 per cent (Surry, 1994). Such a wide variation almost certainly reflects in part the attitude and methodology of the surveyors, and the authors of the most recent survey on perceptions of language proficiency are almost certainly correct when they conclude in a somewhat frustrated tone that perception 'is a two-way phenomenon: it depends on the perceived as much as on the perceiver' (Language Proficiency Perception Survey, 1994: 3). Surveys of language use should distinguish between the spoken and written language, resulting in a four-part matrix.

Philip Bolt and Kingsley Bolton

TABLE 14.1. *Knowledge of English*
in Hong Kong, 1983–1993
(self-reporting)

Response	1983	1993
Not at all	33.1	17.4
Only a few sentences	23.5	21.7
A little	36.2	27.2
Quite well	4.7	26.6
Well	—	3.3
Very well	0.4	3.8

Note: The question asked was 'How well do you know English?'

Within this matrix, the most reliable category is spoken Chinese, which typically means Cantonese in this overwhelmingly Cantonese-speaking city, where we might assume little or no variation in ability. With the other three categories—written Chinese, spoken English, and written English—it is fair to assume that there is a wide range of abilities and proficiencies.

In the case of English, the lowest figure of 12 per cent, for which further details and methodological information are not available, tends to reflect thinking in parts of the business community, where the demand for English seems to have run ahead of supply. This in turn seems to reflect the rather rapid shift in industry from manufacturing to service. The upper estimate quoted above from Bacon-Shone and Bolton (1995) is based on self-reports of proficiency. A comparison of an earlier 1983 (Bolton and Luke, 1985) survey with the 1993 survey is given in Table 14.1 (from Bacon-Shone and Bolton, 1995: 27, table 25).

The problems of interpreting survey results based on self-reports are illustrated here. Categories such as 'a little' and 'quite well' are open to a wide range of interpretation. One clear result that does emerge over the ten-year period, however, is that there is a noticeable drop in the numbers of those claiming no knowledge of English at all. If we take the aggregate total for 'Quite well', 'Well', and 'Very well', we obtain a total percentage of 33.7, which broadly agrees with the census figure mentioned above.

The middle-range estimates of 29 and 20–30 per cent, representing respectively a population-wide census *(Hong Kong Population Census*, 1991) and a very focused group of 7,200 students, educators, graduates, employers, and parents (Language Proficiency Perception Survey, 1994) seem to give two further reasonable indications of the proportion of the Hong Kong population with a better than minimal knowledge of English. By conflating these latter two estimates with the total of 'better' ('Quite well', 'Well', and 'Very well') English users derived from Bacon-Shone and Bolton (1995), we are able to conclude that a figure of about 30–35 per cent of the population represents a realistic estimate of the proportion of educated English users in Hong Kong.

That said, this figure represents the maximum number of possible informants. When it came to the reality of data-collection a series of hurdles existed between identifying who used English and their inclusion in the ICE corpus. The first hurdle was actual, as opposed to simply potential, use of English within one of the ICE categories. The second was the opportunity of recording a text or obtaining copyright to it. The final hurdle was obtaining the permission of the speaker or writer and his or her relevant biographical information. Singularly and collectively, these hurdles have served to reduce the number of informants in practice, because people either elect to use Chinese rather than English, decline to be recorded (or decline to give permission to use material already broadcast), or turn out to have the wrong biographical detail.

3. THE SOURCING OF ICE TEXTS IN HONG KONG

The second assumption we made was that 'this widespread usage [of English] would be reflected in a reasonably straightforward identification of text sources which would match the text categories required by the ICE project.' It was further noted that 'In making these assumptions we were partly right and partly wrong and certainly over-optimistic.' (Bolt, 1994). Throughout the data-collection process in Hong Kong, we encountered a number of rather delicate problems related to individual proficiencies in English and the reluctance of potential participants to co-operate fully in the ICE-HK project. Problems related to real or perceived proficiency were particularly sensitive, since a major aspect of this study is the analysis and comparison of second or foreign language performance in English with the performance of native speakers. In addition, data-collection was not always helped by the constant public, and not necessarily well-informed, debates in the English language press and elsewhere, about the 'decline' in standards and the generally poor level of language proficiency achieved locally.[2]

Complementing the issue of proficiency in English is the parallel issue of the use of English in Hong Kong, i.e. who, of our target group, uses English, under what circumstances, and for what purposes? While recent studies (Bacon-Shone and Bolton, 1995) have recorded some intrusion of English into private life where no non-Cantonese speaking person is present, typically, the 'extended' use of English is found in the formal, public contexts, where, historically, the presence and significance of the non-Cantonese speaker has been greater. The important word here is 'extended' as we have not included 'intermittent' uses of English, as in the case of code-switching and code-mixing, which occur frequently in both spoken and written Chinese. There is undoubtedly a degree of status related to such uses, but the fragmented nature of the language, especially in written text, which tends mainly to involve names or short phrases, does not fit with our focus on the extended use

Philip Bolt and Kingsley Bolton

TABLE 14.2. *ICE text types and data collection in Hong Kong*

Area of use	ICE text categories	Number of examples	
		ICE	Hong Kong
Educational	Class lessons, timed and untimed essays, and learned informational writing	80	80
Government and law	Parliamentary, legal cross-examinations and presentations, administrative and regulatory writing	35	35
Media/publishing	Broadcast interviews and discussions, broadcast news and talks, press reporting and editorials, skills and hobbies, creative writing, and popular informational writing	170	130
Corporate	Business transactions, administrative and regulatory writing, and business letters	30	30
Formal public	All speeches, demonstrations, commentaries, and administrative and regulatory writing	70	70
Private	Private conversations, distanced conversations and social letters	115	105
TOTAL		500	450

of language. The ICE text types may be considered in relation to a number of areas of language use, all reflecting the productive, rather than the receptive, perspective and all embracing both spoken and written forms. These are shown in Table 14.2. Grouping the texts in this way permits an easier discussion of text sourcing in relation to broad areas of use and of the factors which make for easy or difficult text collection. Note that 'administrative and regulatory' appear in both governmental and commercial contexts.

3.1. *Educational*

The claimed medium of instruction in many secondary schools and all post-secondary institutions (with the notable exception of the Chinese (language) University of Hong Kong) is generally English, although this is by no means an absolute policy. The medium of instruction, like the language standard issue, has been the subject of much, still unresolved, discussion for a number of years. A recent study (Language Proficiency Perception Survey, 1994: 6–1) recorded the fact that Cantonese is in fact quite widely used within secondary and tertiary education, increasingly so in the latter case as the group size becomes smaller and the situation less formal. The relevant percentages for language use are given in Table 14.3.

202

TABLE 14.3. *Language use in Hong Kong colleges and universities (%)*

Mode	Cantonese	English	Putonghua	Cantonese and English	Other
Lectures	16	69.3	0.9	12.7	1.1
Small-group teaching	23.6	56.6	0.0	16.0	3.8
Tutorial (sic)	24.5	54.7	0.5	16.0	4.3

Nevertheless, such current shifts in the medium of instruction, if indeed they are current, have had little effect on our collection process, with the consequence that class lessons—which range from being close to monologues to being very interactive—and student essays have been collected in their entirety. The effect of this ease of identification and collection has been to make possible early comparative analyses of student writing in Hong Kong and the United Kingdom.[3] The final text category within education may require some explanation. While class lessons and student essays fit easily into a broad educational area, it should be noted that the 'informational learned' category is also included here, as all such texts that we have collected are written by academics, mainly for an academic audience for publication in journals.

A major issue to be aware of with most of the written data, and this is doubtless true for all ICE teams, is that published texts (including anything which is electronically produced), are almost certainly subject to editing. In particular, it must also be noted that there is a tendency to recycle text in different places, and, for us, it has been necessary to read with some attention to ensure that a particular text was both suitable and original.[4]

3.2. *Government and Law*

The most visible governmental activities are the weekly session of the Legislative Council, its committee sessions, the open committee sessions of other agencies such as the Housing Authority, and the written ordinances and instruments issued by such agencies. Hong Kong is an executive-led government with only rudimentary political parties and little form of government and opposition. Government tends to consist of a mixture of expatriate (mainly British) officials and local officials, while the members of the Legislative Council are, with a small number of notable exceptions, local people within our definition above. The lack of a government-and-opposition framework means that the adversarial style of debate, which is typical of the British parliament, is largely missing in the local legislature, a fact underlined by the very prominent, government-directed role of the President of the Council. Legislative Council sessions are broadcast, albeit only in part, so that this data was easily obtainable, but it is very much on the outer edge of the broad category of dialogue. To offset this, we have also obtained recordings of a number of committee and panel meetings where there is a greater amount of interaction. A further complication with the full Legislative Council sessions is the use of Cantonese, even by those members who are fluent in English. In many cases this is a matter of conscious choice.

The use of English in the judicial system reflects the fact that English law is used and the administration of justice is based largely on English practice. In addition, a relatively large number of participants in the process are native speakers of English—judges, counsel, and jury members. A proficiency in English is a prerequisite for jury service. However, the existence of a substantial proportion of local judges and counsel, who were very helpful in the data-collection process, means that both legal categories have been successfully collected. However, while the legal presentation, as a form of monologue, probably compares with that of other ICE teams, the fact that witnesses and defendants are free to use English or Cantonese, and that most choose the latter, means that our cross-examination dialogues are mostly between the relevant counsel and an interpreter. Of some fifteen cases that we have had access to only one had a witness who spoke in English— and that person declined to be included in our project.

3.3. *Media and Publishing*

The categories of broadcast texts—interviews, discussions, news, talks, and (usually) spontaneous commentaries—illustrate very well the range of issues attached to sourcing spoken English in Hong Kong. Sourcing printed texts illustrates the range of issues associated with the use of multiple editors and authors in the local print media. For the broadcast texts we were able to source, with increasing degrees of difficulty, the ten interviews, the twenty discussions, ten (out of twenty) broadcast news items, ten (out of twenty) talks (but with major qualifications below). In addition, twenty commentaries, but none easily comparable to the prototypical commentary of the sports or ceremonial event, have been collected (below).

Interviews, ranging from short snippets in news programmes to longer in-depth sessions, were relatively easy to obtain. The interesting feature about such interviews, however, is that in almost all texts the interviewer is a native speaker of English and the interviewee a local person. Discussions proved extremely time-consuming to complete, as there were very few sources (and there are even fewer now), and a number of people who appeared on the current affairs programme, 'Newsline', our major source for such discussions, were prominent people who also appeared in other contexts. Our other major source, Metro Radio, only broadcast two suitable programme series over a two-and-a-half year period. Again, however, with the exception of the male host of 'Newsline', the interviewer–interviewee divide is very similar to that found in the interviews. A further practical consideration was that in many discussions not only was the interviewer a native speaker of English (or the regular local presenter of 'Newsline', of whose speech we have restricted ourselves to the 2,000-word individual text amount), but one or more of the other discussants was a native speaker, resulting in a large measure of extra-corpus text.

Television and radio news reading is typically anchored by expatriate presenters who are sometimes western, sometimes Asian, and sometimes overseas-born Chinese. The number of local (in our sense) news-readers is small, and this explains our collection of only half the targeted number of texts. In addition, these are somewhat fragmented texts, and therefore, in common with interviews and discussions, the number of subtexts is inflated in comparison with the comparable texts for those ICE teams where all participants are generally suitable for inclusion in the final corpus. Broadcast talks in which one person speaks uninterruptedly on a subject for any reasonable length of time are very few, 'Letter from Hong Kong' being, until 1995, the only example. This programme has tended to be dominated by expatriates, with only a small proportion of local speakers. In mid-1995 the format was changed so that a previously twelve to fifteen minute independent programme became a segment of an afternoon magazine programme. A small number of part-texts have been obtained from this source. To make up our total of ten texts we have included a number of narratives/voice-overs to current affairs type documentaries.

The range of printed and published material includes press reporting and editorials, popular informational writing, creative writing, and skills and hobbies. As with the broadcast texts, these five categories illustrate many of the relevant sourcing issues and the resultant state of collection. Press (newspaper and magazine or journal) reporting and editorials have both been fully collected. There are now three English-language newspapers and a number of the news reports are by-lined by local people. However, two interesting issues have emerged: first, the comparative use of local reporters in the Asian region in English-language newspaper publishing, and, secondly the extent and nature of editing of writers' copy which is undertaken. One of the authors (Bolt) undertook a study of regional English-language newspapers over a three-day period and it yielded the comparative author information shown in Table 14.4. The far lower percentage of local writers in Hong Kong

TABLE 14.4. *The use of local and foreign reporters in selected English-language dailies*

	Local writer	Foreign writer	Agency reports	Proportion of local writers (%)
South China Morning Post (Hong Kong)	134	292	108	25
Straits Times (Singapore)	203	36	200	46
New Straits Times (Malaysia)	358	55	142	64
Manila Bulletin (the Philippines)	410	3	81	82

is very evident. In addition, local writers in Hong Kong tend to be concentrated in the local and China news sections, very few penetrating other kinds of news stories, non-news features, the arts and entertainment, or sport, while special features are invariably authored by expatriate writers.

The editor of the major local English-language newspaper noted recently that most copy needs more than just a little attention and that the worst copy needs rewriting from top to bottom, commenting that 'Even where the structure and broad style are more or less acceptable, grammatical errors and clumsy expression can demand heavy editing' (Braude, personal communication). Newspaper editorials have usually been written, until recently, by expatriates, or by writers who have had much of their education in an English-speaking country. However, a few local writers have recently begun to produce editorials and some of these have been collected, although the biodata has not been made available. In addition to these, our editorials include an English-language editorial feature from a daily Chinese language newspaper, some from a student publication and others from a number of magazines.

As with 'creative writing' and 'skills and hobbies' (below), sourcing texts for popular informational writing is not simply a case of browsing along the magazine racks or shelves of booksellers. Although a very wide range of magazines are available, very few are relevant because they are either imports, or are written by expatriates, or are in Chinese. A few that do have English along with Chinese articles employ translators to make a parallel text in English, and many of these translators are expatriate. As such, the sources of our popular writing are books, a small number of magazines and a small number of trade journals; for humanities, (only five) books; for technology, magazines and journals; and for the natural science category we have no texts at present.

In the area of creative writing we have identified only three or four published local writers, so we have decided to extend the interpretation of published to 'written to be published' in order to obtain a greater number of texts. This is an area in which there are few easily, publicly identifiable and available texts. Texts in the area of skills and hobbies, written by people having the right biodata, have not been sourced. Many magazines which have an English title or some English text turn out to be not suitable, as either the amount of English is too small, often restricted to names, or they have been authored by someone who is not a Hong Kong person.

3.4. *Corporate*

The relative degrees of difficulty in sourcing business transactions, administrative and regulatory writings, and business letters have provided interesting contrasts. Business transactions in the corporate and commercial world have been very difficult to obtain, issues of confidentiality being the usual barrier. As such, the notion of a business transaction has been interpreted very widely, covering the discussion and exchange of ideas rather than simply monetary issues. As a result of this, two-thirds of our texts have been collected in the education sector—meetings of various degrees of formality, in the areas of research, faculty, and staff/management—with just four from the commercial sector. For written data, the experience has been much happier, such that both categories are almost complete.

3.5. *Formal Public*

Unscripted speeches, scripted, but not broadcast, speeches, demonstrations, and commentaries have been classified here as 'formal public' to reflect the fact that the general context of delivery is in front of an audience whose composition is usually not entirely known in advance. The qualification of 'usually' indicates that a number of our demonstrations have been recorded as part of an ongoing course of sessions, and a small number of speeches have been made to committees whose composition is known in advance.

The distinction between 'scripted' and 'unscripted' has not been easy to apply in practice as there are few occasions when the speaker fails to depart from a prepared text and few occasions where a speech is entirely unscripted, since speakers often resort to memorization or notes (including graphical aids). Of the largest category, unscripted speeches, many of our texts are from industry seminars, some from conferences, and some from organizations such as the Toastmasters' Club.

Demonstrations include computer software, cookery, nursing, and first aid demonstrations. The first fits squarely into the category of not knowing the composition of the audience in advance, whereas, for the latter three the audience was partly known as the session was part of a course. Of these, the cookery demonstration is an especially good example of the genuine use of English, as the audience consisted of Filipina 'amahs' (domestic servants).

Spontaneous commentaries represent an area where we have made our most significant departure from the normal meaning of ICE categories. Sports and ceremonial commentating reflects a sociolinguistic divide, with no local commentators performing in English for the major sport of horse-racing, the reasonably popular sport of tennis, or for minority sports or events such as the dragon boat-racing. Interpreting widely both the individual terms 'spontaneous' and 'commentary' and their combined meaning, our spontaneous commentaries are six tourist guides, seven interpreters for the Legislative Council, and seven interpreters from the high court. Our motivation for using such texts is that the tourist guides are in fact reasonably flexible in what they talk about, even though they follow a fixed itinerary, and there is, in all cases, quite a lot of ad-libbing by the speakers. For the two interpreting situations, it is suggested that although there is no absolute spontaneity involved there is a high degree of having to respond to (linguistic) input in real time and, given the nature of virtually simultaneous interpretation, that this is in fact a form of commentary, if only on meaning and message. In the case of the high court, such interpretation is of vital importance and, on more than one occasion, its accuracy and the possible effects of inaccuracy have been raised. It has, however, proved impossible to obtain the biodata of the speakers for the interpretation, although it is highly unlikely that anyone other than a Cantonese native speaker would be able and likely to do this work. Nevertheless, our spontaneous commentaries as a whole may remain something of a rogue collection.

3.6. *Private*

Private conversations (75) and social letters constitute our collection in the private area. For a number of logistical reasons we have not been able to collect distanced (telephone) conversations; this is somewhat ironic given the immense local popularity of the device, especially the mobile variety. In the case of private conversations, as noted above, without the presence of a non-Cantonese speaker, Cantonese speakers tend to use Cantonese. This meant that to ensure that such conversations were as natural as is possible, given the fact that the speakers knew about the recording in advance, the presence of a non-Cantonese speaker was necessary. In fact this is the case with the majority of our spoken texts. Another important factor to note is that the vast majority of private conversations involve speakers aged between 20 and 30. A similar age-range exists for social letters, where we should also note that approximately half of such texts are email messages. This reflects the popularity of this channel of communication among students and the fact that email is only available in English on campus networks. A number of social letters have also been obtained from Hong Kong students studying abroad.

4. Processing the Data—Tagging and Parsing

What of the nature of the language found, our first motivation? We are not yet able to report global results because of the time it has taken us to complete the data collection. There remains, however, the question of how the data may be further processed, particularly of how it is to be tagged and parsed. The tagging stage is prior to the parsing stage and provides the input for parsing, so much so that a number of ICE word-class categories reflect syntactic patternings, e.g. the various tags for 'it', and the range of transitivity options for verbs. Our problem can be seen from the following output from AUTASYS 3.0 on sentences taken from a business letter, student writing, and an editorial.

Sentence 1		Sentence 2		Sentence 3	
Regarding	v(cxtr,ingp)	Despite	N(com,sing)	If	CONJUNC(subord)
the	ART(def)	in	PREP(ge):1/3	a	ART(indef)
mistake	N(com,sing)	terms	PREP(ge):2/3	lecturer	N(com,sing)
caused	v(montr,edp)	of	PREP(ge):3/3	finds	v(ditr,pres)
by	PREP(ge)	property	N(com,plu):1/2	his	PRON(poss,sing)
our	PRON(poss,plu)	relations	N(com,plu):2/2	superiors	N(com,plu)
staff	N(com,sing)	they	PRON(pers,sing)	involving	v(montr,ingp)
who	PRON(rel)	might	AUX(modal,past)	in	PREP(ge)
was	AUX(pass,past)	have	v(montr,infin)	administrative	ADJ
overlooked	v(montr,edp)	none	PRON(neg,sing)	indiscretions	N(com,plu)
and	CONJUNC(coord)	,	PUNC(com)	and	CONJUNC(coord)
delayed	v(montr,edp)	they	PRON(pers,sing)	having	v(montr,ingp)
the	ART(def)	admire	v(montr,infin)	errors	N(com,plu)
check-in	N(com,sing)	the	ART(def)	of	PREP(ge)
for	PREP(ge)	life	N(com,sing):1/2	judgment	N(com,sing)
the	ART(def)	style	N(com,sing):2/2	,	PUNC(com)
guests	N(com,plu)	of	PREP(ge)	it	CLEFTIT
	PUNC(per)	that	PRON(dem,sing)	is	v(intr,pres)
		of	PREP(ge)	his	PRON(poss,sing)
		the	ART(def)	duties	N(com,plu)
		upper	ADJ	,	PUNC(com)
		class	N(com,sing)	and	CONJUNC(coord)
		and	CONJUNC(coord)	rightly	ADV(ge)
		is	v(cop,pres)	so	CONJUNC(coord)
		in	PREP(ge)	,	PUNC(com)
		attitude	N(com,sing)	to	PRTCL(to)
		conform	v(intr,pres)	report	v(montr,infin)
		to	PREP(ge)	the	ART(def)
		conservative	ADJ	situation	N(com,sing)
		ideas	N(com,plu)	to	PREP(ge)
		and	conjunc(coord)	someone	PRON(ass,sing)
		resistance	N(com,sing)	higher	ADJ(comp)
		to	PRTCL(to)	up	ADV(phras)
		change	v(montr,infin)	in	PREP(ge)
			PUNC(per)	the	ART(def)
				bureaucratic	ADJ
				hierarchy	N(com,sing)
				before	PREP(ge)
				more	PRON(quant)
				damages	N(com,plu)
				are	AUX(pass,pres)
				done	v(montr,edp)
					PUNC(per)

The problem here is not that a few words are incorrectly tagged—*regarding* and *despite* in the first and second sentences respectively might better be labelled as prepositions—and the *it* in the main clause of the third sentence seems

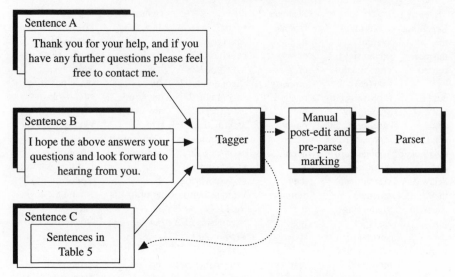

Fɪɢ. 14.1. Output from AUTASYS 3.0 for standard and non-standard written text

uncomfortably classified as a CLEFT. Rather, the problem is that the range of tags available for local tag disambiguation may not provide the best guide for the parsing stage. As opposed to the local—typically three item context—of tagging programs, parsing involves the whole sentence. The constructions of interest in the sentence, phrases and clauses, might not be easily determinable on the basis of the wordclass information given in this output alone. This may be either because such information as provided by the tagger is not the best guide to phrase and clause structure, but can be recovered manually, or because the raw data does not conform to the descriptions of 'standard' English grammar. There are three possible relations between the original sentence, the tagger, and the parser, as shown in Fig. 14.1. For Sentence A, the phrases and clauses of which conform to standard English grammar, the route to a parsed output is relatively straightforward, requiring minimal post-tagger marking, e.g. for clause boundaries, as shown by the directions of the arrows in Fig. 14.1. For Sentence B, again a well-formed sentence but one whose structure forces the tagger into minor mis-labelling, this mis-labelling can be corrected manually between the tagging and parsing stages. Again, the arrows in Fig. 14.1 indicate an onward progression to the post-tagger stage, where the broken line indicates that there is some mis-labelling of one or more word-forms which will require attention as evidenced below.

I	PRON(pers,sing)
hope	V(montr,pres)
the	ART(def)
above	ADJ

answers	N(com,plu)
your	PRON(poss)
questions	N(com,plu)
and	CONJUNC(coord)
look	V(intr,pres)
forward	ADV(ge)
to	PREP(ge)
hearing	N(com,sing)
from	PREP(ge)
you	PRON(pers)
.	PUNC(per)

However, for Sentence C, of which the three sentences displayed above are typical examples, it is not simply the case that some mis-labelling needs to be adjusted prior to parsing. Rather, not only do the original sentences not provide the right input to generate the level of tagging accuracy as produced for sentences A and B, but, more crucially, whatever tagging results are obtained, they cannot be altered sufficiently to provide a sensible input to the parser. It is not a problem with the tagger's efficiency in these instances but with the original sentence, hence the direction of the even more broken and backward-looping arrow in Fig. 14.1. There would seem to be two possible strategies for coping with these sorts of sentences. Either a distinctive tag-set could be created for such sentences, which would incorporate the necessary additional, possibly first-language-specific information needed to produce some semblance of phrase and clause structure, or the sentences could be 'normalized' to bring them syntactically into line with the intention of the writer. Although this latter approach would be relatively simple in the case of sentence 3, neither option is attractive given the comparative objective of ICE.

Although other ICE teams may have syntactically odd constructions, it is anticipated that up to 35 or 40 per cent of our data, including written texts, may have the kind of features shown in these sentences. The decisions regarding how to proceed, therefore, have far-reaching implications, especially as we wish for consistency of labelling and structure with other ICE teams. These issues will be the subject of discussion in the near future.

5. CONCLUSION

The complex and shifting realities of the current sociolinguistic context have had an obvious influence on the process and results of the data collection in Hong Kong. In some cases these have made for easy collection—the use of English in the education system, in government, in the judiciary, in large businesses, and an English-language press and publishing industry—have all made sourcing possible, if not always procedurally straightforward. In other cases, the relative paucity of English use has made for difficulties. In all cases, there has sometimes been the delicate link referred to above between the existence of a text and its author or speaker and its eventual inclusion in ICE-HK.

The dramatic spread of English through younger age-groups in Hong Kong has been commented on by Bacon-Shone and Bolton (1995), who explain this by reference to the huge expansion of secondary education in the 1970s and a similar expansion of university education in the late 1980s and early 1990s. On this they comment that at present 'more people than ever are speaking "good" English, and more people than ever are speaking "bad" English' (33), and we have noted the predominance of younger people in the 'private' category. At the same time, however, counter-tendencies can also be seen, particularly within the public domains of language use, and they have been evident in the data sourcing and collecting stages of the ICE-HK work, especially in the last two years. In particular, there has been a significant increase in the amount of Chinese used, alongside or instead of English. Within the government and the judiciary—which are actively promoting the future use of Chinese—in the meetings of many public bodies, and throughout education—the Education Department has for a long time been trying, without a great deal of success, to persuade more schools to use Chinese as the medium of instruction—the use of Chinese is on the increase. Conversely, English-language television and radio broadcasting seems to be declining rapidly in both scale and importance and we have noted above the comparatively low, in regional terms, local input to the English-language press.[5] In this sense, it may be that our work coincides with a high-water mark in the use of English in Hong Kong and that it will represent the last large-scale exercise of this nature that achieves a near 90 per cent data collection rate across a wide range of contexts.

This reflects the unique geopolitical context of Hong Kong with its scheduled reversion to Chinese sovereignty soon to be completed. With the change from being within the British Commonwealth to being an albeit special part of China it is difficult to imagine a decline in the use of Chinese at the end of the twentieth century, even given the complexities of the varieties of spoken Chinese. Yet English is fairly well-rooted in certain areas of public activity, especially those areas which have an international interface. Those people presently proficient in English are unlikely to lose this facility, even if there is less opportunity to exercise it. However, for those not especially proficient in English or those individuals (and organizations) contemplating language choice, the limitations of time, if not political correctness in its more literal sense, may begin to sharpen perceptions regarding language acquisition and use in the not too distant future.

NOTES

1. Article 9 of the Basic Law, which serves as the proposed constitution for the new Special Administrative Region, gives some, albeit not entirely unambiguous, indication of this

when it declares that: 'In addition to the Chinese language, English may also be used as an official language by the executive authorities, legislative and judicial organs of the Hong Kong Special Administrative Region' (Basic Law, 1991).

2. A recent issue (24 Feb. 1995) of one of the three English language newspapers *Eastern Express* is a not untypical example. There are three items relating to poor standards, one concerning the views of certain New Zealand schools who are worried about the influx of Asian non-English-speaking schoolchildren, one about the comments of a UK academic noting the increasing care which must be taken with language standards of non-maths and science applicants from Hong Kong, and a final letter to the editor containing a blistering attack on the Education Department and the proficiency of students emerging from the education system.

3. Two M.Phil. studies on discourse particles in broadcast interviews in ICE-GB and ICE-HK, and another on student writing in the two corpora are underway.

4. In a recent case a senior academic admitted to using a former teacher's text in a textbook. What made matters worse was the somewhat cavalier fashion in which a more senior academic at the same institution dismissed the use of other people's work in a textbook as 'no big deal'.

5. Interestingly, we note that Pennington and Yue (1994) arrive independently at a similar conclusion on 'countertrends' in the use of languages in official and public domains.

REFERENCES

Bacon-Shone, J. and Bolton, K. (1995), 'Charting Multilingualism: Language Censuses and Language Surveys in Hong Kong', in M. C. Pennington (ed.), 15–24.

Basic Law (1991), *The Basic Law of the Hong Kong Special Administrative Region of the People's Republic of China* (Hong Kong: Joint Publishing Co.).

Bolt, P. (1994), 'The International Corpus of English Project—the Hong Kong Experience', in U. Fries, G. Tottie, and P. Schneider (eds.), *Creating and Using English Language Corpora: Papers from the Fourteenth International Conference on English Language Research on Computerized Corpora* (Amsterdam: Rodopi).

Bolton, K. and Kwok, H. (1990), 'The Dynamics of The Hong Kong Accent: Social Identity and Sociolinguistic Description', *Journal of Asian Pacific Communication*, 1/1: 147–72.

—— and Luke, K. K. (1985), 'The Sociolinguistic Survey of Language in Hong Kong: The Background to Research and Methodological Considerations', *International Journal of the Sociology of Language*, 55: 41–56.

Fu, G. S. (1987), 'The Hong Kong Bilingual', in R. Lord and H. N. L. Cheung (eds.), 27–50.

Hong Kong Population Census: Summary Results (1991) (Hong Kong: Census and Statistics Department).

Language Proficiency Perception Survey (1994), Report prepared by the Education Commission Working Group on Language Proficiency, unpublished mimeo. (Hong Kong: Hong Kong Polytechnic University).

Lord, R. and Cheung, H. N. L. (1987), *Language Education in Hong Kong* (Hong Kong: The Chinese University Press).

Luke, K. K. and Richards, J. C. (1982), 'English in Hong Kong: Functions and Status', *English World-Wide*, 3: 47–63.

213

Philip Bolt and Kingsley Bolton

PENNINGTON, M. C. (1995) (ed.), *Language in Hong Kong at Century's End* (Hong Kong: Hong Kong University Press).

—— and YUE, F. (1994), 'English and Chinese in Hong Kong: Pre-1997 Language Attitudes', *World Englishes*, 13/1: 1–20.

RICHARDS, J. C. and LUKE, K. K. (1982), 'English in Hong Kong: Functions and Status', paper presented at 16th RELC Seminar, Singapore.

SO, W. C. D. (1987), 'Searching for a Bilingual Exit', in R. LORD and H. N. L. CHEUNG (eds.), 249–68.

—— (1992), 'Language-based Bifurcation of Secondary Schools in Hong Kong: Past, Present and Future', in *Into the Twenty First Century: Issues of Language Education in Hong Kong*, 69–95 (Hong Kong: Linguistic Society of Hong Kong).

SURRY, M. (1994), 'English not Spoken Here', *Window*, 1 Apr., 33–7.

PART IV

Applications

15

The Corpus as a Research Domain

GRAEME KENNEDY

The design and development of machine-readable corpora and tools for their analysis has been a major preoccupation of corpus linguistics for more than three decades. During this period there have been massive changes in the capacity and speed of computers, an increasing use of microcomputers with CD-ROM as the basis for storage, the development of new and faster means of text capture through optical scanning, and the development of more sophisticated software packages for the analysis of corpora. At the same time there have been continuing issues in the design and use of corpora. How big should a corpus be to provide a valid and reliable picture of how a language is structured and used? What aspects of a language can be validly and reliably described using a corpus of a particular size? Can a corpus be designed to be a representative sample of a language 'as a whole'? Should particular genres be represented in a corpus and, if so, which genres? What are the respective roles of automatic and manual analysis in corpus-based research?

As Quirk (1992) has noted, machine-readable corpora have grown in size from the one-million-word standard of the Survey of English Usage (SEU) Corpus and the Brown Corpus of the early 1960s to the 100-million-word British National Corpus (BNC) of the 1990s. The most recent developments, including vast monitor corpora of potentially unlimited size and the International Corpus of English (ICE), promise to open up new directions in the use of corpora.

Although there have been numerous corpus-based studies of English completed since 1960, the changes in technology mentioned above and issues in the design and development of corpora have in a sense been necessary prerequisites for systematic corpus-based research. It is just such systematic research, involving comprehensive lexical and grammatical description and comparisons across genres, registers, and major regional varieties which the ICE project will encourage and facilitate. The purpose of this paper is to outline some matters which might be considered part of a research agenda for the ICE corpus.

To a considerable extent, the size, nature, and structure of machine-readable corpora and the associated software, determine the kind of linguistic research which can be undertaken. Obviously, for example, however big a corpus may be, if it includes only written texts, it cannot reasonably be used as a basis for the description of the 'language as a whole' nor for lexical, grammatical, or discourse characteristics of the spoken language. Similarly, a one-million-word corpus (or even a 20-million-word corpus) has limitations for lexical research because it will not be big enough to include the full range of low frequency words in English, nor provide enough occurrences of the words of medium frequency outside the commonest 3,000 words to enable the researcher to get an accurate picture of their range of meanings and how they are used. On the other hand, on the basis of research on the Brown and LOB corpora, researchers can be reasonably confident that a corpus of one million words will be adequate as a basis for describing high frequency vocabulary, the major morphological, syntactic, and discourse processes, and systems of English, and possibly even many of the major collocations (Kjellmer, 1991). Indeed, major descriptions of the collocations in the Brown and LOB Corpora have already been published by Kjellmer (1994) and Johansson and Hofland (1989). A corpus of less than 50,000 words may be entirely adequate for description at the phonological level, although regrettably computer corpora have rarely been transcribed with sufficient delicacy for many types of phonological analysis. Corpus texts which come from spoken sources have up till now typically been subject to the same kinds of lexical, grammatical, and discourse analysis as written texts.

The particular facilities made available by the ICE Corpus Utility Programme (ICECUP), which has been developed for the analysis of the ICE corpora, will also help determine the kinds of research which are undertaken. ICECUP is able to retrieve from text for descriptive and comparative purposes all tokens of particular types, including word forms, parts of words (such as suffixes), punctuation, word-class tags, combinations of words, and combinations of tags. For each of these, basic frequency counts are provided. Furthermore ICECUP has been designed to facilitate searches of subcorpora defined by various sociolinguistic, discoursal, or textual parameters. When subcorpora are large enough, valid and reliable comparative studies will be possible. The value of ICECUP will be further enhanced when later versions incorporate facilities which can indicate whether there are statistically significant differences in the use of linguistic items or strings in various regional, sociolinguistic, register, or genre domains of use.

The ICE Tagset, which includes some 278 lexical word-class, tag combination, and punctuation tags allows for greater delicacy of grammatical analysis than is normally available for machine readable texts. The associated String Description Language, which makes possible the retrieval of all instances of complex sequences of words and tags, should enable researchers to describe the distribution of patterning in English, including patterning which has hitherto remained unnoticed or has not been included in descriptive grammars.

Although the kinds of linguistic research which can be based on a corpus are heavily influenced by whether or not that corpus is grammatically tagged or parsed, even after tagged versions of the Brown and LOB Corpora became available many researchers continued to work with untagged versions. The comprehensive ICAME bibliography (Altenberg, 1991), which records over 700 studies of English based on the available machine-readable corpora beginning in the early 1960s, shows that many of the studies involved the behaviour of individual words. Table 15.1 classifies and summarizes the major topics covered by studies listed in the first ICAME bibliography and in subsequent updates. Even for many of the grammatical studies, the approach has been through lexical items, for example modals or complementizers, including such things as their distribution in a corpus, their function, semantic varieties, and 'the words with which they habitually co-occur.

Table 15.1 shows that a heterogeneous variety of topics or aspects of English have been investigated, most of which were based on analyses of the SEU, Brown, or LOB corpora. However, many of the studies explored only one aspect of a particular linguistic phenomenon and few have been definitive or comprehensive. Some, for example, have been based on the genres of just the spoken part of the Survey of English Usage (the London–Lund Corpus). Others have been based on a single genre, such as Section J (Learned and Scientific) of one or both of American and British written varieties represented in the Brown and LOB corpora. Some have been based on a single genre from a small unpublished corpus of less than 50,000 words. There have been very few studies involving comparisons between genres or between regional varieties.

The ICE project will make available for the first time a set of parallel corpora of the major regional varieties of English, with each corpus being structured to include a carefully designed selection of genres. The systematically structured and grammatically tagged ICE corpora are thus poised to benefit from the 30 years of corpus design and development and should provide the basis for long-overdue, systematic, and comprehensive descriptions and comparative studies of both formal and functional aspects of world Englishes. There are, of course, already corpus-based descriptions of English. Many major dictionaries are now corpus-based in the sense that the types, major meanings, and examples of use are all identified from text databases which are necessarily large to ensure reliable description of less common words. Modern grammatical descriptions of English culminated in the great *Comprehensive Grammar of the English Language* (Quirk *et al.*, 1985) which was informed by the one-million-word Survey of English Usage Corpus. However, as corpus linguistics has developed, it is clear that what makes corpus-based descriptions of a language different from descriptions which are not based on machine-readable corpora is the systematic explicit quantification of items and processes associated with the linguistic description. Unlike other sciences, linguistic description has been curiously uneasy with measurement, but it is the ability of corpus-based research to quantify the occurrence of items of a linguistic system in use which is its most particular contribution to the science of language.

It is no longer enough for the object of research to be a description of the linguistic system we use. Rather, the new ground to be broken is to record the use of the system, and especially what parts are more likely to be used by particular users in particular varieties for particular purposes. A corpus-based description can do more than record that there are auxiliary verbs known as modals, having particular grammatical forms, positions, functions, and meanings. A corpus-based

TABLE 15.1. *A classification of corpus-based research (1960–93) listed in the ICAME bibliographies 1–3*

I. Word class and lexically-focused studies
  1. Verb forms
    • Transitive verbs
    • Infinitives
    • Distribution and use of modals *shall, should, will, would, can, could, may, might, need*
    • *going to, will, is, isn't, is not, have, get, do*
    • Progressive, preterite, perfect, subjunctive, passive voice
    • Verb + particle combinations, prepositional verbs, verbs in *-alise*
  2. Noun phrases
    • NP types
    • Articles, quantifiers, *some, any*
    • *man, one, your, who, whom, what, whose, of which*
    • *both . . . and, neither . . . nor, all but, nothing, no, not*
    • Classifying adjectives
    • Referential pronouns, reciprocal pronouns, pronominal chains
    • Noun phrases with *of*
    • *'s* genitive
  3. Prepositions
    • *around, to, between, through, of*
  4. Adverbials
    • *only, really, literally, directly, closely, increasingly, also, too, -ly* adverbs
    • Adverbial stance types
  5. Miscellaneous
    • *if not, even if, even though, but,* existential *there*
    • High frequency vocabulary, lexical density, cohesive devices, adjective-noun collocations
II. Syntactic processes
  1. NP Complexity
  2. Premodification and postmodification
  3. Subordination
    • Relative clauses
    • Conditional clauses
    • Nominal clauses
    • Causal linking and ordering strategies
    • Temporal *as* clauses
  4. Complementation
    • Infinitival complement clauses
    • *for/to* infinitive clauses
    • *to* + infinitive and *of* + infinitive
  5. Topicalization
    • *Tough*-movement
    • Extraposed gerundial subject clauses
    • Cleft and pseudo-cleft constructions

(TABLE 15.1. Cont'd)

---

6. Ellipsis
   * Conjunction-headed abbreviated clauses
   * Gapping
7. Co-ordination
   * Contrastive linking
8. Adverbial usage
   * Adverbial fronting
   * Sequences of spatial and temporal adverbials
9. Miscellaneous
   * Comparatives
   * Apposition
   * *do*-support
   * Negation
   * *by* agents
   * Tag questions

III. Miscellaneous topics in spoken English
   * Impromptu speech, carry-on signals in conversation, speech rate, turn taking, slips of the tongue, pauses, segmentation, phraseology, contractions, tone units, intonation, prosodic units, tone contrasts, discourse tags, lexical items peculiar to spoken discourse, questions and responses in conversation
   * Discourse particles and hedging devices
      * *sort of, kind of, you know, actually, in fact, anyway, now, just, oh, ah, you see, I mean, to begin with, for example, yes, no, well*

IV. Variation
   * Historical drift in genres
   * Word frequencies in US and UK English
   * Linguistic characteristics of different genre
   * Gender-related differences in spoken English
   * Differences in speech and writing
   * Comparison of UK and US Written English

---

description will also show the relative frequency of use of these word forms in different genres and also the relative frequency of the meanings or functions of each of these forms. A study by Coates (1983) is an outstanding example of such a quantified comparative description of the use of the English modal auxiliaries in different domains, based on an analysis of a small sample from the LOB and London–Lund Corpora.

The research domain in machine-readable corpora such as those which are part of ICE will be as varied and wide-ranging as there are facts about language and language use. However, it is important to distinguish between systematic linguistic description and unmotivated, even trivial research which may in no obvious way contribute to a theory of language or to a descriptively adequate account of a particular language. It may not be of great interest to discover, for example, that *how*-questions are less likely to be used than *why*-questions in radio interviews, or that *learned* rather than *learnt* is the preferred variant in a particular variety of English. On the other hand whether *he* is used more or less than *she* in documents associated with government administration may have important social and political significance.

It is not possible to know with certainty in advance what is worth studying in a corpus. There is always the possibility of discovering new patterning and significant distributions of known patterning. In the first instance, however, it will be useful for many users of descriptions of English to have a systematic, distributionally-based account of the major systems and processes of English, encompassing the levels of language which conventionally form the basis of linguistic description. Because the spoken texts in the ICE corpora are transcribed orthographically without prosodic analysis, and with only pausing and overlapping speech indicated, there are obviously constraints on the kinds of possible analyses of spoken English which can be undertaken.

Table 15.2 outlines the kinds of items which might be part of a research agenda using the corpus, particularly at the grammatical level. The grammar compiled by Quirk *et al.* (1985) based on the Survey of English Usage Corpus provides a more detailed taxonomy of topics for research into the constituents and structures of English at the levels of the phrase, clause, and sentence. In addition to clarifying how these constituents and structures function in particular corpora or parts of corpora, the most notable addition to the information already provided in comprehensive grammars is likely to be quantitative, with frequencies being provided for all items in relation to their use in particular genres, registers and varieties.

By way of illustration, a corpus-based description of adjectives in English will not just show that this modifying word-class can occur attributively within noun phrases or predicatively but will indicate what proportion of adjectives are used in each category and whether adjectives as a whole or particular adjectives are more likely to occur attributively or predicatively. The use and distribution of participle-derived *-ed* or *-ing* adjectives as against other types of adjectives will be shown as also will adjective collocations with nouns and intensifiers in particular genres and the effect of collocation on meaning. *A good cook* and *a good meal* might contribute to *a good time* but the use of *good* to mean either *skilful* or *enjoyable* is context-dependent.

Further, a corpus-based descriptive grammar will not only record that adjectives may be stative or dynamic (and the proportions of each) but may be gradable or non-gradable. The description will show that many adjectives do not have only an absolute form (e.g. *green*, *probable*) but can be marked for comparative or superlative degree (*greener*, *greenest*, *more probable*, *most probable*). Much of this is already well described in non-corpus-based grammars. The new ground broken will be in showing the relative frequency of absolute, comparative, and superlative forms, and the relative frequencies of the *-er/-est* forms and the *more/most* + adjective forms.

TABLE 15.2. *An outline of the units and structures from morpheme to discourse which can be investigated in the ICE corpora*

Word classes
  e.g. adjectives, adverbs, determiners, nouns, prepositions, pronouns, verbs
Word morphology and functions
  e.g. tense, aspect, number
Word types
Lemmas
Collocations
Phrase classes
  e.g. noun phrases, verb phrases, prepositional phrases, adjective phrases, adverb
  phrases
Clause elements
  e.g. subject, direct object, complement, adverbial (adjuncts, conjuncts, disjuncts)
Clause patterns
  e.g. SV, SVO, SVC, SVA, existential constructions
Clause processes
  e.g. extraposition, clefting, passivization, negation (e.g. *no* vs. *not*)
Sentence types
  e.g. declarative, interrogative (*yes/no*, *wh*-), imperative
Complex sentences
  e.g. co-ordination, subordination (nominal clauses, relative clauses, adverbial clauses,
  comparative clauses)
Ways in which information is organized and structured in discourse
Discourse particles
Form and function
  e.g. interrogative vs. questions
Cohesion

Varieties and variation

Lexis, grammar, and discourse in different domains
  speech and writing
  sociolinguistic variation
  register variation
  regional variation

In as much as grammatical processes and systems are ways of realizing or marking semantic or intentional processes, the corpus is an important resource for the investigation of preferred ways of expressing particular semantic functions in a language. The comparative, for example, is one of the ways by which comparisons are made in English, but by no means the only one. Comparisons can be made in terms of superiority, inferiority or equality, and English provides a large number of ways, both morphosyntactic and lexical, of realizing them. Mitchell (1990) outlined a taxonomy of possible semantic relationships in making comparisons. The linguistic devices used to express such relationships include parallel systems for continuous substances and discrete objects as the following examples show.

Superiority
There is/are more X than Y.
The amount/number of X exceeds the amount/number of Y.
There is a larger amount/number of X than Y.
The number of X is greater than the number of Y.

Inferiority
There is/are less/fewer Y than X.
The amount/number of Y is less than the amount/number of X.
There's a smaller amount/number of Y than X.
The amount/number of Y is smaller than the amount/number of X.

Equality (and denial of equality)
There isn't/aren't as much/many Y as X.
The amount/number of Y isn't as large as the amount/number of X.
There is/are as much/many Y as Z.
The amount/number of Y is the same as the amount/number of Z.

These sentences are illustrative of part of the system we use to make comparisons of quantity in English. Our use of the system, however, is not captured in this description. The corpus can be used to describe which of the devices are most likely to be used by particular groups of users in particular contexts or domains of use. This example illustrates the necessary interaction between the ingenuity and judgement of the researcher in identifying the system, and the use of computer software to find and count instances of the items or strings of items in machine-readable corpora. The need for this partnership between the researcher and the machine has been noted by Leech (1991) as being necessary if interesting and worthwhile questions are to be addressed in corpus-based research.

Considering the importance of prepositions, both in terms of frequency and as devices for marking intra-propositional cohesion, surprisingly little is known of their distribution in English. A corpus-based research agenda will set out to describe how the one hundred or so simple and multi-word prepositions of English are used, and will show what proportion of the uses of each preposition have the locative role that is often assumed to be their main function. Sinclair (1991) has shown in his analysis of the most frequent preposition *of* that the conventional wisdom about the grammatical function of this major preposition can be substantially modified on the basis of corpus evidence. The corpus can also be used to show what proportion of the uses of each preposition are devoted to expressing various semantic functions such as location, time, quantification, causation, instrumentality, accompaniment, and agency (Kennedy, 1991). Similarly the corpus can show what proportion of prepositional phrases have an adjectival function modifying nominals, and what proportion have an adverbial function. The major collocates

224

occurring before and after each preposition and the extent to which such collocations may be discontinuous can also be established.

In corpus-based descriptive studies the following questions are likely to be central: what are the linguistic units, patterns, systems, or processes in the language, genre, or text and how often, when, where, why, and with whom are they used?

When completed, the corpora in the ICE project will be ideally placed to facilitate studies which compare use in different genres or in different regional or sociolinguistic varieties. Although the research domain using corpora will potentially cover all aspects of language and language use, the main points of entry are likely to continue to be the following, whether the texts have spoken or written origins:

1. Word-based studies which explore the ecology of lexis. Work by Nattinger and De Carrico (1992), Renouf and Sinclair (1991), Kjellmer (1994) and others suggests that the expansion of lexical studies to include collocations is likely to be one of the most innovative and productive areas of corpus-based research.
2. Studies of the co-occurrence of tags as expressions of syntactic patterning and as the basis for quantitative studies of the use of syntactic structures and processes.
3. Studies of the co-occurrence of groups of items to show by means of factor analysis the characteristics of genre on linguistic grounds. Biber (1988) has pioneered the use of this approach to establish text types.
4. Studies of the structure of discourse, especially of spoken interaction and of the basis of cohesion in spoken and written texts.

The outcomes of corpus-based studies can have important implications for work in descriptive and applied linguistics. Verb forms marking tense, aspect, modality, or voice are very pervasive in that about 20 per cent of all word tokens in a corpus are typically verbs, and almost every sentence has at least one verb form. Earlier corpus studies in the 1960s showed that for English, only six tense and aspect forms account for about 95 per cent of all verb forms in a variety of genres (Kennedy, 1992). For language teaching purposes it matters a great deal to know which these forms are, and there is a need for replication of earlier studies, especially taking account of spoken varieties of English.

The research agenda will of course vary according to the intended use of the outcomes. For those involved in large-scale studies leading to new comprehensive grammars, the agenda will need to cover the whole range of items and processes of the kind outlined in Table 15.2. There will also continue to be an important role for smaller thesis-type studies which characterized most of the corpus-based research over the last 30 years. A study of preferred clause order in complex sentences which express temporal, causal, and conditional relationships can be highly relevant research for teacher education in showing what is normal in different varieties of English and what are stylistic variants. On the other hand, a much more narrowly focused study of the distribution of *different from*, *different to*, and *different than* in varieties of English can teach students or teachers more about the hazards of prescriptivism than many pages of injunctions about the nature of language and language change.

The systematic investigation of new corpora such as ICE to provide up-to-date descriptions of English including distributional characteristics of its use in various contexts should mark a new phase in linguistic description, and add new dimensions to our understanding of language and language use.

REFERENCES

AIJMER, K. and ALTENBERG, B. (1991) (eds.), *English Corpus Linguistics: Studies in Honour of Jan Svartvik* (London: Longman).

ALTENBERG, B. (1991), 'A Bibliography of Publications Relating to English Computer Corpora', in S. JOHANSSON and A.-B. STENSTRÖM (eds.), *English Computer Corpora*, 355–96 (Berlin: Mouton de Gruyter).

BIBER, D. (1988), *Variation Across Speech and Writing* (Cambridge: Cambridge University Press).

COATES, J. (1983), *The Semantics of the Modal Auxiliaries* (London: Croom Helm).

JOHANSSON, S. and HOFLAND, K. (1989), *Frequency Analysis of English Vocabulary and Grammar*, 2 vols. (Oxford: Clarendon Press).

KENNEDY, G. (1991), '*Between* and *Through*: The Company They Keep and the Functions They Serve', in K. AIJMER and B. ALTENBERG (eds.), 95–110.

—— (1992), 'Preferred Ways of Putting Things with Implications for Language Teaching', in J. SVARTVIK (ed.), 335–73.

KJELLMER, G. (1991), 'A Mint of Phrases', in K. AIJMER and B. ALTENBERG (eds.), 111–27.

—— (1994), *A Dictionary of English Collocations based on the Brown Corpus*, 3 vols. (Oxford: Clarendon Press).

LEECH, G. (1991), 'The State of the Art in Corpus Linguistics', in K. AIJMER and B. ALTENBERG (eds.), 8–29.

MITCHELL, K. (1990), 'On Comparisons in a Notional Grammar', *Applied Linguistics*, 11/1: 52–72.

NATTINGER, J. R. and DE CARRICO, J. S. (1992), *Lexical Phrases and Language Teaching* (Oxford: Oxford University Press).

QUIRK, R. (1992), 'On Corpus Principles and Design', in J. SVARTVIK (ed.), 457–69.

—— GREENBAUM, S., LEECH, G., and SVARTVIK, J. (1985), *A Comprehensive Grammar of the English Language* (London: Longman).

RENOUF, A. and SINCLAIR, J. M. (1991), 'Collocational Frameworks in English', in K. AIJMER and B. ALTENBERG (eds.), 128–43.

SINCLAIR, J. M. (1991), *Corpus, Concordance, Collocation* (Oxford: Oxford University Press).

SVARTVIK, J. (1992) (ed.), *Directions in Corpus Linguistics* (Proceedings of Nobel Symposium 82) (Berlin: Mouton de Gruyter).

16

ICE and Teaching

JOHN M. KIRK

1. INTRODUCTION

The British component of the International Corpus of English (hereafter ICE-GB) makes available a new, machine-readable resource to teachers of native-speaker students and foreign learners. The purpose of this paper is to demonstrate possible uses of ICE-GB in both of these teaching contexts. Although ICE-GB is intended to form the basis of authoritative descriptions of British English for years to come, the material lends itself for teaching and for assessment work in its copious supply of fresh data from across a wide range of spoken and written registers.

As far as mother-tongue teaching is concerned, ICE-GB enables students to learn about the structure of English, to develop a descriptive and theoretical vocabulary, and to cultivate a methodology for dealing analytically with, and writing effectively about, language. Following Kirk (1994a), this paper considers the likely use of ICE-GB in terms of three central characteristics of the student approach to language study which I have developed at the Queen's University of Belfast: data, model of analysis, and the analysis itself, which correspond to higher-level issues in corpus linguistic methodology in general, and which receive special emphasis in my course.

As far as teaching foreign learners is concerned, ICE-GB represents the target language and can be used as a source of data and of teaching materials. This paper considers how it can be used in grammatical and lexical teaching, and focuses specifically on aspects of adverb and preposition differentiation, of vocabulary improvement (specifically synonymy, polysemy, lexical differentiation, and collocation), and of affixation and word structure.

2. THE QUEEN'S COURSE

Since 1983 I have taught a course originally called 'Varieties of English' and now called 'Corpus Linguistics: Analysing Spoken and Written English'. Much of this course prepares students for a project which they are required to submit as the sole piece of assessment.

An important function of corpora is their role, for students, as imitative designs and standards of data collection, of transcription types, and of a growing range of annotation and enhancement schemes (such as grammatical tags and parses). A further function is for the study through corpora of the many existing qualitative and quantitative descriptive or taxonomic analyses based on their data as well as the results and conclusions drawn from these investigations. Finally, corpora can also be used as case-studies for testing existing, often general, hypotheses about language, speakers, or texts.

When ICE-GB comes to be used, the teaching goal will be the replication of the general corpus linguistic methodology on an extremely reduced scale, in the form of a project. Students will be encouraged to use a sub-component of ICE of their own choice. In effect, they are creating their own subcorpus. They would be required to use the background information about the data in order to describe the data chosen (e.g. if spoken data, the social characteristics of the speaker and details of the speech situation).

ICE data may be interpreted by general pragmatic models of linguistic use, such as the co-operative principle, speech act theory, or politeness theory. Discourse models of production, performance, and audience design may also be readily applied. Other models might be concerned with semantic and pragmatic interpretation and distribution of specific syntactic classes (such as modal auxiliary verbs or to-infinitive clauses).

Whatever model is adopted, it should be sufficiently discriminatory to yield classificatory results in categorical, qualitative terms as well as in distributional, quantitative terms. For project work, comparisons of quantified data provide the optimum scope, but there are many possibilities for comparisons or dealing with comparisons between disparate data-sets. From their ICE-GB sub-corpus, students will be expected to generate distributional information and compare these results for the same phenomenon in other corpora, if suitable results are already available. Each student's sub-corpus is potentially unique, so that the exercise of rationalizing the differences which emerge from comparison, and of extrapolating to the language (or simply language) as a whole will remain an abiding and continuously renewing challenge. A few examples are given below. Sometimes, comparisons are possible with project data from previous years; more advanced students might wish to compare the same topic in two or more national ICE components, as they become available.

In these ways, students using ICE-GB replicate the corpus linguistics method. They come to assimilate the paradigm and, in an elementary way, they come to make it their own. The comparison of their results with others serves to validate their findings and further their experience of research methodology: if the sets of results are similar, what does this suggest? And if they are different, how can this be explained? Often the results are different, and this has as much to do with differences between ICE data used by the students as with the data used by scholarly investigators. It is thus essential that students should be able to provide a clear descriptive profile of their data because so often there is a direct contingency between the particular data and the particular results. Moreover, students learn to extrapolate from their results—the object of their investigation—to draw conclusions about some underlying issue or concept in language study (such as the universality of discourse strategies or the homogeneity of English between registers and periods).

The final stage of this work is presentation: a project has to be written up clearly, effectively, and attractively. Guidelines, including a general structural format, are issued. Writing up usually proves harder for students than they expected. An early difficulty is a clear description of their data—it is not sufficient to assume it as given. A further recurrent difficulty is the presentation of the chosen model in such terms that it can be used beneficially later in the project. Yet another is distinguishing first in their own minds, and then on paper, between results about the data and conclusions about the general subject under investigation. In the end, after the production of a spiral-bound, word-processed, laser-printed document, there is almost universal satisfaction for, behind the physical object, the results from the students' data and the wider-ranging conclusions usually reflect some genuine originality now proudly attributable to the name on the cover.

2.1. *Data*

Data—real, authentic, attested, and observed data, from continuous natural discourse or continuous, often entire, written texts—form the basis of a corpus linguistics approach. There is no place for introspectively observed sentences, or made-up sentences, not even individual observations, however circumstantially documented. For the student, ICE-GB makes available one million words of continuous running text or transcription in the form of evidence of current British English. A project sub-corpus might comprise between 5,000 and 10,000 words.

Corpora—actually no more than collections of data—have sometimes comprised one single type of text, for which there is some internal, justifiable coherence. The ICE compilers have made a considerable effort to gather a sufficiently wide range of data for their corpora to be deemed representative of mainland, educated British (but predominantly English) English as a whole. Students are stimulated by discussion of corpus design, because it makes them reflect upon the criteria for sampling representativeness and the possible number of varieties, and their attention can also be drawn to some of the discussion—notably by Schmied, 1990 and Leitner, 1992— which preceded ICE decisions about its actual data types. Since students are likely only to exploit a small part for their term paper or course credit assessment, the particular choice of data will require some defence.

Students often think naïvely about English—that language is somehow given, that everything there is to know about it is already known, even that all English is somehow the same, and that there is some kind of unchanging (or unchangeable) English common to, but inseparable from, any particular instance. The study of corpus design makes students aware of the contingency of corpus linguistics findings on the data upon which these findings are based, (*vis-à-vis* the seeming infiniteness of language use), of the inductive nature of empirical corpus research, which moves by inference and induction from the particular to the whole, and of the crucial need for qualification around such extrapolations. Students of ICE-GB will become aware that if their corpus data were changed, the results would be different.

Spoken data have to be collected by audio tape-recording, unless taken off television by video. Students will come to recognize the practical difficulties encountered by the corpus fieldworker: identifying the possible recordings (say of committee or business meetings), making the arrangements for the recordings, undertaking the recordings, securing and ensuring completion of the biodata forms and of the necessary permissions, etc. Since surreptitious recordings are generally considered unethical (if not illegal), none of the ICE components contain them. Students who undertake their own recordings should be warned against the practice, however alluringly mischievous its appeal.

The use of spoken data raises questions about types of transcription in the corpus. Is it merely orthographic? Does it have capitals and punctuation? Is there any indication of tone units or other prosodic features? Are there any phonetic features? Is further transcription—for instance, the direction of tones—necessary for a particular investigation? ICE does not have the full prosodic transcription of the London–Lund Corpus (the spoken component of the SEU (Survey of English Usage) Corpus). ICE includes capitalization as an aid to users. The golden rule for transcription appears to be 'to do as much as is required'; as far as ICE was concerned, it was felt that any researchers needing to consult the prosody could listen to the speech recordings and provide their own transcriptions.

2.2. *Total Accountability*

One of the central procedures within corpus-linguistics methodology is the provision by means of a search program of a list of every token of a particular phenomenon under investigation. This information is usually generated through concordance or corpus utility packages. For ICE, they can use any concordancer available to them, or they can use the project's dedicated retrieval software ICECUP (cf. Chapter 7 in this volume). The creation of a word count or of a full-width concordance display is often a revelation for the student. Students also come to realize, like corpus linguists, that each token of their concordanced data has to be accounted for satisfactorily, without exception or remainder. They are made to understand the principle of total accountability and are challenged to conform to it. Corpus methodology has a rigour which the student is required to negotiate. Because corpus data are finite, it is possible for students to deal with all the tokens of a well-defined data-set. Unlike random examples from casual observation or intuition, corpus data can be shown to be subject to conditioning factors, which students can identify and quantify.

At Queen's University, a final-year undergraduate module lasts for a single semester comprising twelve weeks (the equivalent of twenty-four contact hours) and three weeks assessment. It is usually possible in that time to provide instruction on automatic techniques of text analysis, especially concordancing, and to focus on any of the growing number of enhancements and annotations, such as word-class tagging or parsing, which are currently being developed by corpus linguists. Individual supervision is needed, and at Queen's University the students are entitled to three sessions.

2.3. *Models and Analyses*

Some of the early work in corpus linguistics had among its goals the discovery of distribution patterns (e.g. Coates, 1983 on the sense distributions among modal auxiliary verbs, or Stenström's 1994 work on the structure and vocabulary of discourse and their functions). Such studies show how the corpus linguistic methodology provides progressively better models of linguistic performance than previous methodologies because qualitative distinctions are quantitatively reinforced. (cf. Leech, 1992). Later work in corpus linguistics has been concerned with comparing the results of one corpus with those of another: for example, Coates's results have been compared with modal auxiliaries in Australian English (cf. Collins, 1991*a*, 1991*b*) and in Scottish and Northern Irish English (cf. Kirk, 1987, 1991). Corpus-derived results lend themselves for comparison with those from other corpora; details of existing published studies are conveniently available in the ICAME bibliography, now available on-line from the CORPORA electronic discussion group, and it makes a useful class resource. A popular measurement is a comparison of frequency distributions (e.g. frequencies per 1,000 words). The models which are made best use of by my students present a set of quantified results. Students are expected to replicate the study on their own data, to come up with a new set of statistics (usually frequencies or percentage distributions).

The use of corpus material for detailed syntactic or discourse analysis has proved popular with some students. Students these days prefer to analyse and categorize data than learn by rote a possible classificatory taxonomy. Studies using the London–Lund corpus have proved particularly useful because no students from Northern Ireland identify with the speech sampled in that corpus; besides, some expressions (e.g. *crikey* or *cor blimey*) are conspicuous for having dated, so that in the replication of an original London–Lund study, my students always expect differences. The explanation, however, might not always rest with the obvious external variables of speakers from different areas. With ICE-GB data, students anywhere will be able to make comparisons with the earlier SEU data, and of course with their own data. Teachers are likely to use an electronic corpus a lot more than a hard-copy corpus (such as the SEU), so that for many topics the primary research using ICE may not have been done by the scholars. Students might therefore come to use an existing model and either compare its results with ICE, or use the model for a comparison between ICE and their own data, so in effect comparing two new data-sets. Differences there always will be, but the final challenge to the student rests with the extrapolation of results from imperfect and uneven data into claims about the language as a seemingly undivided whole.

A powerful model of linguistic variation for projects using computer corpora is Biber's (1988) model of register and text-type variation—not least because it is itself corpus-based. Details of Biber's algorithms have never been published, making it impossible to replicate his study directly, but it is possible to get close to replication. For bright students, the negotiation with published statistics for factor analysis is a challenge.

Biber's starting-point was the range of registers and genres which make up the London–Lund Corpus of Spoken English and the Lancaster–Oslo/Bergen Corpus of Written English. It has long been maintained that medium differences (as between spoken and written language) were primarily responsible for differences in the use and distribution of structural features. While these corpora have confirmed medium differences and have also confirmed subvariation within each medium (as between monologic and dialogic speech or between fictional and non-fictional prose), they were used by Biber as evidence for the presence in texts of different patterns and frequencies of features which were functionally important and which cut across spoken and written uses. Biber showed, for instance, that texts with a narrative shared the same features with similar frequencies, whereas texts with no narrative content did the opposite but also behave similarly to each other, regardless of medium. Biber shows that the same holds true for contextual reference—where it is present to the participants and is immediately observable, or whether it has to be created and continually referred to explicitly—either way, patterns and frequencies of language occur. In some studies, Biber has worked with five such functional factors, in others with seven; in either case, he represents his findings for each factor on a graph. Because of the visibility of the results, students replicating the methodology can readily superimpose their findings on the graphs; even if the figures do not match exactly, the relative distributions do have validity so that real comparisons can be made. Because Biber's results cut across all the different types of text in the Lund and LOB corpora, and because his results are organized in terms of the small number of features associated with each factor, students need only choose one type of text but they are able to replicate each of his tests, up to the five or seven possibilities, if need be. They may also choose texts not looked at by Biber and try to fit them. One student thought that his collection of pop song lyrics should match the matter of scripted monologues; his results showed that they matched face-to-face conversations. Such studies do not form scholarly criticism of Biber's work; rather Biber's model is used as the means by which students come to do detailed linguistic analysis over a stretch of text and apply their findings in a meaningful way. Definitive studies of ICE corpora will no doubt be undertaken, but until then students have much to learn from exploiting their own subcorpora.

A third type of model lending itself immediately to student use of ICE is that developed by sociolinguists posing such questions as: do men speak differently from women? How true is it that women use tag questions and colour adjectives more often than men? Do women speak more standardly than men? Are women more polite than men? Who apologizes more or who hesitates more: men or women? Do older people speak differently from younger people? Do people switch styles from one situation to another? ICE is making available data which is not only copious but which is tagged for sex, age, and other social variables. One Lund study refuted all the standard stereotypes by showing that men not only talked more often in mixed party conversations but that when they talked they also did so for longer (cf. Altenberg, 1984). With its many quantifications, Holmes (1995) will almost certainly prove a central model for this type of analysis. More ambitious projects will, through time, be able to compare such questions across national corpora, with a view to establishing genuinely international sociolinguistic universals in the English-speaking world.

Students are required to present their chosen model before applying it to their data. It is this part of the project which most resembles traditional forms of assessment, such as examination questions that invite accounts—or critical accounts—of individual models or papers. But the project goes beyond the presentation of essentially external ideas to engage the students directly. They have each chosen the particular subject-matter, the project data, the model used for analysis, and have then undertaken the study. My role is to facilitate the undertaking of the projects.

2.4. *Results and Conclusions*

One of the distinctions which students learn from their project work is that between results and conclusions. From quantifications, results always emerge—results drawn exclusively from their particular data-set, their delimited corpus, their object of investigation. Conclusions, on the other hand, relate to abstract issues such as the universality or distributive or functional homogeneity of items or functions.

2.5. *Presentation*

The final stage of the project is presentation: a project has to be written up clearly and effectively within the general structural format suggested in the guidelines. Writing up usually proves harder to students than they expected. They gain in self-confidence when finally they see what they have achieved: the project finished, neatly word-processed, and bound together. For the first time, they experience intellectual ownership. For a few, the end proves to be the beginning, the dawn of a realization that they are capable of investigative research.

Many projects would benefit from revision, but either the opportunity is not presented or there simply is not enough time. A few projects have certainly been worthy of publication. I expect this will be true of the best on ICE-GB, too.

John M. Kirk

3. Foreign Student-Learner Teaching

The advent of ICE-GB provides a timely contribution to the growing uses of corpora and concordances in computer-aided language learning or computer-based instruction. The provision of so many spoken transcriptions of educated speech makes it eminently favourable as a resource which authentically represents the learner's target. It is also a resource which both the learner and the teacher can interact with and exploit.

Central to the use of the computer in foreign-language teaching is the concordancer—whether ICECUP or a commercial product designed with language teaching needs in mind, such as MicroConcord or the Longman Mini-Concordancer. The benefits of concordancing—inescapability, detextualization, and visibility of the data —are well-known and need not be discussed here (cf. Kirk, 1994*b*). Concordance output and the patterns which emerge from it (e.g. usually all tokens of an item or group of items and all their contexts) makes the user focus on the language rather than the 'text'. Nowadays, concordancers operate very quickly (in seconds), reliably, upon demand, and good packages allow the user to interact with the output or to input it to further processing (word-processing or databases). Once inside the word processor, the concordanced output can be enhanced with font sizes and styles, and with different arrangements of page layout; in addition blank spaces or nonsense words can be inserted for key words in the creation of teaching material.

The use of concordances in language teaching has created a new orientation in language teaching. Students are given direct access to authentic data immediately, without the intervention of teachers or other intermediaries; the approach is applicable at every level or grade. Starting with concordanced data, it is an inductive process directed towards observing similarities and differences, and then towards classification and hypothesis testing. This orientation is quite the opposite from traditional deductive approaches, which proceed from teacher-given rules to their application to data. In this new approach—labelled by Tim Johns (1991) as 'data-driven learning'—learners are discoverers of the foreign language. Through the concordancer, they investigate the language by posing queries in the form of concordance searches, so that the concordance, in providing answers, takes on the role of a special kind of informant. Specifically, the concordancer enables learners to see patterns in the target language (e.g. by lemmatized groups of items) and then to form generalizations which account for that patterning.

In a data-driven approach, according to Johns, the role of the teacher changes too; teachers become providers of resources (including equipment and software) and facilitators of the searches. They thus function in a context in which strategies for discovery can be developed; they become directors or co-ordinators of student-initiated research. In short, corpus-based data-driven learning re-evaluates the place of vocabulary and grammar in language-learning and language-teaching. Goals are needed more than ever, so that teachers need to have strategies into which the use of ICE-GB and its exploitation by a concordancer will fit. At the same time, the

234

teacher is at liberty to use the corpus as a copious supply of good examples for incorporation into any part of the syllabus.

4. TARGET LANGUAGE TEACHING

For teaching purposes, concordanced ICE-GB output provides fresh authentic data, particularly of the spoken language. Concordanced output is a highly illustrative medium, with high visibility, yielding no shortage of good examples of contexts in which the selected items operate. Because familiarity is now widespread, examples for mere examples' sake need not detain us here. Using concordances, teachers can demonstrate to students how each example listed in the concordance works, how items as a whole or even how the exponence of more abstract phenomena operate (how do people express apologies, or give and receive thanks, or deal with unwanted impositions, and so on?). Alternatively, concordances can be used to test the student's existing knowledge about the operation or functioning of items. In this way, the limits of student knowledge will soon emerge. By effective monitoring of these techniques, teachers can begin to monitor student's actual learning process (Philip Shaw, personal communication).

A common problem with advanced learners is vocabulary improvement (cf. papers in Milton and Tong, 1992; Pemberton and Tsang, 1993; Flowerdew and Tong, 1994; and the papers at the Symposium on Learner Corpora, Louvain-La-Neuve, January 1995). ICE-GB will readily generate material on individual lexical and grammatical items, on their synonyms, and on collocations. ICE-GB is applicable at any level: for core syllabus vocabulary, for the development of phrases and idioms; for advanced collocations; and for specialized text or field uses (e.g. in scientific discourse or newspaper reporting). Like the Collins COBUILD project, ICE, too, has the potential (if suitable arrangements are made) for publishing reference grammars (Greenbaum's *Oxford English Grammar* (1996) is an example), course books, guides to individual grammatical topics, and as a lexicographical resource. ICE is fully automated, and it is conceivable that in due course teachers and students will be able to log on directly to the corpus data for searching and outputting and for on-line retrieval. Unlike other projects, ICE not only has the potential of producing such material for each of its national corpora but also for uniting it into one global variety of truly international English.

Three main uses of concordances for vocabulary improvement are for gap-and-filler exercises, for substitution exercises, and for lexical enhancement, as in the identification of individual senses in polysemic words. ICE-GB represents one of the finest current sources of British English for these teaching purposes; in due course, other national varieties will become available. Their mere generation as evidence is not the only purpose behind concordances; since the arrival of user-friendly packages like OUP's MicroConcord, language teachers are now skilled at blanking out the concordanced (or KWIC) item and immediately creating a set of gapped exercises out of the remaining material. The purpose of such exercises is to get the student to re-insert the missing item into the right slot (or possibly group of slots, if identical items are grouped together). An alternative, more challenging version of the same exercise would be the underlining of whatever collocations helped determine the choice: was it the context before or after the missing item, or what?

Considered more widely, ICE-GB provides copious material for testing synonymy, easily confused words, and false friends across a wide range of semantic areas. How, for instance, are verbs like *realize* and *recognize* distinguished? Or *realize* and *understand*? Or the nouns *difficulty*, *dilemma*, and *predicament*? Or the participial adjectives *frightened* and *afraid*? Lemmatized concordances from ICE could be generated to provide, with the search word blanked out, a ready-made gap-and-filler exercise. ICE also provides copious material for testing similarly behaving grammatical items, such as how the general temporal adverbs *still*, *yet*, and *already* differ. The search words could yet again be blanked and the lines reordered for an effective gap-and-filler exercise. Further grammatical questions could be tested: are any stative verbs marked for continuous aspect? In what texts do passives occur and are there patterns to agent deletion? ICE-GB also provides evidence for collocations (Are there patterns to the co-occurrences with vague quantifiers like *heaps of* and *loads of*? What significance can be attached to repetitions (such as *yes, yes* or *no, no* or even *yes, yes, yes* or *no, no, no*?), for connotations (do adverbs like *utterly* or participial adjectives like *fixed* carry negative overtones?), and for interlingual false friends (does *actually* in English behave like its cognate form in other European languages or is it quite different?).

A different use of ICE-GB for a learning strategy would be in the development of collocations of specific words, such as *develop, develops, developed, developing, development*, etc., particularly if a lemmatized search is first undertaken, so that all possible forms of a word are used in the exercises. Who or what *develops*? Who or what *is developed*? With what words does *develop* regularly collocate? Do these collocations have any striking semantic features? Are there senses of the verb *develop* not covered by the nominalization *development* or vice versa?

A further use of ICE-GB for strategies of vocabulary improvement would be to compare the concordanced output with the dictionary entry for a polysemic, multifunctional word so that each token becomes associated with a particular dictionary sense. The task for the student is to discover the distribution of the dictionary senses in the corpus and in particular those senses not evidenced in the corpus. As most advanced learner dictionaries are now based on corpus data, it may be less of a question whether the dictionary lists each use of an item as evidenced in ICE-GB but rather which senses of the word listed in the dictionary are not evidenced in the ICE-GB data. Examples might be words like *account, favour, spite*, or *view*, which are members of different speech classes, or two-word verbs such as *go in* or *go on*, which have many senses depending on the types of subject and complementation.

236

Other obvious areas where ICE-GB could be applied would be in the study of words with specific affixal or derivational structures, drawing attention to the productivity of the vocabulary and the semantics of frequent affixes. ICE-GB can also be searched for more complex words such as *-ed* participles used as general adjectives and beginning, for instance, with *re-* or *un-*. ICE may therefore prove to the teacher to be particularly useful for identifying national trends in contemporary patterns of word formation.

I have suggested that ICE-GB provides for the foreign language teacher authentic target language data which can readily be applied to particular learning goals by manipulating concordance output. The speed of present-generation concordancers makes ICE-GB a classroom resource; on its basis, queries are immediately answerable. As this chapter shows, the learning strategy is not restricted to closed category items but can be applied just as readily to polysemy, synonymy, and collocations in the development of vocabulary. Learning strategies can be devised around individual lexical items and word-class tags, either separately or in groups or in combinations with each other. As classroom concordancing and data-driven learning continue to develop, ICE is assured a central role as a major witness of the use of the language.

References

ALTENBERG, B. (1984), 'Lexical and Sex-related Differences in Spoken English', in H. RINGBOM and M. RISSANEN (eds.), *Proceedings from the Second Nordic Conference for English Studies, Hanasaari/Hanaholmen, 19–21 May 1983*, 279–98 (Abo: Publications of the Research Institute of the Abo Akademi Foundation, no. 2).

BIBER, D. (1988), *Variation across Speech and Writing* (Cambridge: Cambridge University Press).

COATES, J. (1983), *The Semantics of the Modal Auxiliaries* (London: Croom Helm).

COLLINS, P. (1991a), 'The Modals of Obligation and Necessity in Australian English', in K. AIJMER and B. ALTENBERG (eds.), *English Corpus Linguistics: Papers in Honour of Jan Svartvik*, 145–65 (London: Longman).

—— (1991b), 'Will and Shall in Australian English', in S. JOHANSSON and A.-B. STENSTRÖM (eds.), *English Computer Corpora: Selected Papers and Research Guide*, 181–99 (Berlin: Mouton de Gruyter).

FLOWERDEW, L. and TONG, K. K. (1994), *Entering Text* (Hong Kong: Language Centre, Hong Kong University of Science and Technology).

GREENBAUM, S. (1996), *The Oxford English Grammar* (Oxford: Oxford University Press).

HOLMES, J. (1995), *Women, Men and Politeness* (London: Longman).

JOHNS, T. (1991), 'From Printout to Handout: Grammar and Vocabulary Teaching in the Context of Data-driven Learning', in T. JOHNS and P. KING (eds.), *Classroom Concordancing*, 27–45 (Centre for English Language Studies, University of Birmingham).

KIRK, J. M. (1987), 'The Heteronomy of Scots with Standard English', in C. MACAFEE and I. MACLEOD (eds.), *The Nuttis Schell: Essays on the Scots Language Presented to Professor A. J. AITKEN*, 166–81 (Aberdeen: Aberdeen University Press).

—— (1991), 'Modal Verbs and the Dialectologist', paper presented at the Annual Meeting of the American Dialect Society, San Francisco.

—— (1994*a*), 'Teaching and Language Corpora: The Queen's Approach', in A. WILSON and A. MCENERY (eds.), *Teaching and Language Corpora*, 29–51 (University of Lancaster Department of Modern English Language and Linguistics Technical Reports).

—— (1994*b*), 'Corpus—Concordance—Database—VARBRUL', *Literary and Linguistic Computing*, 9/4: 259–66.

LEECH, G. (1992), 'Corpora and Theories of Linguistic Performance', in J. SVARTVIK (ed.), *Directions in Corpus Linguistics: Proceedings of Nobel Symposium 82, Stockholm, 4–8 August 1991*, 105–22, Trends in Linguistics, Studies and Monographs no. 65 (Berlin: Mouton de Gruyter).

LEITNER, G. (1992), 'International Corpus of English: Corpus Design—Problems and Suggested Solutions', in G. LEITNER, (ed.), *New Directions in English Language Corpora: Methodology, Results, Software Developments*, 33–64 (Berlin: Mouton de Gruyter).

MILTON, J. and TONG, K. S. T. (1992), *Test Analysis in Computer Assisted Language Learning* (Hong Kong: Hong Kong University of Science and Technology and City Polytechnic of Hong Kong).

PEMBERTON, R. and TSANG, E. S. C. (1993), *Studies in Lexis: Working Papers from a Seminar* (Hong Kong: Hong Kong University of Science and Technology).

SCHMIED, J. (1990), 'Corpus Linguistics and Non-Native Varieties of English', in *World Englishes*, 9: 255–68.

STENSTRÖM, A.-B. (1994), *Introduction to Spoken Interaction* (London: Longman).

17

The Sociolinguistics of English in Nigeria and the ICE Project

AYO BANJO

1. ENGLISH AS A MODERNIZING AGENT

The amalgamation in 1914 of the Northern and Southern Protectorates to form the Colony and Protectorates of Nigeria can be taken as marking the first step in the modernization process of Nigeria, for the aim of amalgamation was to render the territory more amenable to development—initially, to be sure, for the benefit of the colonizing power. But the process of exploitation inevitably benefited sections of the local populace as well, giving them more economic power, and exposing them to precisely those modern ideas that were to help them, after barely fifty years, to terminate the colonial status of the country.

It is possible to see modernization process as taking place simultaneously in two interlocking domains, namely the public and the private. The English language —and often the literacy skills of that language—plays a prominent role in both domains.

In the public domain, we can identify politics, administration, the judiciary, education, commerce, the media, and the arts. The role of English in Nigerian politics tends to be subsumed under the role of the language in other sub-domains—notably administration and the media. But true as it may be that politics does find expression in these two other areas, there are other aspects of the use of English in politics which deserve independent examination.

Before 1960 Nigerian politics had mainly been concerned with the struggle for independence. The advent of party politics from 1950 onwards had introduced a new dimension to the use of English in Nigeria. Of the three regions, the North alone had a *lingua franca* in the Hausa language. The West was almost linguistically homogeneous, with the majority of the citizens speaking Yoruba as a first or second language. But there were, in addition, important languages in the eastern part of the region. Similarly in the East, the majority of the citizens were Igbo-speaking, with other languages spoken in the southern and south-eastern parts of the Region. In the south, therefore, English was, from the beginning, the language of politics. But since, later on, all politicians had to compete for power at the centre and therefore campaign in areas outside their own regions, English necessarily became the national language of politics. The scope thus opened to Nigerianisms in the English language is obvious, as are the opportunities for code-switch and language-mixing. At the same time, the need for a national language was indicated.

By the same token, the official language of administration, of the judiciary, and of international commerce is English in the absence of a common indigenous language. Here, more than in the political sub-domain, what is called for is an internationally intelligible variety of English, and in any case, English had been entrenched here since the colonial period. Generally speaking, as Adesanoye (1973) has found in the case of the judiciary, performance can be correlated with level of education. Adesanoye's method is essentially an error-analysis one, in which the written performance of the various officers of the nation's judiciary is contrasted with standard (British) written English in a comparable field. Deviations from this model are noted, and Adesanoye discovers that his data reveal a cline of density of deviations which varies from the highest in respect of the most modestly educated, to the lowest in respect of the most highly educated. The field represented by the data makes the incidence of Nigerianisms virtually impossible, and the performance of the most highly educated participants is generally taken as illustrating the standard variety of technical written English in Nigeria. As for the media and the literary Arts, English is the predominant language, and these sub-domains do lend themselves to the processes of nativization of the language.

All the foregoing reflects the use of English in the modernization process in Nigeria in the public domain. But in the absence of an endoglossic *lingua franca*, English is also widely used in the private domain in inter-personal communication, in the writing of personal letters (English being often preferred in letter-writing even when the writer and his addressee are literate in a common indigenous language), and as the language of personal diaries. As is well-known, a number of Nigerians have also distinguished themselves in the use of English for creative writing. All this has implications for language planning, a matter that came to the fore soon after the country's attainment of independence but in which so far little headway has been made.

2. ENGLISH IN LANGUAGE PLANNING

An ideal approach to language planning in Nigeria would seek to allocate the available languages for the maximum efficiency of the country and of its citizens. Such an approach has proved very hard because of the difficulty of choosing a national language. Ideally, Nigerians would prefer such a language to be endoglossic, but this is at the moment not feasible because of the emotional nature of the subject. The speakers of none of the three major languages—Hausa, Igbo, and Yoruba—are at the moment prepared to concede the status of national language to either of the others. Each of these major languages has no less than ten million speakers, with Hausa having the highest number, followed by Yoruba, but none of them is spoken by a clear majority of Nigerians either as mother tongue or second language. On the other hand, even if English were to be chosen, it would be found to be spoken in any form at the moment by perhaps just about 20 per cent of the population. A more deliberate effort would therefore be required to promote the learning of the language throughout the country, although even now, it would be true to say that, thanks to the spread of education, English is probably the fastest-growing language in the country. Inevitably, the language has been acquiring a number of characteristics of its own in the country, and the notion that it is a totally foreign language is being increasingly questioned.

Still, most people would prefer a language that has grown completely out of the soil, and even Nigerian Pidgin, which is more widely spoken and understood than English, suffers, as it were, from the English connection in this regard. In the circumstances, it has not been possible to make a direct approach to language planning in Nigeria. Meanwhile, English continues to occupy a strategic position in the national life because it is in the interest of the ruling élite (cf. Cooper, 1989), which is not disposed to make any concessions on the choice of an indigenous language.

There have, therefore, to date been only two cautious attempts at language planning in Nigeria, both of them in the public domain. The first was the national language policy in education, first legislated in 1977 and revised in 1981, by which English was to be taught as a subject from the first day of the primary school and then was to become the medium of instruction from the fourth year onwards. This confirmed the position of English as the language of literacy and of education in the country, for pupils were expected to be literate by the end of their primary school career, and educated by the end of their secondary school career. Interestingly, one of the indicators most readily pointed to in the charge of falling standards in education generally is the falling standard in English, particularly written English, which has tended to be cultivated to the exclusion of spoken English. As for the indigenous languages, anyone literate in any of them but illiterate in English is hardly regarded as literate at all, and those erudite in any of them, or even in Arabic, without being literate in English, tend to be at best grudgingly regarded as being educated.

If this policy were to be faithfully implemented in the context of the prevailing universal primary education—and, even more particularly, of the proposed free education for the first nine years of every pupil's education—the result, ultimately, would be the emergence of English as the country's effective *lingua franca*—at worst perhaps one of two *lingua francas*—as well as official language. But unfortunately, there are few indications that the policy is being seriously pursued. Nevertheless, it is the current policy, and it has profound implications for the teaching of English at all three levels of Nigerian education.

The other piece of legislation is to be found in the country's constitution, which confers the status of official language of business at the federal legislature on the nation's three major languages—Hausa, Igbo, and Yoruba—in addition to English. The state legislatures were, at the same time, expected to take their cue from the federal legislature. Since the legislatures can be regarded as Nigeria's engines of modernization, it can be assumed that the intention of this piece of legislation was to enable the nation's three major languages to participate with English in the modernization process, as a prelude, most people would hope, to one of them taking over from English ultimately as the national language and *lingua franca*. Unfortunately, the political climate in the country since this provision was first made in the constitution in 1979 has made it impossible for it to be implemented. The result is that, officially, English remains the unchallenged language of modernization, though at other levels, the development of the indigenous languages to enable them to cope with modern demands has continued. For example, tertiary books have been written in Yoruba by Bamgbose (1990), Olatunji (1988), and Owolabi (1989).

The use of English in the private domain in Nigeria arises partly from the fact that there is no endoglossic *lingua franca* to serve the needs of the citizens of a country where as many as 400 languages are spoken, and partly from the personal development that the use of English offers the individual. The inter-personal use of English in the country is conditioned by a number of factors. Nigerian English-speaking bilinguals do have from time to time to interact with other bilinguals with whom they do not share the same mother tongue. In such circumstances, the use of English is indicated, though in some cases, Pidgin, if available to both interlocutors, may be used. But even with bilinguals who do share the same mother tongue, the formality of an occasion would dictate the use of English. Marriage across ethnic boundaries also results in the use of English as the language of some homes, so that the children have English as their first language chronologically before, if ever, learning to speak the language of either or both of the parents, and retain it as the dominant language for the rest of their lives.

With bilinguals who do share the same mother tongue, the choice of language is determined by the variable factors of field, mode, and tenor (cf. Enkvist *et al.*, 1964). Interaction in the scientific field, and in areas of modernity generally, would almost certainly call for the use of English—interspersed, perhaps, with code-switching and language-mixing—even between such bilingual interlocutors. Similarly, even when such bilinguals are able to interact orally in the mother tongue on even the most non-technical subjects, the moment the interaction takes place in writing, English is automatically chosen. Finally, tenor also plays a part in the choice of English, used, as it often is, by a superior-feeling interlocutor to distance him or herself from a perceived inferior one, or by both interlocutors because they are unsure of their relative status or age. Among Yoruba bilinguals, for instance, the use of English in the latter situation helps to solve the problem of having to decide whether to use the plural second person pronoun of respect, or the singular of familiarity.

---

3. A MODEL OF ENGLISH IN NIGERIAN EDUCATION

Since, for the great majority of Nigerians, the school provides the medium for the acquisition of English, with varying degrees of outside reinforcement, it follows that the effective use of the language in both the public and private domains depends ultimately on the efficiency of teaching the language within the educational system. The realization of this fact must, indeed, have prompted the government in 1977 and 1981 to introduce the national policy on language in education.

Given the increasing load that English has to carry as any country's second language (cf. Platt *et al.*, 1984: 2) and the perceived deterioration in the performance of candidates in the school examinations in English, a point was soon reached in Nigeria, in the mid-1960s, when attention was turned to the possible use of an endonormative model for the teaching of the language within the nation's educational system. Grieve (1966) was the first to put forward this novel idea, and was immediately supported by Walsh (1967), among others. But a number of other scholars, notably Salami (1968), objected to the idea. Grieve's argument had been based generally on the position of English as a second, rather than foreign, language in the country, but more immediately on deteriorating levels of performance by candidates in the English paper of the School Certificate examinations. Salami's objections, on the other hand, related to the lack of a formal description of the new standard being proposed. The idea of such a standard has now been generally accepted, but the adoption is far from being an easy one. The central problem is that even though individuals may have subjective ideas about what constitutes standard Nigerian English, a comprehensive formal description of such a variety is not yet available. Such a formal description is, in turn, impossible without an agreement as to a definition of the individuals who speak this standard variety. This, in turn, has led to a lively interest in the varieties of English spoken and written in the country and in the correlation of each variety with sociological categories. This area has been increasingly researched in recent years (cf. Banjo, 1971, 1993; Jibril, 1986; Jowitt, 1991; Bamgbose, 1992). The consensus at present is that three social dialects of English are identifiable in Nigeria (leaving aside a variety of English spoken as mother tongue by a small group of Nigerians) loosely correlated with educational attainment. There is, of course, additionally, the geographical dimension to be taken into consideration, as Jibril's work has shown.

If the grammar of Standard Nigerian English is to be written, reliable informants have to be identified, and since the standard variety must also be the educated variety, it seems justifiable to look for the informants among people with at least a secondary education. Banjo (1971, 1993) has suggested that the standard variety must satisfy two conditions based on the needs analysis of the language in the country: namely, social acceptability and international intelligibility. Tiffen (1974), Obanya *et al.* (1979), and Ekong (1980) have tested potential informants for one or the other of these two requirements and, among other findings, have established that there is a variety of Nigerian spoken English which is as efficient as RP, strictly in terms of international intelligibility. A similar case for written Nigerian English has been rather more easily made by Adesanoye (1973).

However, it must be conceded that all the investigations carried out so far constitute little more than pilot studies, given the narrow range of sampling (although this is sometimes supplemented with careful introspection), and extrapolations have therefore to be cautiously made. Although there is greater unanimity today than thirty years ago about the necessity for an endonormative model of English, particularly for pedagogical purposes, there is still lingering scepticism about the adoption of such a model in the absence of a clear definition. ICE offers an ideal setting for confirming or rejecting previous findings, as well as a more scientific approach to data collection, storage, retrieval, and analysis. Besides, it provides a framework and a database within which future studies of Nigerian English in all its ramifications can be pursued on a strictly scientific basis.

4. ICE IN THE NIGERIAN CONTEXT

'The principal idea of ICE', as Schmied (1995) has noted,

is to compile machine-readable corpora of English from the United Kingdom, the USA, Jamaica, Canada, Australia, New Zealand, Hong Kong, the Philippines, Singapore, India, Nigeria, countries in East Africa and possibly from other countries. Each national corpus will be composed of 250 spoken and 250 written texts of approximately 2,000 words each, and will thus amount to one million words.

Such a representative corpus—for the text categories aim at comprehensiveness—can be expected to be put to various uses to solve various problems in the participating countries, but Greenbaum (1988) summarized the aims at the beginning as being:

(1) to sample national varieties from other countries where English is the first language, for example Canada and Australia; (2) to sample national varieties from countries where English is an official additional language, for example India and Nigeria; and (3) to include spoken and manuscript English as well as printed English.

These aims are well suited to the present preoccupations of Nigerian linguists in English studies, for they provide a way for them to monitor what is going on both in the first-language countries, with which Nigeria has to continue to be in communion, and also in countries in a similar situation to Nigeria, with which communication is also important but which, additionally, provide new perspectives on the phenomenon of nativization. Greenbaum's third aim is also very relevant to the Nigerian situation because, as already noted, English is nationally used in Nigeria in the spoken and written modes in the public and private domains. Comparability with other national corpora is ensured by the use of a common tagset (see Greenbaum, 1993; Greenbaum and Ni Yibin, 1994).

Current research on the English language in Nigeria tends to emphasize varieties differentiation and the definition of a standard, and it is easy to see how these efforts can be greatly facilitated by ICE. Published studies in varieties differentiation have already been referred to above, but as already indicated, these studies, to the extent that they are empirical, have been conducted on too small a scale to make generalizations valid. The ICE corpus would make such generalizations more reliable.

As for the identification and description of a standard variety, most of the works cited above have also been concerned with these, and a solution to the question of appropriate informants has been attempted, as we have seen, through tests of social acceptability and international intelligibility. ICE provides a neater way of going about the investigation through the use of a fairly large number of text categories and the provision of the ICE Bibliographical and Biographical Data sheet. The correlation of the standard with sociological categories would thus be enhanced. Above all, ICE, being machine-oriented, would constitute a vast improvement on present methods, once the hardware and software become available.

ICE-Nigeria is at the very initial stage, and therefore all that can be said about it at present is programmatic. At the time of writing, four centres for the project are being set up: in Lagos, where the co-ordination of the entire project will also take place, Ibadan (in the west), Kano (in the north), and Nsukka (in the east). In this way, the entire country, which is a vast one of about 80 million people, will be more conveniently covered, and regional variations can be more easily observed. In addition, an advisory committee for the project has been established.

Studies emanating from the corpus are expected to be applied in two areas: first, in language planning, and secondly, in English language teaching, particularly in the provision of reliable endonormative grammars and dictionaries. The former would allow us to define more clearly the role of the English language in the national life and the regional differences in the emphasis placed on the language as well as relative proficiency in it. The second is expected to lay to rest finally the objections commonly made to the use in schools of an endonormative model. Lexical and collocational peculiarities in that standard variety would feature in a possible scholarly dictionary of Nigerian English usage. Other dictionaries aimed at the various levels of the educational system are also expected to be produced, as are various pedagogical grammars.

As Nigeria is starting later than the other participating countries, a number of issues will have to be resolved. For purposes of comparison, it is important that the corpora should cover the same period, the suggested one being 1990 to 1994. To a large extent, the Nigerian team will still be able to gather written and spoken (recorded) texts covering this period, but unfortunately, live performances will have to fall outside the agreed period, although a difference of two or three years will not be significant. At any rate, the Nigerian corpus would presumably want to exceed one million words in an attempt to obtain more data. The ICE corpus itself will presumably have to be updated periodically in the future, and ICE-Nigeria would participate in such updating, but perhaps what many Nigerian participants would like to see developing is a comprehensive project like the Survey of English Usage directed by Greenbaum. The current ICE project can serve as a nucleus of that bigger project.

5. Conclusion

A sociolinguistic study of the English language in Nigeria indicates that the literacy skills of the language have always been more highly prized than the oracy skills. A large proportion of books read in Nigeria are imported from other English-speaking countries, notably Britain and the USA. At the same time, publishing activity within the country itself has greatly increased in the last decade, and some of these publications are also read in other parts of the world. International intelligibility of Nigerian written English is therefore of great importance. The ICE project will enable Nigerians and the rest of the world to see in exactly what ways Nigerian written English differs from other national standards of written English. With regard to lexis, for example, international scholarly dictionaries would thus be able to reflect distinctly Nigerian usage which it would be helpful for users of English in other parts of the world to know about. Görlach (1989) has discussed the feature of heteronymy in international English, and it would be useful to know the extent to which Nigeria has already been contributing to this phenomenon. This is all the more important in view of the growing prominence of Nigerian creative writers of English expression.

Moreover, as English is the language of scholarship in Nigeria, the cultivation of an internationally intelligible variety of written English in Nigeria is important throughout the educational system. ICE will help in this respect by making it possible for teaching materials to be based on data gathered and analysed on strictly scientific principles.

The other more general role of English is in the modernization process, and here, attention has to be paid to both written and spoken English. Improved communication systems—air travel, radio and cable or satellite television—mean that more and more Nigerians are now exposed to varieties of spoken English from other parts of the world while at the same time Nigerian spoken English is also increasingly heard in other parts of the world. Above all, debates and discussions over the modernization process take place almost exclusively in English, in spite of recent attempts to bring the three major languages—Hausa, Igbo, and Yoruba—into this role. Thus the need for an internationally intelligible Nigerian variety of spoken English also arises; but such a variety also has to be socially acceptable, while regional differences have to be tolerated. It is important to remember that English plays a strong unifying role internally in the country, as a *lingua franca* in diglossic relation to Nigerian Pidgin, and it is precisely this role that has given the language a distinctly Nigerian character. In the solution of all these problems, the ICE project is expected to provide a reliable database, with the analyses having, again, a salutary backwash effect on all three tiers of the educational system. Hopefully, Nigerian linguists will thus be able to play a more dynamic role in solving the language problems of the country.

REFERENCES

ADESANOYE, F. (1973), 'A Study of Varieties of Written English in Nigeria', Ph.D. thesis (Ibadan).

BAMGBOSE, A. (1990), *Fonólójì àti Gírámà Yoruba* (Ibadan: University Press Ltd.).

—— (1992), 'Standard Nigerian English: Issues of Identification', in B. KACHRU (ed.), *The Other Tongue: English Across Cultures* (Urbana: University of Illinois Press), 99–111.

BANJO, A. (1971), 'Towards a Definition of "Standard Nigerian Spoken English"', *Actes du 8me Congres International de Linguistique Africaine* (Abidjan), 161–75.

—— (1993), 'An Endonormative Model for the Teaching of the English Language in Nigeria', *International Journal of Applied Linguistics*, 3/2: 261–75.

COOPER, R. L. (1989), *Language Planning and Social Change* (Cambridge: Cambridge University Press).

EKONG, P. A. (1980), 'Investigation Into the Intelligibility of a Possible Standard Model for Nigerian Spoken English', *Journal of Language Arts and Communication*, 1/1: 1–11.

ENKVIST, N., SPENCER, J., and GREGORY, M. (1964), *Linguistics and Style* (London: Oxford University Press).

GÖRLACH, M. (1989), 'Heteronymy in International English' (mimeo).

GREENBAUM, S. (1988), 'A Proposal for an International Computerized Corpus of English', *World Englishes*, 7/3: 315.

—— (1993), 'The Tagset for the International Corpus of English', in C. SOUTER and E. ATWELL (eds.), *Corpus-Based Computational Linguistics*, 11–24 (Amsterdam: Rodopi).

—— and YIBIN, N. (1994), 'Tagging the British ICE Corpus: English Word Classes', in N. OOSTDIJK and P. DE HAAN (eds.), *Corpus-Based Research into Language*, 33–45 (Amsterdam: Rodopi).

GRIEVE, D. G. (1996), *English Language Examining* (Lagos: West African Examinations Council).

JIBRIL, M. (1986), 'Sociolinguistic Variation in Nigerian English', *English World Wide*, 7/1: 47–74.

JOWITT, D. (1991), *Nigerian English Usage: An Introduction*. (Lagos: Longman).

OBANYA, P., DADA, A., and ODERINDE, T. (1979), 'An Empirical Study of the Acceptability of Four Nigerian Accents of Spoken English in Nigeria', in E. UBAHAKWE (ed.), *Varieties and Functions of English in Nigeria* (Lagos: African Universities Press), 242–56.

OLATUNJI, O. (1988), *Yoruba: A Language in Transition: Ìdàgbàsókè Èkó Ìmò ìjìnlè Yoruba* (J. F. ODUNJO Memorial Lectures).

OWOLABI, K. (1989), *Ìjìnlè Ìtúpalè Èdè Yoruba (1) Fonétíkì àti Fonólójì* (Ibadan: Onibonoje Press).

PLATT, J., WEBER, H., and Ho, M. L. (1984), *The New Englishes* (London: Routledge).

SALAMI, A. (1968), 'Defining a Standard Nigerian English', *Journal of the Nigeria English Studies Association*, 2/2: 99–106.

SCHMIED, J. (1995), 'National Standards and the International Corpus of English', in BAMGBOSE, A., BANJO, A., and THOMAS, A. (eds.), *New Englishes: A West African Perspective*, 337–48 (Ibadan: Mosuro).

TIFFEN, B. (1974), 'The Intelligibility of Nigerian English', Ph.D. thesis (London).

WALSH, N. G. (1967), 'Distinguishing Types and Varieties of English in Nigeria', *Journal of the Nigeria English Studies Association*, 2: 3–15.

18

Why a Fiji Corpus?

JAN TENT and FRANCE MUGLER

The linguistic situation in Fiji is unique and complex. Of the three major languages spoken in Fiji (Fijian, Fiji Hindi, and English[1]) English is the first language of only a tiny section of the population. Yet its influence on the lives of Fiji's people is very significant. Over the last 200 years, its role has evolved from being merely a source language for foreign loanwords to the language of government, education, and commerce. In no other South Pacific nation is English used in so many domains as it is in Fiji. This paper presents a profile of the development and status of Fiji English, and argues for its inclusion in ICE.

1. HISTORICAL BACKGROUND

The history of English in Fiji can be divided into six distinct periods.

1.1. *Pre-European Contact*

The history begins roughly 30 or 40 years before the arrival of the first European settlers in about 1805. From Cook's time, and perhaps before, a number of English words found their way into Fijian, introduced by the Tongans, who had well-established trade relations with the Fijians; e.g. *kapa* 'sheet metal' < 'copper', *kote* < 'coat', and *pusi* (now *vusi*), 'cat' < 'pussy' (Geraghty, 1989: 380 and personal communication).[2]

1.2. *Beachcombers and Traders in Sandalwood and* Bêche-de-mer

The first Europeans to settle in Fiji were mainly deserters and marooned sailors who became beachcombers. However, their impact on the linguistic situation was negligible, as they adopted the Fijian way of life and learned Fijian. Indeed, they often acted as interpreters and intermediaries between ships' captains and the Fijian chiefs under whose protection they lived (Derrick, 1950: 41). Fijians did not learn English, with the notable exception of Cokānauto (more commonly known as Phillips to the English), a chief of Rewa who learned to speak English reasonably well (Derrick, 1950: 96).

European contact steadily increased in the first three decades of the century, with the subsequent arrival of sandalwood and *bêche-de-mer* traders, and regular visits by whaling ships. Loans from English that most likely date from this era include *vinivō* 'dress' < 'pinafore', *tapako* < 'tobacco', *kaloko* < 'clock', *bisikete* < 'biscuit', *vōkete* < 'bucket', and *sēlō* < 'sail ho!' (Geraghty, 1989: 380).

1.3. *Methodist Missionaries*

The second influx of Europeans had a much greater impact. In 1835 Methodist missionaries arrived, with specific instructions to learn Fijian, devise an orthography, and ultimately publish the scriptures in Fijian. They established churches and schools in which Fijian was the medium of instruction. Many of the English borrowings from this period are associated with religion and education: *same* < 'psalm', *Kosipeli* < 'gospel', *pepa* < 'paper', *peni* < 'pen', *fika* 'arithmetic' < 'figure' (Geraghty, 1989: 383–4).

1.4. *Cession*

In 1874 the leading Fijian chiefs ceded Fiji to Great Britain. Fijian was generally the medium of communication in the colonial administration, and a new category of English loanwords entered the language, relating to government and administration: *sitaba* < 'stamp', *lawa* < 'law', *laiseni* < 'licence', and *kōvana* < 'governor' (Geraghty, 1989: 388).

1.5. *Catholic Mission Schools*

The situation changed dramatically when, in 1894, the Marist Brothers opened a school near Levuka, on the island of Ovalau (the main European settlement at that time), and introduced the formal teaching of English to Fijians. Such was the success of the school that it was swamped with Methodists wanting to learn English. The fight for Fijian souls had now entered the classroom, with English as its principal weapon (Geraghty, 1984: 38). In 1899 the Methodist senate resolved to introduce English into their school curriculum as well (Macnaught, 1975: 173). Several provincial government schools were established soon after, and they also included English as part of their curriculum. In 1906 the Queen Victoria School was opened, and its pupils (mainly sons of prominent Fijian chiefs) received their lessons entirely in English (Siegel, 1989: 51).

From 1876 to 1916 labourers were brought to Fiji from India under the indenture system to work on sugar-cane plantations, and their presence added to the richness and complexity of the country's linguistic and cultural make-up. The 1909 Education Commission—despite strong opposition from most Europeans—recommended that English be taught as a foreign language in Indian and Fijian schools. However, this policy was not implemented until the 1930s.

Few Indians received any formal education until the end of indenture in the 1920s, when they established their own schools. The record of the colonial government with respect to education is clear from the 1911 census rates for literacy in any language: 9.4 per cent for Indians compared with 52.8 per cent for Fijians and 86.5 per cent for Europeans (Gillion, 1962: 160). English played a prominent role in Indian schools, since indentured labourers and their descendants saw the learning of English as their only means of economic and professional advancement. Fijians, on the other hand, were encouraged by the paternalistic colonial government to remain sheltered from modern life in their villages, and did not, therefore, feel as much of a need to learn English. The fact that missionaries almost always preferred to evangelize in Fijian rather than English also contributed to this.

Until the 1930s Fijian was still almost exclusively used as the language of instruction in Fijian schools, and as the language of government and for communications between the government and the people. The British government required its officials to learn Fijian (and after 1928, either Fijian or Hindi), and a gratuity was given if both languages were learned (Siegel, 1989: 50). Although English speakers had been in Fiji for some 120 years, the use of English was still almost entirely restricted to Europeans. The principal medium of communication during this period remained Fijian or Hindi.

1.6. *The New Zealand Education System*

In the 1930s there was a reversal in the colonial administration's policy when the New Zealand education authorities were given the responsibility for education in Fiji (Geraghty, 1989: 390). One of the main reasons for this change was the colonial authorities' belief that a *lingua franca* was needed to allow Fijians and Indo-Fijians to live together harmoniously. Cyril Cato, a prominent educator at the time, asserted: 'In a country where many races and languages mingle as they do in Fiji, a common language is essential. Fijian can never become this, for its poverty of ideas and expressions is such that it cannot meet the modern demands upon such a language.' (cited in Geraghty, 1984: 41). It was during this time that many schools started insisting that only English be used at school, whilst strictly forbidding the use of the vernaculars. The teaching and learning of English was henceforth heavily promoted, so much so that English became the second language for the majority of Fiji citizens.

2. THE CURRENT ROLE OF ENGLISH IN FIJI

English in Fiji is a *de facto* official language, the major language of government, administration, the courts, and business; the major, sometimes the only, medium of instruction in the education system; and an important *lingua franca* among people with different first languages.

Although the 1990 Constitution makes no mention of language, the provisions of the 1970 Constitution are still followed, in so far as, for instance, the official language of parliament is English, although members of both houses may address the chamber in Fijian or Hindi. Fijian and Hindi can also be used in the courts, with interpreters being provided when needed. Although English is also used in government departments and official government correspondence, education, and commerce, its use is far greater in written than in oral communication. Much of the everyday work in either government or business circles is conducted through oral exchanges, a substantial proportion of which are in Fijian and/or Fiji Hindi, although code-switching is also frequent. In classes in which the medium of instruction is supposed to be English, teachers faced with a seeming lack of understanding on the part of their pupils often resort to Fijian or Hindi. Furthermore, schools have traditionally been organized along ethnic lines and the trend towards multi-ethnic schools, which favour the use of English, is a relatively recent one.

The main language of the media is English. There are seven radio stations in Fiji, three of which broadcast exclusively in English, three in Hindi, and one in Fijian. Television was introduced in 1991, and all programmes, including the local news and locally produced programmes, are in English. Advertisements are also in English, with an occasional one in Hindi or Fijian. Advertisements in Hindi, though rare, are more frequent than those in Fijian, since some are imported from India, while Fijian advertisements have to be produced locally. The linguistic situation with regard to television is constantly evolving, however, and for the past year or so interviews in Fijian or Fiji Hindi have started being featured on the news, whether of political figures or ordinary citizens in the street. Initially, such interviews were either voiced-over or subtitled in English, but in the past few months, stretches of interviews have been left in without any translation.

For a small nation, Fiji has a quite a large number of serials; two daily tabloids (both in English), three weekly tabloids (two in Fijian and one in Hindi), and five monthly publications (all in English). The audited circulation figures for these are shown in Table 18.1.[3]

While English is a *de facto* official language in most of the Pacific, nowhere is it used as a *lingua franca* to a greater extent than in Fiji.[4] This is due to the country's unique mix of languages and peoples. In Polynesia, typically, each country has one indigenous language, which is known by nearly everyone, and English is used as a medium of communication only with foreign residents who do not know the national language. Almost everyone who lives in Tonga knows Tongan, for instance. In Western Samoa even foreign residents, including those in the country for the medium term, tend to acquire enough Samoan to be able to communicate with Samoans in the national language rather than in English.

Melanesia, on the other hand, is characterized by extreme multilingualism. The Solomon Islands has over sixty indigenous languages for a population of 375,000, and Papua New Guinea over 850 languages for 4.173 million people. Vanuatu, with about 105 languages for 168,000 people, has the highest language density in the

TABLE 18.1. *Fiji serials: average circulation per issue at March 1995*

Publication	Daily publication	Weekly publication	Monthly publication
The Fiji Times	35,000[a]	—	—
The Daily Post	17–18,000	—	—
Volasiga (Fijian)		14,000	
Nai Lalakai (Fijian)		8–9,000[b]	
Shanti Dut (Hindi)		8,500[c]	
Fiji Business Week		6,500	
Pacific Islands Monthly			1,000
Islands Business Magazine			2,000
Enquirer			2,000
The Review			11–12,000

[a] The 1984 average daily circulation figure was 25,000 (Geraghty, 1984: 60).
[b] The 1984 average weekly circulation figure was 17,000 (Geraghty, 1984: 60).
[c] The 1984 average weekly circulation figure was 7,000 (Geraghty, 1984: 60).
Note: The 1995 figures show a 40% increase in readership of the *Fiji Times* since 1984, and an approximate 53–47% decrease in readership of the Fijian weekly *Nai Lalakai* over the same period. The readership of the Hindi weekly *Shanti Dut*, on the other hand, has had a 21% increase since 1984.

world, roughly one language for every 1,600 speakers.[5] In these three countries, multilingualism is the norm, and many children grow up speaking several languages. The languages of both parents may often be different, and although in each country English has official status, it is Melanesian Pidgin which is the major *lingua franca*.[6] Melanesian Pidgin, in fact, serves as a *lingua franca* between these three countries as well as within them.

The population of Fiji consists mainly of two groups: Fijians and Indo-Fijians (or 'Fiji Indians'). Currently, the Indo-Fijian population is estimated at 47 per cent, and Fijians at 49 per cent. English is often used as a *lingua franca* between these two groups and with the smaller groups of Chinese, Europeans, part-Europeans, and other Pacific islanders, although many people know enough of the language of the other major group to be able to communicate. Many part-Europeans know Fijian, for instance, as do many Indo-Fijians, especially in the rural areas. Conversely, many Fijians know some Fiji Hindi, particularly in the sugar-cane belt, on the Western side of the main island of Viti Levu, and in the North of the second largest island of Vanua Levu, where these two communities often work side-by-side.

English, however, tends to be used as a *lingua franca* to a greater degree in urban areas, where it is used to varying degrees in the workplace. Thus, while it is only one of the languages people with different mother tongues use to communicate, English serves as a *lingua franca* in Fiji to a far greater extent than anywhere else in the Pacific.

3. Surveys of Language Use and Attitudes

Few surveys on language use and attitudes have been conducted in Fiji. A 1950 Fiji Department of Education survey showed that a majority of parents of school-aged children advocated the use of English as the main language in schools (Adam, 1958). Interviewing residents of a low-income neighbourhood in Suva, White (1971) found that English was the home language in a surprisingly high number of households and that it was the main language used for communication between the two major ethnic groups, although bilingualism in Fijian and Fiji Hindi was also present and was, he claimed, a typical urban phenomenon. A survey of urban Indo-Fijians in the Nadi area revealed that English was displacing Standard Hindi for most formal language functions, such as reading, writing, and public speaking (Siegel, 1973). Siegel also found that most Indo-Fijians used Fijian, rather than English, to communicate with Fijians, and that, contrary to White's findings, bilingualism in Fijian and Fiji Hindi was not only an urban phenomenon. Thus, the pattern of language use is often quite complex, while language shift is not limited to a simple gain by English. In a Suva survey of speakers' perceptions of their language skills, the answers to a few preliminary questions concerning language use indicate a shift by younger people towards greater use of English in the home (May, 1990).

In 1993 a survey on language use and attitudes in Fiji was carried out (Mugler and Tent, 1995). As part of this survey 252 Fijians and 252 Indo-Fijians living in Suva were interviewed. The results of this component of the survey, some of which are given below, reveal the significant role English plays in the lives of urban dwellers. For instance, 92.5 per cent of Fijians and 87 per cent of Indo-Fijians interviewed claimed that they regularly read one or more of the two English language tabloids, whereas only 54 per cent of Fijians and 36 per cent of Indo-Fijians regularly read one or more of the three vernacular tabloids.

Geraghty (1984: 45) reports that 'small sections of all races have abandoned their traditional home language for English'. This encroachment of English in the home environment, also noted by Siegel (1989: 57), is reflected in the fact that 55 per cent of Fijians and 48 per cent of Indo-Fijians state that they use English for one or more purposes in the home. Furthermore, 34 per cent of Fijian parents and a remarkable 67.5 per cent of Indo-Fijian parents say that they regularly use English at home when talking with their children. Geraghty (personal communication) believes the high incidence of English use in the home reported by White (1971) and Siegel (1989) is largely due to a confounding factor. There is a pervading attitude among Fijians and Indo-Fijians alike, that the vernaculars are inferior to English, and that the only way to economic and social advancement in the modern world is to be a good speaker of English. The origin of this belief can be traced back to the New Zealand Education System established in the 1930s. According to Geraghty, English use in the average Fijian or Indo-Fijian home is much less than is actually reported. To declare that you speak English at home is to show education and sophistication.

Another reflection of the spread of English is found in the number of respondents who declare that they learned English at home rather than at school: 20 per cent of Fijians and 26 per cent of Indo-Fijians. According to Geraghty (1989: 393–4), one of the reasons for the intrusion of English into the private and domestic domains, at least in the written mode, is the awkwardness of Old High Fijian.[7] Geraghty claims that Fijians who know even a smattering of English prefer to read an English translation of the Bible rather than the Fijian version, as the English is much clearer. Furthermore, 'Fijians who would talk to each other in Fijian frequently correspond in English' (Geraghty, 1989: 393–4). This is supported by the results of the 1993 survey, in which 9 per cent of Fijians report that the last time they wrote a letter to a relative, it was in English, and 40 per cent say the last time they wrote a letter to a Fijian friend, it was in English. The figures for the Indo-Fijian informants were even more startling, with 88 per cent claiming they wrote their last letter to a relative in English, and 90 per cent using English when they last wrote to an Indo-Fijian friend. The higher Indo-Fijian figures may be partly due to the lower literacy rate in Hindi (68 per cent claimed ability to write Hindi in Roman script, and 61 per cent in Devanagari script), while 94 per cent of Fijians claim to be able to write in Fijian. This lower rate of literacy is in turn due in large part to the fact that a different script is used for Hindi, while Fijian shares with English the Roman script. Although most Indo-Fijian children learn Standard Hindi in school, few seem to develop or maintain into adulthood a comfortable level of competence in the language, and particularly in the script.[8]

Not surprisingly, the vast majority of informants (95 per cent of Fijians and 96 per cent of Indo-Fijians) state it is important to be 'good' in English, as English is now seen by both Fijians and Indo-Fijians alike as the main—if not the only—means to occupational and economic advancement. In the 1993 survey, informants were given the option of having the interview conducted in English or in their own vernacular: 42 per cent of Fijians and 56 per cent of Indo-Fijians opted to have it carried out in English. Secondly, 52 per cent of Fijians and again a surprising 76 per cent of Indo-Fijians said they didn't consider someone from their own linguistic community to be showing off if that person spoke to them in English. These results confirm that English is considered important by members of both major communities, and is making inroads into the private lives of people from both groups, more so among Indo-Fijians than Fijians.

4. STUDIES OF FIJI ENGLISH

Only two small empirical studies of Fiji English exist. In the mid 1970s Sister Francis Kelly (1975) recorded the playground conversation of a group of teenage schoolgirls of mixed ethnic backgrounds. She noted numerous phonological, lexical, and grammatical features that were both unique to these girls' 'dialect' (a basilectal variety), and were shared by non-standard varieties of English found elsewhere. Siegel (1991) extended the work of Kelly by recording two samples of conversational speech: one of a group of first-year high-school girls (representing nearly every ethnic group present in Fiji), and one of a group of young Fijian and part-European boys. The salient features of Fiji English noted in these two studies are described in the next section.

4.1. *Some Features of Fiji English*

The notion of a 'Fiji English' seems to have been taken for granted. But are there in fact recurring linguistic features that distinguish the English spoken in Fiji from other varieties? As we have seen, Fiji has a culturally and linguistically diverse population. Indo-Fijians exhibit phonological, lexical, and grammatical characteristics in their English that are quite distinct from those of Fijians, not to mention those of Rotumans, Chinese, part-Europeans, Europeans, or other Pacific Islanders. And within each of these groups speakers can be placed along a continuum, characterized by features that go from basilectal to acrolectal. As in any language, then, Fiji English is a cover term for a number of sociolects and, as in many countries where English is a second language, some features of Fiji English vary according to the speaker's first language.

There are, however, a number of features that are shared by most, if not all, varieties. They are mainly lexical, and include a large number of words for objects or concepts typical of Fiji or Fijian culture, for which there are no appropriate English equivalents, such as *tabua* (whale's tooth), *tānoa* (wooden kava bowl), *yagona* (kava), *dalo* (taro), *bele* (leafy green vegetable), *bure* (Fijian-style house), *kokoda* (fish pickled in lime juice and coconut milk), *sevusevu* (ceremonial presentation of kava). Hindi items are fewer, most of them being names of Indian foods or religious terms: *bhajan* (devotional song), *Diwali* (Hindu festival of lights), *roti* (unleavened bread), *bhuja* (salty and spicy snack). There is also a large set of English expressions that have shifted or restricted meaning which are used mostly by basilectal speakers. Some of the more common ones (which are also known by speakers of the acrolect) are *a European* (any Caucasian person), *set* (OK, ready), *grog* (kava), *plain tyres* (bald tyres), *plastic* (a plastic bag), and *girmit* < 'agreement' (the indenture period or experience).

One phonological feature that seems common to all speakers is the deletion of /j/ ('yod'), with no evidence of coalescence before alveolar stops, in words such as *regular, fabulous, annual, educate*. In most other varieties of English, yod deletion is not very common after velars or labials, or in weakly stressed syllables (Wells, 1982: 207, 247).

A number of grammatical features of Fiji English are also found in other New Englishes or in non-standard varieties. These include:

1. The use of non-count nouns as count nouns: 'Fiji will draft *a legislation* . . .' (FNVC TV News, 22 July 1993); 'They were treated for dehydration, lacerations, *sunburns* and fatigue and have been admitted for observation.' (*The Fiji*

Times, 22 July 1994, p. 1); 'The irritating voice could only come from an idiot. Also, the advertisement shows *a disrespect* for women.' (J. B., Letters to the Editor, *Fiji Times*, 29 July 1994, p. 6).

2. The use of *one* as an indefinite article: 'I have *one* brother who work in *one* factory in Sydney.'; '*One* Indian man come to the door just now'.
3. The omission of determiners: 'I met them *in Civic Centre* one time.'; 'Kava has a great place of importance among *Fijian and Indian hierarchy* . . . The money in grog keep *wheels* of economy rolling.' (K. N., Letters to the Editor, *Daily Post*, 8 August 1994, p. 9).
4. The use of *the thing* as the third person singular pronoun with [–human] referents: 'You going to start *the thing* up?' (referring to a bulldozer).
5. The use of *gang* as a plural marker with personal pronouns: 'Sorry, us *gang* can't come at that time.'; 'Us *gang* own this store . . . you *gang* don't belong here!'
6. The use of verbal particles as verbs: 'I been come down and *off* the light and do the washing up'; 'You want me to *on* the alarm?'
7. The use of *been* as a pre-verbal past tense marker: 'I *been* study all week.'; and example in 6.
8. The use of *full* as an intensifying adverb: 'That man, he was *full* running.'; 'Us two (first person dual inclusive) get *full* drunk tomorrow next' (i.e. the day after tomorrow).

The extent to which these features are shared remains to be ascertained, however, and a systematic study of Fiji English is much needed to determine, among other things, whether it is indeed legitimate to speak of a 'Fiji English'.[9]

5. FIJI'S PLACE IN THE PACIFIC

The Pacific Ocean spans approximately one quarter of the Earth's surface, and scattered over its 3 million square miles of ocean lie several thousand islands. Over 8 million people live in the Pacific, yet both islands and people are often forgotten by the rest of the world, as if this ocean were devoid of human habitation. The current catch-phrase 'the Pacific century' invariably turns out to refer to the predicted growing importance of the economies of the countries on the Pacific rim, usually with no mention of the island nations which lie in the middle of that ocean. The invisibility of Pacific island nations is reflected in their lack of participation to date in the ICE project. The nearest representatives are Hong Kong, the Philippines, Australia, New Zealand, USA, and Canada—all, typically, Pacific rim countries.

Fiji is at the heart of the Pacific and, thus, at the centre of cross-currents of influences both within the country and beyond—across the entire region. Geographically, linguistically, and culturally, Fiji is the meeting-point between Melanesia and Polynesia. Fiji is also the hub of the South Pacific, thanks to its central location and its relative size. Next to Papua New Guinea, Fiji has the largest population of all Pacific island nations, with about 768,600 inhabitants. The next largest nation, the Solomon Islands, is far behind, with only about half that number. Most of the other island nations in the Pacific have populations in the tens of thousands (e.g. the Cook Islands, Kiribati, or the Marshall Islands), or even in the thousands (e.g. Niue, Nauru, Tuvalu).

Fiji's central location in the Pacific makes its capital the natural choice for the seats of many regional organizations, such as the South Pacific Forum and the South Pacific Commission, whose members regularly gather in Suva. The diplomatic missions of a number of nations (e.g. Australia, New Zealand, USA, Japan, Israel, Germany) have their South Pacific headquarters in Suva. The University of the South Pacific, with its twelve Pacific island member countries, is the meeting place and training ground for the educated. The University exerts a great influence on the students from the region (who spend three or more years on its main campus in Suva), from developing a taste for the popular Indo-Fijian curry to acquiring a smattering of Fijian, from gaining an understanding and respect of other cultures to picking up bits of Fiji English.

Given Fiji's centrality and importance in the Pacific, its 200-year history of English, and its continuing importance, both as a *de facto* official language and as a *lingua franca*, it is clear that Fiji English is the most appropriate representative of Pacific English, and Fiji the most rational choice for an ICE component in the region.

6. ICE-FJ IMPLICATIONS

As in every other ICE project, an ICE-FJ corpus will be an invaluable resource for linguists interested in comparative studies of English in the world. It will also be indispensable to those already working on Fiji English, who will be able not only to analyse the corpus but to extend it, and who will be best placed to take into account the unique characteristics of the sociolinguistic situation in the country. A corpus of English as it is actually used will naturally be helpful in many areas of language planning in Fiji, particularly in education, where a variety of international English is currently used extensively, with little reference to the home-grown variety.

The sociolinguistic characteristics of the Fiji English setting, and in particular the fact that, in Fiji, English is not the first language of the majority of the population but rather a *de facto* official language and a *lingua franca*, mean that an ICE-FJ project may make a valuable contribution to the theoretical model of data-gathering and analysis currently used in ICE. The use of English in Fiji has more in common with the situation in, say, India, Zambia, or Singapore, than with that in the USA, Britain, or New Zealand. While there are undoubtedly variations in each country in the sociolinguistic pattern of use of English, the distinction between first-language and second-language settings is fundamental, and the possibility of evolving an alternative model with different categories of use for countries where English is not a first language cannot be discounted.[10]

An ICE-FJ component will also provide a model for an eventual expansion of data-gathering in other countries of the Pacific. It is hoped also that the project may inspire Pacific linguists to build corpora—with suitable modifications—in, say, Fijian and Fiji Hindi in Fiji, and in other languages in the rest of the Pacific.

NOTES

1. Fijian is characterized by a great deal of regional diversity, with about 300 communalects, a communalect being 'a variety spoken by people who claim they use the same speech' (Geraghty, 1983: 18). We use 'Fijian' here as a cover term for these communalects. Fiji Hindi is a local variety of Hindi, which has evolved from a koine of various dialects of the Hindustani *lingua franca* of North India (Siegel, 1987: 187–203).

2. Fijian words are given in the usual Fijian spelling. Vowels are pronounced approximately as in German, Spanish, Italian, etc.

   Consonant pronunciation guide:

Symbol	IPA
b	^{m}b
d	^{n}d
q	^{ŋ}g
g	ŋ
j	ʧ
c	ð
v	ß

3. Figures were supplied by the publishers. The monthly publications *Pacific Islands Monthly*, *Islands Business*, and *The Review* are also circulated in other Pacific countries (including the Rim). The figures given here represent only the Fiji readership. Unless otherwise indicated, publications are in English.

4. While English is the official language of government, administration and the media, as well as either the only or the major medium of instruction in the majority of the countries in the Pacific, this function is fulfilled by French in the French Overseas Territories of New Caledonia, French Polynesia, and Wallis and Futuna. In Vanuatu, which was governed jointly as a condominium by Britain and France until independence in 1980, both French and English were, and continue to be, official languages. Bislama, a variety of Melanesian Pidgin, is the third official language, and is used extensively in government, administration, and the media. Paradoxically however, it is banned from the educational sphere, even though it is also the national language of Vanuatu.

5. All population figures quoted in this article are the latest estimates of the South Pacific Commission (Doyle *et al.*, 1993: 41).

6. Melanesian Pidgin can be considered a single language with three regional dialects, as the varieties spoken in the three countries of Melanesia are mutually intelligible (*Tok Pisin* in Papua New Guinea, *Pijin* in the Solomon Islands, and *Bislama* in Vanuatu).

7. Old High Fijian is the creation of the early Methodists missionaries. It is a literary form

of Fijian heavily influenced by early renditions of Lauan, foreigner talk, and Eurocentric notions of 'correctness' (Geraghty, 1989: 384–5). (The Lau group of islands is in eastern Fiji, where the first missionaries were initially based.)

8. This includes many of the most highly educated Indo-Fijians (including colleagues at the University of the South Pacific), who are fluent speakers of Fiji Hindi but freely admit that they rarely read anything in the Devanagari script, as they find it difficult to read.

9. The examples listed in this section have been collected by Jan Tent, who is currently working on a Ph.D. dissertation on Fiji English.

10. A Fijian project would have to include categories such as ceremonial usage, *meke* Fijian (roughly, 'action song' or 'poetry perfomance'); while a Fiji Hindi corpus would comprise, for instance, *bhajan* (religious songs), recitations of the Ramayana, and challenge songs.

REFERENCES

ADAM, R. S. (1958), 'Social Factors in Second Language Learning', Ph.D. thesis (London).

CHESHIRE, J. (1991) (ed.), *English Around the World: Sociolinguistic Perspectives* (Cambridge: Cambridge University Press).

DERRICK, R. A. (1950), *A History of Fiji*, i (Suva: Government Press).

DOYLE, B., WICHMAN, V., and JIMMY, P. M. (1993), *South Pacific Economies Statistical Summary: SPESS*, no. 13 (Noumea: South Pacific Commission).

FODOR, I. and HAGÈGE, C. (1989) (eds.), *Language Reform: History and Future*, iv (Hamburg: Helmut Buske Verlag).

GERAGHTY, P. (1983), *The History of the Fijian Languages* (Honolulu: University of Hawaii Press).

—— (1984), 'Language Policy in Fiji and Rotuma', *Duivosavosa: Fiji's languages: Their Use and their Future*, Fiji Museum Bulletin no. 8, 32–84 (Suva: Fiji Museum).

—— (1989), 'Language Reform: History and Future of Fijian', in I. FODOR and C. HAGÈGE (eds.), 377–95.

GILLION, K. L. (1962), *Fiji's Indian Migrants* (Melbourne: Oxford University Press).

KELLY, SR. F. (1975), 'The English Spoken Colloquially by a Group of Adolescents in Suva', *Fiji English Teachers Journal*, 11: 19–43.

MACNAUGHT, T. J. (1975), 'From Mainstream to Millpond? The Fijian Political Experience 1897–1940', Ph.D. thesis (Canberra: Australian National University).

MAY, T. (1990), 'Language in Suva: Language Use and Literacy in an Urban Pacific Community', paper delivered at the Australian Linguistics Society Conference, August.

MUGLER, F. and TENT, J. (1995), 'A Survey of Language Use in Fiji', paper presented at the Second International Conference on Oceanic Linguistics, University of the South Pacific, Suva, 3–7 July; to be published as 'A Survey of Language Use and Attitudes in Fiji', in F. MUGLER and J. TENT (eds.), *Language Contact: Proceedings of the Second International Conference on Oceanic Linguistics* (Series C Books), Pacific Linguistics, ANU.

SIEGEL, J. (1973), 'A Survey of Language Use in the Indian Speech Community in Fiji', unpublished paper (Honolulu: East-West Center Resource Materials Collection, Institute of Culture and Communication).

—— (1987), *Language Contact in a Plantation Environment: A Sociolinguistic History of Fiji* (Cambridge: Cambridge University Press).

—— (1989), 'English in Fiji', *World Englishes*, 8/1: 47–58.

—— (1991), 'Variation in Fiji English', in Cheshire, 664–74.

WELLS, J. C. (1982), *Accents of English*, i. *An Introduction* (Cambridge: Cambridge University Press).

WHITE, R. V. (1971), 'Language Use in a South Pacific Urban Community', *Anthropological Linguistics*, 13/8: 361–84.

19

PROSICE: A Spoken English Database for Prosody Research

MARK HUCKVALE and ALEX CHENGYU FANG

1. INTRODUCTION

Prosody—the study of the intonation, stress, and rhythm of speech—is now assuming a greater importance in phonetics, phonology, and speech technology than ever before. Once regarded as subservient to studies of segmental structure, it is now being seen as providing the 'framework' which holds different levels of phonetic description together. The recent past has seen novel views of the phonology of intonation (e.g. Pierrehumbert, 1980), a new interest in prosodic phrase structure and prominence (e.g. Liberman and Prince, 1977) and the rise of autosegmental or non-linear accounts of phonetic description which integrate metrical structure with phonetic substance (e.g. Clements and Keyser, 1983). The role of prosody is also changing in speech synthesis and recognition. In speech synthesis, the success of concatenative systems—whereby recorded segments of speech are glued together to make novel utterances—has meant that the key issues have changed from segmental to supra-segmental quality (Klatt, 1987). In speech recognition the increasing emphasis on dialogue systems has meant more research is taking place into the automatic determination of prosodic structure for the purposes of utterance disambiguation (e.g. Wightman and Ostendorf, 1995).

Contemporaneous with the development of prosody research has been the increasing influence of corpus-based research throughout speech technology and experimental phonetics. This has been driven by the huge appetite of current speech recognition research for large quantities of controlled recordings. As an example of this trend in prosody, the prediction of segment durations in speech synthesis is now commonly generated from a multiple regression analysis performed upon a database of transcribed spoken speech (van Santen, 1993).

The combination of these two trends has created a demand for publicly available corpora of spoken recordings for the scientific research and technological application of prosody. In this chapter we look at the requirements and existing corpora and describe a new spoken English database with novel characteristics. Our database is derived from ICE-GB, the British component of the International Corpus of English (ICE).

2. REQUIREMENTS FOR PROSODY RESEARCH

The prosodic elements of main interest (above the level of the syllable) are of three kinds: *prosodic phrase structure*, which describes how words are grouped into prosodic units, and which is strongly related to the syntactic structure of utterances; *phrasal prominence*, which describes how components gain particular emphasis or focus in an utterance, and which is related to semantic and discourse structure; and *intonation markers*, which describe the particular tune types which are related to discourse functions. Hence prosody research requires speech recordings with a particularly wide range of linguistic annotations—from discourse functions, through semantic and syntactic annotations, to phonetic properties of pitch, duration, and loudness. Scientific studies are currently involved in relating higher-level linguistic annotations to phonological models, and phonological models to phonetic realizations, while technological studies are perhaps more concerned with a simple means of determining 'neutral' readings of texts, possibly moving from a shallow syntactic analysis directly to phonetic values of duration and pitch.

While each type of study will have its own specialist requirements, a corpus for prosodic analysis is often associated with high-quality recordings of naturally produced speech, with fundamental frequency tracks, and with phonetic and linguistic annotations.[1] Surprisingly, very few databases of British English currently meet these requirements.

These are the most relevant corpora that are currently available:

- SCRIBE contains passages of spontaneous speech that were recorded in an anechoic chamber with a simultaneous laryngograph recording which provides a robust fundamental frequency trace.
- EUROM0 (Fourcin and Gibbon, 1994) contains four readings of a two-minute passage, which have been phonetically annotated to fine detail, and also have laryngographic signals.
- SEC (Knowles, 1993, 1994) contains transcriptions of broadcast material of about 20,000 words with prosodic annotations. MARSEC (Knowles, 1995) adds to this material phonological intonation marking, word-class labels, and phrase-level syntactic analyses.
- The London–Lund Corpus (LLC) of Spoken English (Svartvik and Quirk, 1979) contains transcribed spoken speech with prosodic markings.

However, these speech databases form a rather strange picture. The EUROM0 corpus has fine phonetic detail and fundamental frequency, but no prosodic or syntactic analysis. The SCRIBE corpus contains spontaneous speech, but it is not annotated at all. The LLC corpus has manually transcribed prosodic annotations, but no quality annotated signals. The SEC corpus does not have time-aligned annotations, while the MARSEC corpus, which is otherwise the most sophisticated, has prosodic and grammatical annotations, but is based on a rather limited syntactic analysis of a mixed group of speakers. Furthermore the broadcast medium and the mixture of speakers makes fundamental frequency analysis in MARSEC difficult. Of these, only the LLC corpus has been used extensively for prosodic research so far (Altenberg, 1987; Svartvik, 1990).

3. DESIGN AIMS

Our objective with the PROSICE corpus has been to combine the best features of existing databases to generate recordings with a complete set of characteristics appropriate for prosody research, within certain resource limitations. This chapter describes the first component, PROSICE-1, which is based on read speech from a single speaker.

The design objectives of PROSICE-1 were:

• High-quality recordings
• Accurate fundamental frequency information
• Genuine spoken texts
• Annotations at both word-class and syntactic levels linked to signal
• Relevant phonetic annotations

The resource constraints were:

• The use of existing texts and grammatical analysis
• No manual annotation
• The size of a single CD-ROM for distribution

The impracticality of performing manual annotation has meant that we could not provide a phonological level of prosodic annotation. This limitation is potentially very serious in that it precludes the typical division of levels found in scientific research in prosody (e.g. Altenberg, 1987), where syntactic information is projected onto phonological levels of prosody. However, we feel that such phonological level marking is in itself rather limiting. First, prosodic annotations, such as those found in the LLC corpus for example, bring with them particular theoretical models of prosody—they mark 'tone units', implying a certain definition of intonational phrasing; and secondly, they are subjective, resulting in a level of disagreement between annotators. As far as technological applications are concerned, an intermediate representation between words and phonetic realization of prosody introduces the requirement for two mapping processes rather than one. Furthermore the trend in speech recognition is for the phonological model to be in the application rather than in the data. It is reasonable to incorporate prosodic phrasing and phrasal prominence as features of a realization process, but the free parameters in such a system should be calculated from the phonetic evidence directly. Speech recognition systems use phonological segments to model the functions of the sounds in words, but they do not require the training data to be phonologically annotated.

We have based PROSICE-1 on recordings in a form which guarantees the highest acoustic quality, and then indexed them for access via time-aligned annotation at both word-class and syntactic levels.[2] In Section 6 below, we describe the levels of phonetic annotation that we have been able to provide for PROSICE-1. We hope that other workers will be able to provide some phonological annotations, particularly to allow comparisons between applications of prosody corpora.

4. CHOICE OF TEXTS

The choice of the texts to record was primarily decided by the immediate applications of PROSICE-1 in the design of text-to-speech systems. Thus a few guidelines in text selection can be easily formulated. First of all, the texts should have their origins in the written genre. Secondly, they should be written mainly for spoken delivery. It is also desirable that texts for this study should be diversified in both style and subject-matter. These considerations naturally led us to the scripted texts in the ICE-GB corpus, which are further divided into *broadcast news*, *broadcast talks*, and *non-broadcast speeches*. These three categories range from *S2B-001* to *S2B-050*, covering fifty texts totalling about 100,000 words. For detailed descriptions of the ICE text categories, see Chapter 3 in this volume.

Our next question was which of those three categories best serves our purpose. We left out *non-broadcast speeches*, which largely consists of university public lectures, where speakers hesitate, stutter, or correct themselves in a conscious effort to try to 'talk' to the audience, instead of simply 'reading' from their scripts. As a result, such texts, or rather transcriptions, are usually characterized by self-corrections and voiced pauses, and thus are not suitable for this study. We then opted for *broadcast talks*, a sub-category where, unlike *broadcast news*, speakers are the actual composers of their deliveries, where the prosodic phrasing and phrasal prominences have their intended meanings. New recordings of the texts from this group might also enable an interesting comparison with the original recordings.

There are twenty texts in this category, coded sequentially from *S2B-021* to *S2B-040*. Table 19.1 lists their titles, sources, and dates in text-code order. The column labelled *Text Nos.* indicates the number and the sequence of extracts in a composite text.[3] For instance, *S2B-022* has two components: the first one was transcribed from *The River Times* on ITV recorded on 21 June 1991 and the second from *Nature* on BBC 2 TV produced on 5 March 1991. Those without such number indications are non-composite texts.

5. RECORDING

The texts were re-recorded in the anechoic chamber at the Department of Phonetics and Linguistics at UCL. Recording of the sound pressure signal was made using a B&K 2231 microphone positioned 50cm in front of and 10cm to the side of the

TABLE 19.1. *A list of texts in broadcast talks*

Text Code	Text Nos.	Title	Source	Date
S2B-021	1–4	Journalists' monologues on presidential wealth	LBC Radio	07/07/91
S2B-022	1	The River Times	ITV	21/06/91
S2B-022	2	Nature	BBC 2 TV	05/03/91
S2B-023	1	Can You Steal It?	BBC Radio 1	02/03/91
S2B-023	2	Spirit Level	Radio Oxford	20/01/91
S2B-023	3	From Our Own Correspondent	BBC Radio 4	27/04/91
S2B-024	1	Viewpoint '91: Poles Apart	ITV	30/04/91
S2B-024	2	40 Minutes	BBC 2 TV	08/11/90
S2B-025		For He Is an Englishman	BBC Radio 4	05/02/91
S2B-026		The World of William	BBC Radio 4	05/11/90
S2B-027		Castles Abroad	ITV	21/06/91
S2B-028	1	Lent Observed	BBC Radio 4	19/03/91
S2B-028	2	Lent Observed	BBC Radio 4	26/02/91
S2B-029		The Reith Lecture, No. 2	BBC Radio 4	21/11/90
S2B-030	1	Address to the Nation	BBC Radio 4	17/01/91
S2B-030	2	Address to the Nation,	BBC Radio 4	18/01/91
S2B-030	3	Labour Party Political Broadcast	BBC 1 TV	13/03/91
S2B-030	4	Social Democratic Party Political Broadcast	Channel 4	13/03/91
S2B-031	1–2	The Police Debate	BBC Radio 4	10/02/91
S2B-031	3	The Week's Good Cause	BBC Radio 4	30/03/91
S2B-032	1	Opinion: King or Country	BBC Radio 4	07/11/90
S2B-032	2	The Police Debate	BBC Radio 4	10/02/91
S2B-033		Barry Norman's film '91	BBC 1 TV	12/03/91
S2B-034		Analysis	BBC Radio 4	16/05/91
S2B-035	1–2	The Class Debate	BBC Radio 4	24/02/91
S2B-036	1–2	The Class Debate	BBC Radio 4	24/02/91
S2B-037		The Scarman Report	BBC Radio 4	16/06/91
S2B-038	1	Medicine Now	BBC Radio 4	12/03/91
S2B-038	2	Medicine Now	BBC Radio 4	19/03/91
S2B-038	3	The Week's Good Cause	BBC Radio 4	17/03/91
S2B-039	1–3	From Our Own Correspondent	BBC Radio 4	02/04/91
S2B-040	1–3	From Our Own Correspondent	BBC Radio 4	27/04/91

speaker's mouth. A simultaneous laryngograph signal was also recorded, using surface electrodes placed on the neck at the level of the thyroid cartilage. The laryngograph maintains a small current through the neck, and is able to provide an indication of vocal fold contact area (Fourcin and Abberton, 1971). In Fig. 19.1 you can see that the laryngograph signal is greatest when the vocal fold contact is greatest, immediately after a vocal fold closure.

The two signals were amplified, filtered and digitally recorded directly onto computer disk with 16-bit linear quantization at 20,000 samples/second. The recorded signals were also captured on digital audio tape for archival purposes. The selection of the 20,000 samples/second sampling rate was chosen as a suitable compromise between audio bandwidth and the capacity of the publication CD-ROM. At this sample rate, we could expect to hold eight texts on one CD-ROM. At the full CD-audio sample rate of 44,100 samples/second, we would only have been able to store half as much. The 20,000 samples/second rate is also very common for spoken language databases (it was used, for example, in the eight-language EUROM1 database).

To prompt the speaker, the printed texts were inserted into soft plastic wallets, which considerably reduced the amount of noise created by page turning. We investigated, but rejected, the possibility of teleprompting via a computer monitor —we felt that this would compromise the speed and prosody of the delivery. Either the prompter must be controlled by the speaker—which adds to his cognitive task —or by an assistant. In the latter case the speaker may be confused by the jerkiness of the scrolling text.

Misreadings and corrections are natural consequences of reading a text out loud. We did not perform any editing on the finished signal, so all deviations from the text are marked and annotated. The speaker read through each text three times before the recording—the aim was to make sure that there were no surprises for the speaker, but to avoid a carefully rehearsed intonation (the speaker did not listen to the original broadcast recording).

6. PHONETIC ANNOTATION

6.1. *Orthographic Alignment*

To form the necessary connection between signal and syntactic structure, it was desirable to find the temporal location of each word unit in the parse tree. We addressed this problem in a novel way. From each text as it was actually spoken (including corrections), we collated all the different words (typically 800 different words for a 2,000-word text).[4] The list of words was entered into a tele-prompting system and the speaker re-recorded the words individually in the anechoic chamber. Alongside the speech pressure signal and the laryngograph signal, a third signal generated by the prompting system was recorded. This prompting signal comprised 'clicks' made by the prompting system as each prompt word was displayed. Thus for each text, we finished with a recording of about half an hour of individual words. These recordings were first made onto an eight-channel digital audio recorder at 44,100 samples/sec and later transferred to computer disk at 20,000 samples/second.

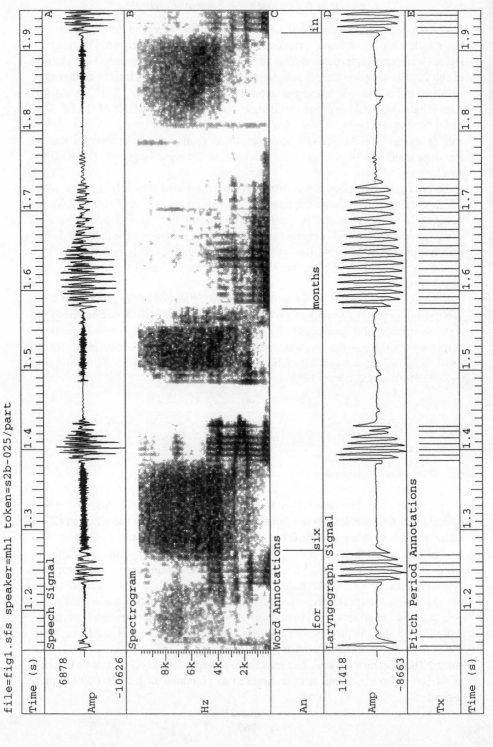

file=fig1.sfs speaker=mh1 token=s2b-025/part

The presence of the prompting signal combined with the list of words in the order recorded (chosen to be random) allowed the identification of the position of each individual word in this second recording. A small amount of hand-editing was required to tidy up some mistakes made during this recording—less than 2 per cent of words. From the identified individual words, we then constructed a procedure to identify the positions of words in the original recording as follows.

We first formed a frequency-domain representation of both sets of data using a 26-channel filterbank analyser (this was based on an extension of the 19-channel vocoder described by Holmes (1980)). This analyser provides a vector of 26 log energies every 10ms from the speech pressure signals. The actual alignment was made using this representation. This type of analysis is highly suitable for our purposes because a simple Euclidean distance function can be computed between any two spectral vectors which will give a direct measure of the similarity between any two 10ms speech segments. The filterbank output can be seen in a grey-level representation of energy in Fig. 19.2.

The alignment of the individual words with the passage can be performed using a procedure called dynamic programming (DP). The aim here is to find a suitable compression or extension of the concatenated individual words such that the total distance between the aligned spectral vectors is at a minimum. The DP method guarantees that the alignment found will have the lowest possible cumulative distance. The actual implementation is a modified version of the 'one-pass' DP algorithm used for speech recognition by Bridle and Brown (1979).

Although the alignment could have been computed over the whole passage, there were good reasons for arbitrarily segmenting the original passage and performing the alignment over smaller regions: less computer time and memory are required; and alignment errors cannot extend beyond one alignment region.

The segmentation of the original passage was performed automatically on the basis of 'major pauses' in the signal. A program located regions of the signal delimited by major pauses and by prompting the operator allowed the word-string for each region to be identified. Each region could then be aligned by DP separately (see Fig. 19.2). The criteria for the identification of a major pause are given in the next section.

From the identified regions, the text word-string, and recordings of the individual words in the string, the DP algorithm finds the best alignment and hence the start and stop time for each word. Each alignment is actually made starting from the middle of the pause preceding the region to the middle of the pause closing the region. This allows the DP algorithm to determine the starting and ending times of the region to within 10ms (whereas the pause-finding algorithm only locates regions within 50ms).

FIG. 19.1. (*Opposite*) A short section of a recorded passage showing (A) speech pressure signal (B) spectrogram (C) aligned word annotations (D) laryngograph signal and (E) pitch period annotations

269

file=fig2.sfs speaker=mh1 token=s2b-025/part

Time (s)

Speech Signal

A

9793

Amp

-14287

26-Channel Filterbank

B

7728
5700
4277
3315
2670
2198
1796
1445
1136
859
603
360
120

Word Annotations

An   GAP: putme out action   six   months   innineteenfifty two   GAP: as
                         of for   and

C

Segment Annotations

An   GAP: put_me_out_of_action_for_six_months_in_nineteen_fifty_two   GAP: and

D

Pitch Trace

E

300

200

Hz

100

Time (s)   0.0   0.5   1.0   1.5   2.0   2.5   3.0   3.5

6.2. *Pauses*

Major pauses are defined as regions of the signal either having energy less than 60dB lower than the peak energy for the whole recording; or extending over at least 250ms. In practice this was done by computing the signal energy in 50ms frames over the whole signal and then smoothing this using a triangular weighting filter 250ms wide. The smoothed energy in the signal was then used to set a gap threshold at −60dB relative to peak. Pauses were then regions of 250ms or longer which consisted of frames below this threshold (the use of 250ms is compatible with the definition by Goldman-Eisler (1972)). As will be seen below, such pauses were highly correlated with major clause boundaries.

Minor pauses were taken to be regions of silence of between 50 and 250ms that occurred between words. It is impossible to locate such pauses simply by looking at the speech signal, because stop-gaps (silent regions caused by oral closures prior to a plosive burst) may commonly be of such durations. Thus pauses of 100ms or greater are very common inside words. We addressed the problem of locating minor pauses by integrating it into the word alignment procedure. Using the one-pass DP algorithm, it is a simple matter to allow optional pauses to be inserted between words if this helps the overall alignment score. Thus only in circumstances—between words—where a small silent gap would aid alignment is a minor gap inserted. A typical 2,000-word text provided 260 major gaps and 65 minor gaps with this procedure.

6.3. *Fundamental Frequency Contour*

For the determination of the pitch of the signal, the laryngograph output was processed. First, it was filtered with a zero-phase non-recursive digital band-pass filter operating between 40 and 2,000Hz to remove low-frequency energy due to gross larynx movement and residual high-frequency noise. A peak-following algorithm—which was allowed to rise as fast as the signal but decay at a restricted rate—was used to locate and measure individual pitch periods (see Fig. 19.1).

The pitch period markers give an accurate and instantaneous measurement of fundamental frequency (Fx). However, since the onsets and offsets of voicing can produce false period values (as the vocal folds start or cease vibration) the fundamental frequency trace calculated from the pitch period data was subjected to a five-point median filter (equivalent to 25ms). This removed glitches without compromising the measured frequency values at other times. A contour is shown in Fig. 19.2.

FIG. 19.2. (*Opposite*) A long section of a recorded passage showing (A) speech pressure signal (B) 26-channel filterbank output (C) aligned word annotations (D) major pause and alignment region annotation and (E) fundamental frequency contour

6.4. *Pitch Accents*

While the fundamental frequency contour provides a value of the pitch of the signal every 5ms, it is also useful to have some characterization of the pitch through an entire word. This would make it easier to relate the higher level labelling to phrasal prominence. The aim is to determine a set of parameters which are related to the size and nature of any pitch accent occurring within a word. The parameters chosen are: (i) mean Fx through the word (ii) the standard deviation of Fx (iii) the mean rate of change of Fx (iv) the standard deviation of (iii) and (v) the mean acceleration of Fx. Together these parameters identify words that have unnaturally high or low Fx or have large changes in Fx, they identify whether words have largely rising or falling contours and whether these are rapid or extended in time, and they also differentiate between a rise–fall contour and a fall–rise contour. The measurements are only made on the voiced regions of a word as located by the orthographic alignment. The fundamental frequency units used were in *cents*, one hundredths of an octave, with the median Fx value for the passage taken to be zero.

7. ALIGNING SYNTACTIC ANALYSIS TO SPEECH SIGNALS

The word alignment process generates a file which indexes the graphic word to its temporal location in the acoustic signal file. The next task was to align these references to the syntactic tree structure of the sentence,[5] a necessary integration that enables cross-references between the acoustic recording, the graphic word, and the corresponding syntactic category and function. Table 19.2 shows a sample of the two separate files before the alignment.

In the time-word file, upper-case words bound within colons (:) are not lexical items. They are special mark-up symbols that indicate pauses, coughs, etc. So far, we have found the following indications necessary:

`:CLICK:`	Discernible noise.
`:COUGH:`	Cough.
`:ERR:`	Misreading of the original script during recording. Each item in the misreading is preceded by this symbol.
`:GAP:`	Major pauses.
`:MGAP:`	Minor pauses.
`:?:`	Unclear utterance.

A computer program was written in C to align and merge the two files automatically. The final output takes the format as shown in the displayed text, below.

TABLE 19.2. *A sample of time-word and syntactic tree files*

Temporal File	Syntactic File
54.10000 It	PU S (act, decl, indic, cop, past, unm)
54.90000 looked	SU NP ()
55.16000 interesting	NPHD PRON (pers, sing) {It}
55.79000 GAP:	V VP (act, indic, cop, past)
56.16000 even	MVB V (cop, past) {looked}
56.35000 if	CS AJP (ingp)
56.47000 underpaid	AJHD ADJ (ingp) {interesting}
57.17000 :GAP:	A AVP (add)
	AVHD ADV (add) {even}
	A CL (-su, indic, montr, pass, pastp, sub, unm)
	SUB SUBP ()
	SBHD CONJUNC (subord) {if}
	V VP (indic, montr, pass, edp)
	MVB V (montr, edp) {underpaid}

```
<#5> 14 6
PU S(act,decl,indic,cop,past,unm)
 SU NP()
  NPHD PRON(pers,sing) 1
    {It 54.10000}
 V VP(act,indic,cop,past)
  MVB V(cop,past) 1
    {looked 54.90000}
 CS AJP(ingp)
  AJHD ADJ(ingp) 1
    {interesting 55.16000}
 A AVP(add)
  AVHD ADV(add) 1
    {:GAP: 55.79000}
    {even 56.16000}
 A CL(-su,indic,montr,pass,edp,sub,unm)
  SUB SUBP()
   SBHD CONJUNC(subord) 1
     {if 56.35000}
  V VP(indic,montr,pass,edp)
   MVB V(montr,edp) 1
     {underpaid 56.47000}
     {:GAP: 57.17000}
```

Each aligned syntactic tree is preceded by three numbers indicating: serial number, number of nodes, and number of leaves. For instance, we can read that this tree is the fifth in the whole text (<#5>), that there are fourteen nodes altogether, and that there are six leaf nodes. Each leaf node is annotated with a digit indicating the number of lexical items occupying this node. This indication is especially helpful in the case of compound nouns (*Judge Meyer, The Hague*), complex prepositions (*in accordance with, by means of*), certain conjunctions (*rather than, as if*), certain marginal modal auxiliaries (*need to, ought to*), and semi-auxiliaries (*appear to, be about to*), which are treated as single units and ditto-tagged according to the ICE word-class annotation scheme (cf. Chapter 8 in this volume). Each item in the leaf node is followed by a time value that indicates its position in the actual digital recording and also indexes the other phonetic annotations.

8. CORRELATIONS BETWEEN SYNTACTIC CATEGORIES AND PAUSES

Pauses in speech are by no means of random occurrence, since they tend to divide up the stream of speech into grammatically and lexically relevant chunks (Quirk *et al.*, 1985: II.19). Extensive studies have been carried out to investigate their correlation with syntactic units. It has been established that pauses in read speech are mainly due to the influence of graphic arrangements in the text (Stenström, 1990: 211). It has also been established that pauses specifically mark the sentence and the clause (Goldman-Eisler, 1972). There has also been an emphasis on the use of pauses to identify 'information units' larger than the clause (Brotherton, 1979; Beattie, 1983; and Chafe, 1987; cf. Stenström, 1990: 213). As the only automatically measurable property of read speech that strongly correlates with syntactic units, pauses have been recommended as an anchor-point for the integration of orthographic transcriptions and the digitized acoustic file to create a time-aligned speech database (Knowles, 1994: 97).

In this section, we describe an investigation of pauses in PROSICE-1. The primary aim of this experiment was to test if correlation with syntactic structures was shown by the automatically determined pause annotations. A secondary aim was to find out to what extent clause elements apart from the sentence and the clause coincide with pauses. The clause elements considered in this experiment include five phrases— adjective phrase, adverb phrase, noun phrase, prepositional phrase, and verb phrase— in addition to the clause and the sentence.

The experiment was based on the first re-recorded text, *S2B-025*, which is entitled *For He Is an Englishman*, broadcast on BBC Radio 4, on 5 November 1990. This text has 2,014 running words (tokens), or 843 different word forms (types), which fall into 132 parsing units (PU).[6] We can thus calculate that there are roughly 15.25 words per parsing unit. Except for three (one interjection and two noun phrases), all parsing units correspond to the sentence in terms of structure.[7] The actual recording of this text covers a duration of 11 minutes or 660 seconds,

PROSICE: A Database for Prosody Research

TABLE 19.3. *Frequency distribution of pauses among major syntactic categories*

Category	Frequency		Percentage	
Sentence	150	150	100.00	48.5
Clause	106	38	35.8	12.3
Verb phrase	273	38	13.9	12.3
Prepositional phrase	197	20	10.2	6.5
Adverb phrase	109	9	8.3	2.9
Adjective phrase	161	8	5.0	2.6
Noun phrase	581	28	4.8	9.1
Others		18		5.8
TOTAL	1577	309		100.00

representing a speech rate of 3.05 words per second, or 183.09 words per minute.[8] Altogether, there are 309 pauses, both major and minor, yielding an average of approximately 6.5 words per pause.

Table 19.3 lists the frequency distribution of pauses in relation to the syntactic categories. The first column, *Category*, lists the types of syntactic categories, i.e. sentence, clause, etc. *Frequency* is divided into two columns: the first column indicates the observed frequency of a certain category and the second column the frequency of that category with initiating pauses. *Percentage* also has two columns, the first one displaying the percentage of a certain category that has initiating pauses and the second indicating the proportion of pauses falling into that category. Thus, we can read, for instance, that there are altogether 161 adjective phrases, eight of which have initiating pauses. These eight occurrences occupy 5 per cent of the total number of adjective phrases and 2.6 per cent of the total number of pauses.

We observe that of all the pauses in the text, only 18 (5.8 per cent) coincided with the start of elements other than the seven categories, or 94.2 per cent of all the pauses correspond to syntactic structures. The results confirm that pauses are in general a reliable indication of the start of a canonical syntactic structure. The predominant correlation is between the sentence start and the pause. All the sentence starts in the recording correlate with pauses, accounting for nearly half (48.5 per cent) of all the pauses. This result strongly confirms the finding of previous studies that sentences are marked by their temporal cohesion in reading (Goldman-Eisler, 1972: 103), but not clauses; of the 106 clauses in our text, only 38 (35.8 per cent) are found co-occurring with pauses.[9] To quote Goldman-Eisler (1972: 110), 'the speaker who thinks on his feet organizes his message in highly cohesive sentence units with a clear hierarchical structure whereby constituent clauses are temporally integrated into the sentence frame . . . to a far greater extent than sentences are into the whole discourse.'

Clause elements, accordingly, show an even greater integration into the sentence. Of the five phrases, the verb phrase has the highest correlation with pauses (13.9

per cent), with the noun phrase having only 4.8 per cent. None the less, these five phrases also reveal a varying degree of temporal integration: the verb phrase and the prepositional phrase both demonstrate an integration stronger than the sentence and the clause but looser than the other three phrases. Considering that both of these two phrases generally require nominal complementation and are thus more complex than the other three, we could hypothesize that while sentence demarcation remains the more prominent function of pauses in read speech, some rhetoric pauses are needed with complex phrase structures that demand complements. Manual inspection of the text revealed that verb phrases with initiating pauses typically begin with the word *be*,[10] which occurred sixteen times out of thirty-eight. Here are a few examples.

[1] :GAP: A two-thirds majority but no appeal :GAP: *was* needed for a lamp post in a street [S2B-025-47]

[2] :GAP: One of the difficulties :GAP: *was* that there was no reliable book on the subject [S2B-025-51]

[3] :GAP: One :MGAP: by-product of this essentially rural work :GAP: *was* that with the late Robert Ayckman :GAP: I became and remain :GAP: a waterways revivalist [S2B-025-57]

[4] :GAP: The pre-nineteen :MGAP: fourteen Canal Commissions' admirable report :GAP: *was* wholly ignored [S2B-025-62]

These four examples demonstrate two characteristics that probably explain the occurrences of pauses. The first is a heavy subject, as in examples [1] and [4]. The second characteristic is a heavy subject complement as in [2] and [3], where *be* introduces *that*-clauses as subject complements. [3] actually has both a heavy subject (*one by-product of this essentially rural work*) and a heavy subject complement (*that with the late Robert Ayckman I became and remain a waterways revivalist*). Whether these two observations can be generalized needs to be tested on more data. Preposition phrases with initiating pauses, on the other hand, are typically those that can be termed as complex prepositions ([5] and [6]) and complex conjunctions as in [7]:

[5] :GAP: The latter feared the boroughs :GAP: *because of* their masses of urban voters :GAP: and were looking for allies [S2B-025-28]

[6] :GAP: :COUGH: :GAP: Commons are common :MGAP: only to certain individuals who happen to share rights in the land :GAP: *in common with* some other individuals [S2B-025-76]

[7] :GAP: These ways were left out of the act :GAP: *with the result that* astute gravel merchants and estate developers :GAP: exploit loopholes in the law :GAP: to discommon and ravage [S2B-025-124]

The relatively high proportion of adverb phrases with initiating pauses could be conveniently explained by the use of adverbs as sentential disjuncts. Disjuncts 'have a superior role as compared with the sentence elements; they are syntactically more detached and in some respects "superordinate", in that they seem to have a scope that extends over the sentence as a whole' (Quirk *et al.*, 1985: 8.121).

In conclusion, we can say that this experiment confirmed pauses to be a reliable demarcation of the conventional sentence in fluent read speech. Though often similar to the sentence in terms of syntactic structure, clauses are much less characterized by initiating pauses and thus generally demonstrate subordination to the sentence. We would therefore expect that phrases, which are clause elements, would co-occur with pauses much less often than do clauses. However, nearly half of the pauses (46 per cent) fell on the five phrases considered in the experiment. While we may account for some of their occurrences in the one text, a detailed separate study with substantial data is necessary for any sound generalization.

9. Further Work

PROSICE-1 is a novel database for prosody research. Its level and quality of syntactic analysis go beyond other spoken corpora. It has very high-quality audio speech signals, very accurate fundamental frequency information derived from the simultaneous laryngograph recording, and accurate word annotations derived from whole-word alignment and a number of other phonetic annotations. It is also a corpus of a good size, comprising over 16,000 words and nearly two hours of speech. We intend to make the whole database available on CD-ROM at nominal cost to researchers.

We hope to develop PROSICE in a number of ways. First, we expect to add more annotation to the database by, for example, relating to phrasal prominence the semantic features encoded in the ICE grammatical annotation scheme. Secondly, we hope to make new recordings of spontaneous speech and analyse and present them in a similar way. Thirdly, we hope that other workers will join with us in providing further annotations: phonological annotations such as the TOBI system (Silverman *et al.*, 1992), or phonetic segment annotations which will allow the identification of segment duration changes adjacent to prosodic boundaries.

Notes

1. The database should also be accompanied by a clear statement about intellectual property rights. It is still very common to see private databases unavailable to the scientific world at large.
2. For detailed descriptions of ICE word-class and syntactic annotation schemes, see relevant chapters in this volume.
3. Composite texts are those comprising separate extracts from a single source or from different sources.
4. A word here was defined as a string having a word-class label in the syntactic analysis.

Mark Huckvale and Alex Chengyu Fang

5. For a description of the ICE syntactic parsing scheme, see Chapter 11 in this volume.
6. An ICE parsing unit roughly corresponds to the conventional notion of *sentence*, though there are cases where a parsing unit is only a syntactic phrase.
7. We distinguish the sentence from the clause. A sentence consists of either one sentence or a number of co-ordinated sentences. In this treatment, clauses—whether finite or non-finite—are always subordinate.
8. In comparison, Lumley (1933) noted an average rate of 1.8 words per second for politicians, 2.7 words per second for educators, 2.9 words per second for preachers, and 3.2 words per second for reporters (cf. Altenberg, 1987: 16). Altenberg (1987: 22) found an average of 2.4 words per second for the LLC Corpus.
9. In Stenström, 1990, nearly half (48 per cent) of the clauses in spontaneous speech have initiating pauses, revealing the effect of the cognitive process of planning and selecting.
10. The word *be* is grouped into various uses by the ICE tagging scheme. The four examples include *be* as the passive auxiliary ([1] and [4]) and the copula ([2] and [3]).

REFERENCES

ALTENBERG, B. (1987), *Prosodic Patterns in Spoken English—Studies in the Correlation between Prosody and Grammar for Text-to-Speech Conversion* (Lund: Lund University Press).
BEATTIE, G. (1983), *Talk* (Milton Keynes: Open University Press).
BRIDLE, J. S. and BROWN, M. D. (1979), 'Connected Word Recognition Using Whole Word Templates', in *Proceedings of the Institute of Acoustics Autumn Conference, Windermere, November 1979*, 25–8 (St Albans: Institute of Acoustics).
BROTHERTON, P. (1979), 'Speaking and Not Speaking: Process for Translating Ideas into Speech', in Siegman and Feldstein, 179–209.
CHAFE, W. (1987), 'Cognitive Constraints on Information Flow', in R. TOMLIN (ed.), 21–51.
CLEMENTS, G. N. and KEYSER, S. J. (1983), *CV Phonology: A Generative Theory of the Syllable* (Cambridge, Mass.: MIT Press).
FOURCIN, A. J. and ABBERTON, E. (1971), 'First Applications of a New Laryngograph', *Medical and Biological Illustration*, 21: 172–82.
FOURCIN, A. J. and GIBBON, D. (1994), 'Spoken Language Assessment in the European Context', *Literary and Linguistic Computing*, 9: 79–86.
GOLDMAN-EISLER, F. (1972), 'Pauses, Clauses, Sentences', *Language and Speech*, 15: 103–13.
HOLMES, J. N. (1980), 'The JSRU Vocoder', in *IEE Proceedings 127*, Part F., No. 1 (London: Institute for Electrical Engineers).
KLATT, D. H. (1987), 'Review of Text-to-Speech Conversion for English', *Journal of the American Scientific Association*, 82: 737–93.
KNOWLES, G. (1993), 'From Text to Waveform: Converting the Lancaster/IBM Spoken English Corpus into a Speech Database', in C. SOUTER and E. ATWELL (eds.), 47–58.
KNOWLES, G. (1994), 'Annotating Large Speech Corpora: Building on the Experience of Marsec', *Journal of Linguistics*, 13: 87–98.
KNOWLES, G. (1995), 'Recycling an Old Corpus: Converting the SEC into the MARSEC Database', in G. N. LEECH, G. MYERS, and J. A. THOMAS (eds.), 208–19.

LEECH, G. N., MYERS, G., and THOMAS, J. A. (1995) (eds.), *Spoken English on Computer: Transcription and Mark-up* (London: Longman).

LIBERMAN, M. Y. and PRINCE, A. (1977), 'On Stress and Linguistic Rhythm', in *Linguistic Inquiry*, 8: 249–336.

LUMLEY, F. H. (1933), 'Rates of Speech in Radio Speaking', *Quarterley Journal of Speech*, 8: 393–403.

PIERREHUMBERT, J. B. (1980), 'The Phonology and Phonetics of English Intonation', Ph.D. thesis (MIT).

QUIRK, R., GREENBAUM, S., LEECH, G., and SVARTVIK, J. (1985), *A Comprehensive Grammar of the English Language* (London: Longman).

SIEGMAN, A. W. and FELDSTEIN, S. (1979) (eds.), *Of Speech and Time: Temporal Speech Patterns in Interpersonal Contexts* (Hillsdale, NJ: Laurence Erlbaum).

SILVERMAN, K., BECKMAN, M., PITRELLI, J., OSTENDORF, M., WIGHTMAN, C., PRICE, P., PIERREHUMBERT, J., and HIRSCHBERG, J. (1992), 'ToBI: A Standard for Labelling English Prosody', in *Proceedings of the 1992 International Conference on Speech and Language Processing, Banff, Canada*.

SOUTER, C. and ATWELL, E. (1993) (eds.), *Corpus-based Computational Linguistics* (Amsterdam: Rodopi).

STENSTRÖM, A.-B. (1990), 'Pauses in Monologue and Dialogue', in J. SVARTVIK (ed.), 211–52.

SVARTVIK, J. (1990) (ed.), *The London-Lund Corpus of Spoken English—Description and Research* (Lund: Lund University Press).

—— and QUIRK, R. (1979), *A Corpus of English Conversation* (Lund: CWK Gleerup).

TOMLIN, R. (1987) (ed.), *Coherence and Grounding in Discourse* (Amsterdam/Philadelphia: John Benjamins).

VAN SANTEN, J. P. H. (1993), 'Timing in Text-to-Speech Systems', in *Proceedings of EuroSPEECH-93, Berlin*, 1397–1406 (Berlin: European Speech Association).

WIGHTMAN, C. W. and OSTENDORF, M. (1995), 'Automatic Labeling of Prosodic Patterns', in *IEEE Trans. Speech and Audio Processing*, 2: 469–81 (New York: Institute for Electrical and Electronics Engineers).

INDEX

Abberton, E. 266
Abeille, A. 150
acceptability 193
accountability 230
Adam, R. S. 254
Adesanoye, F. 244
Altenberg, B. 218, 233, 264, 278
ANLT parser 154
Asher, R. E. 182
asyndetic co-ordination 131
Atwell, E. 110, 119, 142
Australia 4
AUTASYS **110–24**, 152, 208

background information sheets 171–2, 174,
    176, 180–1
Bacon-Shone, J. 198, 199, 200, 201, 212
Bamgbose, A. 242, 243
Banjo, Ayo 243
Bauer, L. 163, 177
Baumgardner, R. 193
Beattie, G. 274
Beckman, M. 277
Biber, D. 21, 225, 231
biographical information 44
Bishop, K. 150
Black, E. 142
Bolt, P. 198, 199, 201, 205
Bolton, K. 198, 199, 200, 201, 212
Bridle, J. S. 269
Brill, E. 154
Briscoe, T. 142, 154, 157
British National Corpus 217
Brotherton, P. 274
Brown, M. D. 269
Brown corpus 163, 164, 182, 188, 217, 218,
    219
Bungarten, T. 192
Burchfield, R. 183
Burnard, L. 63

c++ 80
CA, see contrastive analysis
Canada 4
Caribbean 183, 186, 195
Carroll, J. 142, 154
Chafe, W. 63, 274
CHECKMUP 36
Chen, X. 111
Cheung, H. N. L. 198

CIA, see contrastive interlanguage analysis
clause features 127–30
clause functions 127
clauses 126–30
CLAWS 115, 116
Clear, J. 183
Clements, G. N. 262
Coates, J. 221, 231
Cocke, J. 142
collecting:
    lectures and tutorials 167
    natural conversations 169–71
    spoken data 166–71
    telephone conversations 169
    texts 201–8
    transactions 168
Collins, P. 231
collocations 155
collocations in learner writing 19, 21
complex-transitives 122
composite texts 27, 45
compounds 68, 98
concordances in language teaching 234–7
connectors in learner writing 19
Conrad, S. 21
context display 84–5
contrastive analysis 17–18, 22
contrastive interlanguage analysis 17–19
control of tagging quality 117–18
Cooper, R. L. 241
co-ordination **130–3**
    category 131
    of predicates 131
    of verb phrases 136
Copestake, A. 157
copyright 30, **33–4**, 174–5
core corpus 5
corpus, see British National, Brown, core,
    expanded, ICE, Fiji, LOB, London-Lund,
    Kolhapur, monitor, New Zealand,
    Nigeria, nonstandard, representative,
    second-language, specialized, Survey
corpus-based research 217–26
corpus-based studies of English 219–21
corpus linguistics 182, 191, 193–4, 227–8
corpus size 217–18
Cote, S. 150
Coulthard, M. 172
Crystal, D. 172
Cumming, S. 172

281

Dada, A. 243
Davy, D. 172
De Carrico, J. S. 225
De Kadt, E. 186
De Paiva, V. 157
default 128, 129
dependent clauses 126, 127, 128
DeRose, S. 110, 116, 118
Derrick, R. A. 249
detached function 135, 138
diglossia 184
discourse marker 130
disparate co-ordination 126, 131, 134
Doran, C. 150, 156
Du Bois, J. 63, 172

educated English, *see* standard English
Egedi, D. 150, 156
Ekong, P. A. 243
elements as objects 56
Ellis, R. 15
English:
  acquired in English-speaking country 14
  as first language 4
  as foreign language 4–5, 14, 182, 199
  as international language 182
  as native language 182, 191–2
  as official second language 4, 14
  as second language 182–3, 191–2, 193, 197, 199
  in language planning in Nigeria 240–2
  language teaching 193–4
Enkvist, N. 242
errors in learner writing 19, 20
ethnicity representation 165
EUROM0 263
Evans, R. 150, 157
expanded corpus 6
expanding circle, *see* English as foreign language
extra-corpus text 38

Fang, A. C. 110–11, 118, 124, 152, 155
Fang, X. 163
Fiji **249–61**
  language use and attitude in 254–5
Fiji English:
  grammatical features 256–7
  history of 249–51
  lexical features 256
  phonological feature 256
  role of English in 251–3
  studies of 255–6
file headers 42–3, 44–5, 49–52
finiteness features 128, 129
Flowerdew, L. 235
foreign words 37–8
Fourcin, A. J. 263, 266

Francis, W. N. 110
Fu, G. S. 198
Fujisaki, T. 142

Garside, R. 110, 116, 119, 142
Gazdar, G. 150, 155, 157
gender representation 165
Geraghty, P. 249, 250, 251, 254, 255, 259, 260
Gibbon, D. 263
Gillion, K. L. 251
Goldman-Eisler, F. 271, 274, 275
Görlach, M. 246
grammaticality 193
Graphical User Interface 67, 77
Greenbaum, S. 13, 27, 29, 93, 96, 110, 111, 119, 139, 146, 156, 163, 165, 219, 222, 235, 244, 246, 274, 277
Greene, B. 110
Gregory, M. 242
Grieve, D. G. 243

have 120–3
hesitations 42
Hindle, D. 154
Hirschberg, J. 277
Ho, M. L. 243
Hockey, B. A. 150, 156
Hofland, K. 218
Holmes, J. 163, 233
Holmes, J. N. 269
Hong Kong 183, **197–214**
Hong Kong texts:
  from business 206–7
  from education 202–3
  from formal public speech 207–8
  from government and law 203–4
  from media and publishing 204–6
  from private conversations and letters 208
Huang, R. J. 110
Hudson-Ettle, D. 190, 194
hypertext help system 80, 90–1

ICE:
  annotation tools 65–78
  design of ICE corpora 5–6, **27–35**
  corpus 112–13
  editions 6
  markup assistant 54, 55, **65–7**
  markup speech grammar 60–1
  markup structural grammar 56–7, 58, 60
  parsing scheme 147–8
  tags 111, 113, 118, 119, 144–5, 149–50, 152
  tagset **92–109**, 119–21, 218
  text categories, culture-specific aspects 187–91
  uses of 10–11
  see also research using ICE

ICE-Fiji corpus 258–9
ICE-GB 3, 9–10, 73, 83, 84, 85, 89, 93, 110,
    122, 124, 125, 142, 148, 149, 152, 185–6,
    188, 190, 213, 227, 234–7, 262, 265
  broadcast talks in 265, 266
  teaching with 227–38
ICECUBE 36, **89–91**
ICECUP 44–5, 53, 79–89, 94, 218, 230, 234
ICEHELP 138
ICEMARK **71–4**
ICETREE 74–7, 94, 125, 138
ICLE 5, **13–24**, 182
  variables controlled in 15–16
incomplete feature 138
India 183, 187, 189
indigenous words 38
inner circle, *see* English as first language
interlanguage 17
Interleaf 54–5
intonation markers 263

Jamaica 4
Jeffery, C. 184
Jellinek, K. 142
Jibril, M. 243
Johansson, J. 110, 119
Johansson, S. 218
Johns, T. 234
Joshi, A. 150
Jowitt, D. 243

Kachru, B. 13, 14
Kelly, Sr F. 255
Kennedy, G. 21, 22, 163, 224, 225
Kenya 187
Keyser, S. J. 262
Kingscott, G. 23
Kirk, J. M. 227, 231, 234
Kjellmer, G. 22, 218, 225
Klatt, D. H. 262
Klein, E. 155
knowledge of English 199–201
Knowles, G. 174, 263, 274
Kolhapur corpus 188
KWIC concordances 84
Kwok, H. 198

Labov, W. 166
Leech, G. 93, 94, 96, 110, 116, 119, 139, 142,
    156, 174, 194, 219, 222, 223, 231, 274,
    277
Leitner, G. 185, 192, 229
Leverhulme project 10
Levy, L. 150
lexical phrases in learner writing 19, 21
Lexicalized Tree Adjoining Grammar, *see* LTAG
Liberman, M. Y. 262

LOB:
  corpus 163, 164, 182, 188, 218, 219, 231
  tags 111, 113, 118, 119
  tagset 119, 120–1
London–Lund corpus 163, 219, 229, 231, 232,
    263–4
Lord, R. 198
LTAG 150, 156
Luke, K. K. 198, 200
Lumley, F. H. 278

McArthur, T. 13, 14
Macnaught, T. J. 250
Magerman, D. 142, 156
main clauses 126, 127–9
Mair, C. 95, 156, 186, 195
Malawi 189–90
Maori lexis 173–4
Maori representation 165, 167
mapping LOB to ICE 119–23
markedness features 128, 129
markup **54–64**
  as data 55
  bibliographical and biographical markup
    42–4
  codes as objects 55
  display 85, 87
  filters 88
  symbols 47–8
  text unit 65
  textual 7, **36–42**, 44, 66
  see also spoken texts, markup in; written
    texts, markup in
MARKUP ASSISTANT 54, 55, 56, **65–7**
MARSEC 263–4
Marshall, I. 110
May, T. 254
Microsoft Windows 67, 80
Milroy, L. 170
Milton, J. 235
misspellings 42
Mitchell, K. 223
monitor corpus 7
mood features 128, 129
morphological derivations 155
Mugler, F. 254
multi-queries 83

Nation, P. 163
Nattinger, J. R. 225
Nelson, G. 111
New Zealand ICE corpus 163–81
New Zealanders 164–5
Ni, Y. 93, 110, 111, 244
Nigeria 239–48
  English as official language 240
  English in creative writing 240

Nigeria (*cont.*):
  English in education 243–4
  English in politics 239–40
  English in private domain 240
  ICE-Nigeria in English language teaching 245
  ICE-Nigeria in language planning 245
  standard Nigerian English 243, 245
Nishino, T. 142
nonclauses 126, 130
non-count nouns 96
non-native Englishes, *see* English as foreign language, English as second official language
non-standard corpora 7
normalizations 41–2, 66–7, 73
noun phrase 136, 137

Obanya, P. 243
Oberinde, T. 243
observer's paradox 166
Ochs, E. 172
Odlin, T. 15
Olantunji, O. 242
Oostdijk, N. 110
Ostendorf, M. 262, 277
outer circle, *see* English as official second language
overlapping speech 40–1, 61–2
Owolabi, K. 242

Paolino, D. 172
parataxis 135, 137
parse analysis 74–6
parse trees 74, 76, 78, 125–6, 127, 130, 132, 134, 136, 137, 147–8, 149, 150, 151, 153
parser 98–9
parsing 66–7, 71
parsing unit 126
pauses 40–1, 67
Pemberton, R. 235
Pennington, M. C. 214
phrasal prominence 263
phrase structure:
  cluster rules 149, 150, 151, 152, 153
  clusters 150, 152
  rules 149–50, 151, 152
  structures 150, 152
phrases 133, 135
Pierrehumbert, J. 262, 277
Pitrelli, J. 277
Platt, J. 243
Poplack, S. 172, 173
population of texts 28
predicate element 131
predicate group 131, 134

Price, P. 277
Prince, A. 262
processing recorded material 175–7
PROSICE 262–79
PROSICE-1: 264–77
  aligning syntactic analysis to speech signals 272–4
  choice of texts for 265
  design objectives 264
  dynamic programming for 269
  fundamental frequency contour for 270, 271
  laryngograph signals for 266–7, 268, 270, 271
  orthographic alignment in 267–70, 271, 272
  pauses in 271, 274–7
  pitch accents in 272
  prompting signals in 267, 269
  recording of 265–7
  resource constraints 264
  spectograms for 268, 270
  speech pressure signals in 265–7, 268, 270, 271
prosodic annotation 264
prosodic phrase structure 263
prosody research 262–4
PS rules, *see* phrase structure rules
PSC rules, *see* phrase structure cluster rules
Pullum, G. 155

Queen's course 227–33
Quirk, R. 93, 96, 139, 156, 217, 219, 222, 263, 274, 277
quotations 38–9

Ratnaparkhi, A. 154
recording instructions 179
Renouf, A. 225
repetitions 41
Reppen, R. 21
representative corpus 192
research using ICE 222–6
Resnik, P. 154
Richards, J. C. 198
Rooth, M. 154
Rosta, A. 36
Roukos, S. 154
RP 244
Rubin, G. 110

's 93–4
Sag, I. 155
Salami, A. 243
Sampson, G. 110, 116
Schabes, Y. 150
Schlesinger, I. 156
Schmied, J. 183, 185, 190, 191, 193, 194, 195, 229, 244

Schuetze-Coburn, S. 172
Scotton, C. M. 186
SCRIBE 263
SDL 81–3
search display 83
SEC 263
second language acquisition 14, 15
second-language corpora 182–96
self-corrections 41–2
Selinker, L. 17
SEU, *see* Survey of English Usage
SGML 55–6, 60, 65, 79, 80, 89, 111, 112
Shastri, S. V. 188, 189
Shaw, P. 235
Shields, K. 192
Siegel, J. 250, 251, 254, 256, 259
Silverman, K. 277
Sinclair, J. M. 21, 94, 224, 225
Singapore 183
SKELETON tags 111
So, W. C. D. 198
sociolinguistic context 198–201
South Africa 183, 184, 186
specialized corpus 7
speech recognition 262, 264
speech synthesis 262
Spencer, J. 242
Sperberg-McQueen, C. M. 63
spoken texts **30–1**, 67, 230
  collection of 34
  markup in 39
Sridhar, K. K. 18–19
Sridhar, S. N. 18–19
Srinivas, B. 150, 156
standard English 5, 192
Stenström, A.-B. 231, 274, 278
string description language, *see* SDL
Stubbs, M. 172
subcorpus selection 88–9
subtexts 45
Survey corpus 111, 112, 182, 217, 219, 222,
  229, 231
Survey of English Usage 3, 9–10, 91, 92, 94,
  110, 119, 123–4, 125, 149, 154–5, 246
Survey parser 9, 125, **142–60**, 152, 154, 156
Survey parsing scheme 125–41
surveys of language use 199–201
Svartvik, J. 93, 94, 96, 139, 156, 182, 219,
  222, 263, 264, 274, 277
Swaziland 183
syndetic co-ordination 131
syntactic markers **71–4**
syntactico-semantics 155

tagged text formats 113–14
tagging 208–11
TAGHELP 94

tags 67–71, 72–3, 74, **92–109**
  assignment of 115–16
  disambiguation of tags 116–17
  discontinuous tags 98
  ditto tags 98–9, 112
  see also ICE tags; LOB tags; TESS tags
TAGSELECT **67–71**, 94
Takahashi, M. 150
Tanzania 183, 185, 187, 189
teaching of English as a foreign language
  234–7
tense features 128, 129
Tent, J. 254, 260
TESS tags 119
text:
  categories 28–33
  collection 34–5
  description 43
  information 53, 85, 86
  internals 43
  selection 27–8
  source 43
text unit 37
text unit markup 65
textual markup 66
Thompson, S. A. 63
Tiffen, B. 243
Tong, K. K. 235
Tong, K. S. T. 235
topics for ICE research into English 222–6
TOSCA 8–9, 92, 98–9, 115
TOSCA parser 125, 142, 148
TQUERY 149
transcription 7–8, 172–4, 176
transitive 93, 138
transitivity features 128, 129, 145–6
Tsang, E. S. C. 235

Uganda 186
UMB MARKUP ASSISTANT 54–64
United Kingdom 4
United States 4
UNTAG 96–7
use of English 201–2, 204, 207, 212

van Santen, J. P. H. 262
variables for language analysis 191–3
verb phrase 129, 130
videoing 167–8
View Text Window 85, 86
voice features 128, 129

Wall Street Journal 111, 112, 113,
  114–15
Walsh, N. G. 243
WCNZE 163, 177
WCSNZE 164

Weber, H. 242
Weir, D. 150, 157
West Africa 186
White, R. V. 254
Wightman, C. W. 262, 277
Wikberg, K. 188
word-class tags, *see* tags
word classes 92
word partials 82–3, 96

WordPerfect 65
written texts **31–3**
  collection of 34
  markup in 39

Young, D. 184
Yue, F. 214

Zaidel, M. 150